CU00695224

'This very readable book provides a unique persp¢
'voice' of prisoners themselves combined with iı
commentary. It is an important addition to pris¢   ,------,
become a 'must read' for anyone who wishes to understand the actual 'reality'
of the prisoner experience'.

Michael Spurr, *Chief Executive Officer, National Offender Management Service,*
England & Wales

'Despite it having risen to become one of the major issues of public concern in
the UK over the past twenty years or so the reality of prison life remains largely
a mystery for most people in this country. Equally mysterious are the inhabitants
of our prisons. Who are they? And more importantly what motivates them? With
its sensitive balance of prisoner voices and expert analysis this timely, intelligent
book does a peerless job of providing the answers.'

Erwin James, *Guardian columnist and former prisoner*

The Prisoner

Little of what we know about prisons comes from the mouths of prisoners, and very few academic accounts manage to convey some of its most profound and important features: its daily pressures and frustrations, the culture of the wings and landings, and the relationships which shape the everyday experience of being imprisoned.

The Prisoner aims to redress this by foregrounding prisoners' own accounts of prison life in what is an original and penetrating edited collection. Each of its chapters explores a particular prisoner sub-group or an important aspect of prisoners' lives, and each is divided into two sections: extended extracts from interviews with prisoners, followed by academic commentary and analysis written by a leading scholar or practitioner. This structure allows prisoners' voices to speak for themselves, while situating what they say in a wider discussion of research, policy and practice. The result is a rich and evocative portrayal of the lived reality of imprisonment and a poignant insight into prisoners' lives.

The book aims to bring to life key penological issues and provide an accessible text for anyone interested in prisons, including students, practitioners and a general audience. It seeks to represent and humanise a group that is often silent in discussions of imprisonment, and to shine a light on a world that is generally hidden from view.

Ben Crewe is Deputy Director of the Prisons Research Centre at the Institute of Criminology, University of Cambridge. He has published on various aspects of prison life, including staff–prisoner relationships, the drugs economy within prison, the 'inmate code' and public–private sector comparisons. His most recent book, *The Prisoner Society: Power, Adaptation, and Social Life in an English Prison*, was published in 2009.

Jamie Bennett has worked for 15 years as a prison manager and has held senior positions including Governor of HMP Morton Hall. He is also Editor of *Prison Service Journal* and has written widely on criminal justice matters including prison management, the media representation of prisons, and the relationship between crime and inequality. He has published two previous books: *Understanding Prison Staff* (with Ben Crewe and Azrini Wahidin, 2008) and *Dictionary of Prisons and Punishment* (with Yvonne Jewkes, 2008).

The Prisoner

Edited by Ben Crewe and Jamie Bennett

LONDON AND NEW YORK

First published 2012
by Routledge
2 Park Square, Milton Park, Abingdon, Oxon, OX14 4RN

Simultaneously published in the USA and Canada
by Routledge
711 Third Avenue, New York, NY 10017

Routledge is an imprint of the Taylor & Francis Group, an informa business

British Library Cataloguing in Publication Data
A catalogue record for this book is available from the British Library.

Library of Congress Cataloging-in-Publication Data
The prisoner/edited by Ben Crewe and Jamie Bennett.
p. cm.
1. Prisoners--Great Britain. 2. Prisons--Great Britain. 3. Prison Psychology--
Great Britain. I. Crewe, Ben. II. Bennett, Jamie.
HV9647.P747 2012
365'.60941--dc23
2011022925

ISBN: 978-0-415-66865-1 (hbk)
ISBN: 978-0-415-66866-8 (pbk)
ISBN: 978-0-203-15382-6 (ebk)

Typeset in Times New Roman
by GCS, Leighton Buzzard, Bedfordshire

Contents

Contributors

Steve Barlow has worked in the field of education for over 30 years, including seven years as a teacher in a New South Wales prison. He has conducted research for the NSW Department of Corrective Services into educational initiatives within NSW prisons, as well as PhD research into how prisoners indicate their readiness for positive life change. Although no longer working full-time in prison education, Steve maintains an ongoing interest in helping ex-offenders reintegrate into the community.

Jamie Bennett is a prison governor and also Editor of *Prison Service Journal*. He has written widely on criminal justice issues including prison management, crime and inequality, and prisons in the media. He has published two previous books: *Understanding Prison Staff* (with Ben Crewe and Azrini Wahidin, 2008) and *Dictionary of Prisons and Punishment* (with Yvonne Jewkes, 2008).

Rachel Condry is a lecturer at the Centre for Criminology, University of Oxford, and a Fellow of St Hilda's College. She has previously been a lecturer in criminology and a British Academy Postdoctoral Fellow at the London School of Economics, and a lecturer in criminology at the University of Surrey. Her research focuses broadly on the intersections between crime and the family. Her research interests include families of offenders and victims, family violence, the family in youth justice, secondary victimisation, narrative accounts, shame and stigma, and the state regulation of parenting and family life. She is the author of a book about the families of serious offenders, *Families Shamed: The Consequences of Crime for Relatives of Serious Offenders* (Willan, 2007), and is currently conducting two research projects. The first, funded by the ESRC, examines the problem of adolescent-to-parent violence and the second, funded by the British Academy, explores parenting expertise in youth justice.

Andrew Coyle is Emeritus Professor of Prison Studies in the University of London, Visiting Professor in the University of Essex and Director of the International Centre for Prison Studies. Previously he worked for 25 years at a senior level in the prison services of the United Kingdom where he governed several major prisons. He is a prisons adviser to the UN High Commissioner for Human Rights, the UN Latin American Institute, the Council of Europe, including its Committee for the Prevention of Torture, and several national governments. He has a PhD in criminology from the Faculty of Law at the University of Edinburgh and is a Fellow of King's College London. In 2000 he was appointed an Honorary Professor in the Academy of Law and Management, Ryazan, Russia. His books include *The Prisons We Deserve, Managing Prisons in a Time of Change, A Human Rights Approach to Prison Management* (published in 16 languages), *Humanity in Prison* and *Understanding Prisons: Key Issues in Policy and Practice*. He was appointed a Companion of the Order of St Michael and St George in 2003 for his contribution to international penal reform.

Ben Crewe is Deputy Director of the Prisons Research Centre at the Institute of Criminology, University of Cambridge. He has published on various aspects of prison life, including staff–prisoner relationships, the drugs economy within prison, the 'inmate code' and public–private sector comparisons. His most recent book, *The Prisoner Society: Power, Adaptation and Social Life in an English Prison*, was published in 2009.

Rod Earle is a lecturer in the Department of Health and Social Care at the Open University. He is Academic Lead for the Youth Justice courses and a member of the International Centre for Comparative Criminological Research at the Open University. Working with Coretta Phillips, he recently conducted a two-year study of identity, ethnicity and social relations in two men's prisons in southern England. Before working as an academic Rod spent over ten years with Lambeth Social Services in south London trying to help children and young people in trouble with the law.

Yvonne Jewkes is Professor of Criminology at the University of Leicester. She has published several books on prisons and imprisonment including *Prisons and Punishment* (Sage, 2008), *Handbook on Prisons* (Willan, 2007), *Captive Audience: Media, Masculinity and Power in Prisons* (Willan, 2002) and, with Helen Johnston, *Prison Readings: A Critical Introduction to Prisons and Imprisonment* (Willan, 2006).

Alison Liebling is Professor of Criminology and Criminal Justice and Director of the Prisons Research Centre at the University of Cambridge. She has carried out research on young offender throughcare, suicides in prison, staff–prisoner relationships, the work of prison officers, small units for difficult prisoners, incentives and earned privileges, prison privatisation, secure training centres, and measuring the quality of prison life. She has published several books, including *Suicides in Prison* (1992), *Prisons and their Moral Performance: A Study of Values, Quality and Prison Life* (2004) and *The Effects of Imprisonment* (with Shadd Maruna, 2005). She is currently completing a repeat of a study she first conducted in 1998, of staff–prisoner relationships at Whitemoor prison. She has published widely in criminological journals, and is currently co-editor in chief (with Dirk van Zyl Smit) of *Punishment and Society: The International Journal of Penology*.

Natalie Mann is a criminology lecturer at Anglia Ruskin University, Cambridge, having previously been a teaching fellow in the Sociology Department at the University of Essex, where she completed her PhD in 2008, entitled *Doing Harder Time? The Experiences of an Ageing Male Prison Population in England and Wales*. The research investigated the ways in which ageing men cope with imprisonment, and the unique problems they experience. Her more recent work has focused on ageing child sex offenders. She is currently writing a manuscript based on her PhD, to be published by Ashgate.

Shadd Maruna is Director of the Institute of Criminology and Criminal Justice at Queen's University Belfast where he is also Professor of Justice Studies and Human Development. Previously, he has been a lecturer at the University of Cambridge and the State University of New York. His book *Making Good: How Ex-Convicts Reform and Rebuild Their Lives* (American Psychological Association, 2001) was named the 'Outstanding Contribution to Criminology' by the American Society of Criminology in 2001.

Rod Morgan is Professor Emeritus, University of Bristol and Visiting Professor at the LSE and Cardiff University. He is a Ministry of Justice appointed advisor to the five criminal justice inspectorates and was formerly Chairman of the Youth Justice Board for England and Wales (2004–7), HM Chief Inspector of Probation (2001–4) and Assessor to Lord Woolf's Inquiry into the 1990 Prison Disturbances. Among his many publications is his co-editorship of the *Oxford Handbook of Criminology* (OUP), the 5th edition of which is in preparation.

Coretta Phillips is Senior Lecturer in Social Policy at the London School of Economics and Political Science. She has published widely in the field of ethnicities, racism and criminal justice, including *Racism, Crime and Justice* (with Ben Bowling, Longman, 2002). Most recently, her research interests have included examining the resettlement needs of black, Asian, and minority ethnic offenders, and she is also writing up the study on which her chapter is based for a book entitled *The Multicultural Prison*. Coretta is a member of the Independent Equalities Advisory Group for NOMS.

Abigail Rowe is Lecturer in Criminology at the Open University. She has worked on research projects on social exclusion, maximum-security men's imprisonment and conducted ethnographic research in women's prisons in England. She has published on various aspects of imprisonment, including private prisons and women's imprisonment.

Sarah Tait received her doctorate from the Institute of Criminology, Cambridge University in 2008. She has published on prison officer culture, gender and prison officer work, suicide and self-harm in prisons, and the role of care in staff–prisoner relationships. After completing an ESRC post-doctoral fellowship in 2010, she returned to Canada and has taught gender and work and the sociology of punishment at the University of Toronto and the University of Waterloo. She currently lives in Ottawa, Ontario.

Jason Warr has had an unusual pathway into academia. He was incarcerated between 1992 and 2004, during which time he studied in a haphazard fashion. He was eventually inspired to take his studying seriously by Alan Smith, his philosophy teacher at HMP Wellingborough. In April 2004, while awaiting release on life licence, he attended a conference at Cambridge where he met John Irwin, Shadd Maruna, Alison Liebling, Pat Carlen and Ben Crewe, all of whom encouraged him to pursue an academic path that he had never imagined would be open to him. Since his release he has completed a BSc in Philosophy, Logic and Scientific Method at LSE, an MPhil in Criminological Research at the Institute of Criminology University of Cambridge and is currently in the final stages of his doctoral research. As well as working on his PhD and various articles and chapters for publication he is currently working on his autobiography – *There and Back Again: A Con's Tale.*

Foreword

Andrew Coyle

In the world of prisons, terminology has a particular resonance and alternative terms are frequently used to soften the reality. Prisons have been described as jails, penitentiaries and correctional institutions. Over the years prison staff have been referred to as warders, guards, prison officers and correctional officers. Those who are held in prisons have been described variously as convicts, prisoners, detainees and inmates.

Part of the explanation for these variations lies in continuing uncertainty about what the law intends in deciding that some persons who have committed crimes should be sent to prison. Are they sent there merely to be detained (hence, jails and guards), or as punishment (penitentiaries), or in the expectation that they will be reformed by the experience (corrections)? The use of a particular term often denotes the priority that a jurisdiction accords to these places, a priority not necessarily reflected in what actually goes on within them on a day-to-day basis.

When considering these matters it is helpful to go back to first principles, which, in terms of imprisonment, are to be found in the criminal law. In England and Wales, the relevant law is to be found in Section 152(2) of the Criminal Justice Act 2003, which sets out 'General restrictions on imposing discretionary custodial sentences':

> The court must not pass a custodial sentence unless it is of the opinion that the offence, or the combination of the offence and one or more offences associated with it, was so serious that neither a fine alone nor a community sentence can be justified for the offence.

Hence, the law leaves little doubt. Individuals are sent to prison because the court judges that the offence of which the person has been convicted is so serious that no other sentence can be justified. In other words, for persons who have been convicted, it is not a question of whether there are alternatives to imprisonment; rather, it is that imprisonment is the alternative when no other sentence can be justified. Imprisonment is the most serious punishment available to a court following a criminal conviction and the basis of that punishment is the deprivation of liberty. This reality has always been understood by those who are sent to prison; they know that, however anyone else may describe them, they are prisoners. It has also been understood by prison officers.

Generally speaking, those who are responsible for the prison system in England and Wales have also understood and accepted this legal reality. For a short period in the second half of the last century there was an attempt to describe those held in prison as 'inmates', a term with medical overtones, but this was soon discarded. Similarly, at the turn of the century, there was an attempt to introduce the term 'corrections', with the government going so far as to appoint a Commissioner of Correctional Services; but this proved to be a transitory and short-lived diversion.

Clarity of terminology in the prison context is not simply a matter of pedantry or of legal nicety. It goes to the heart of how men and women held in prison are to be treated. They are not objects to be 'corrected', like crooked trees that need to be placed in splints until their direction of growth is corrected. Nor are they merely 'offenders', to be defined by one particular aspect of their behaviour, with all other aspects of their humanity to be viewed through the prism of 'offending behaviour'.

While people are held in prison they should be given every encouragement and incentive to maintain and to develop positive family relationships, to acquire skills that will help them to earn a living after release and to find employment in which they can use these skills, to ensure that they have somewhere to live when they leave prison, to change features of their lives, such as drug and alcohol abuse, and to get help for medical needs, not least mental health problems. At the same time, it is important always to be conscious of the fact that these aspects of personal development and maturity must be based on the choice and determination of the individual. They cannot be imposed from without.

To some extent it is an inevitable feature of prison life that prisoners are regarded, in the words of one author, as 'objects' rather than 'subjects':[1] things are to be done to them and for them, rather than *with* them and *by* them. The inevitability of that stems from the legal reality of prison, as described above. Prisons are primarily places of detention, in which the demands of security and good order will invariably trump all others. That is what Alexander Paterson meant by his famous dictum that people cannot be trained for freedom in conditions of captivity.[2] That is not to say that prisons should be places of despair and inhumanity. On the contrary, recent heads of the Prison Service of England and Wales have pursued with vigour the notion that prisons should be places of decency and humanity.

However, the ethos of prison remains one in which prisoners are treated as passive respondents rather than active participants. This philosophical foundation stone was never more clearly exposed than in the establishment of the National Offender Management Service.[3] This gave explicit articulation to the notion that those in prison were to be dealt with first and foremost as offenders and that they were to be 'managed'. This was to be done in a manner which was decent but which absolutely reinforced the notion of the prisoner as 'object', subjected to 'end-to-end management' delivered in a 'seamless' fashion. This was the logical conclusion to an approach that saw the prisoner as an object to be observed by criminologists, to be assessed according to a 'criminogenic'[4] template invented by psychologists, and to be managed within a world of key performance indicators and targets, with the measure of success to be a 'reduction in reoffending'.

The 'offender management' approach is based on an unsound premise. It acknowledges the need to recognise that prisoners are individual human beings while at the same time implying that their individual humanity is circumscribed by the fact that they are prisoners. One consequence of this dissonance is the assumption that this individual approach can be implemented within institutions which, to borrow a term from one of the Carter reports,[5] are increasingly titanic in size and are of necessity organised on a homogeneous and monolithic basis.

The significance of the chapters in this book lies in the fact that they attempt to portray those who are in prison as subjects rather than as objects. It gives them voices that underline their individuality as human beings. While not seeking to diminish the seriousness of the crimes that many of them have committed, it also opens a window on to who they are as persons and how their life experiences prior to imprisonment have been a factor in the path their lives have taken. The life stories that are recounted are each peculiar to the individual, yet in no case was it inevitable that the person would end up in prison. In our own experiences many of us will have come across people who have faced situations not dissimilar to those recounted in this book, yet who have reacted differently and more positively. In Chapter 1 Alan analyses his young life with a considerable degree of insight:

> The way I see it, it was out of my control, because it was something that was confronted at me and I just made the wrong choice. I had two paths to take and I just took the wrong one every time. I just didn't learn from my mistakes.

Reading his story, it is not entirely surprising that he took the wrong path. Jeremiah in Chapter 6 describes how he tries to balance the need to do what is required of him in prison ('I've addressed everything that I'm supposed to address') with what is really important to him as he comes to the end of his sentence: the wish to become a full member of his family. He understands that his imprisonment is in some respects harder for his partner then it is for him:

> ...I've left her out there to struggle ... standing at the bus stop with my son late at night, and I phone her and she's crying and it's cold and she's waiting for the bus to come home ... I've left her to defend herself with a young child when she was young herself.

One wonders which box that ticked in his OASys (Offender Assessment System) form.[6] In the same chapter Luke also emphasises the importance of family relationships and the difficulty of maintaining them in prison, acknowledging that his drug addiction further complicates his attempts to do so. He has spent much of his adult life in prison and comments without self-pity on the pointlessness of much of his daily life:

> You should be able to work in prison and earn your keep, you know what I mean? ... You can't tell me that a prison couldn't set up a scheme where we are working within a prison, earning decent money, doing anything?

Many politicians and newspaper editors would echo that sentiment.

Most prisoners are adult males and in all countries prisons and prison systems are built and managed with the needs of the majority in mind, with little thought given to the different needs of other groups. One thinks back to the mid-1990s, when following high-profile escapes from male high security prisons the order went out that henceforth every prisoner being taken out of prison (for example, to hospital) should be handcuffed to an officer. The literal interpretation of that order led to the obscenity of pregnant women being shackled even in the labour suites of maternity hospitals. Chapters 7 to 10 of this book remind us of the different experiences of women and young people in prison, of the problems faced by the increasing number of old prisoners, and of those who are of a different culture or race from the majority. Kirsty's story is of a young drug addict who had suffered abuse at the hands of foster parents and was now coping with the distress of having her infant child taken away from her because others, including her mother, had decided that it was best that the baby should be looked after by her grandmother. This may well have been the correct decision but there seems to have been little attempt to assist Kirsty to cope with what she saw as a new failure, that of motherhood, on her part.

Wayne an 18-year-old of mixed race, describes how he feels safer inside prison than outside. He is virtually resigned to the inevitability of a life spent going through the revolving doorway of the prison, yet wanting to break out of this cycle:

> My biggest concern about getting out of jail is coming back, that will always be number one. That feeling of letting everyone down, letting down everyone that has tried to help you again. It comes to a point where people walk away.

The overriding sense when reading this book is that although prisons may be homogenous, prisoners are not. They are individual human beings, each with his or her own story to tell, most of them seeking their own path to a life free of crime and of prison. The prison system we have today rarely helps the individual in that search, despite the best efforts of those who work within it.

It was an official publication from the Thatcher government which noted that when used inappropriately prison can be 'an expensive way of making bad people worse'.[7] Few people today dispute that, with 85,000 people in prison in England and Wales, it is often used inappropriately. It may be that instead of repeatedly attempting to make prison more efficient, we should be looking not at alternatives to prison but to an alternative to the prison, an alternative that would more effectively divert people from a life of crime, that would increase public feelings of safety, and reduce the number of victims. It may be that in giving prisoners a voice in the way it does this book will encourage us to look for such an alternative.

Notes

1 Duguid, S. (2000) *Can Prisons Work? The Prisoner as Object and Subject in Modern Corrections*. Toronto: University of Toronto Press.
2 Ruck, S. (ed.) (1951) *Paterson on Prisons: Being the Collected Papers of Sir Alexander Paterson*. London: Frederick Muller Ltd.
3 Carter, P. (2003) *Managing Offenders, Reducing Crime: A New Approach*. London: Strategy Unit.
4 I am always reassured by the fact that on each occasion I type this word my computer spell check refuses to recognise it.
5 Carter, P. (2007) *Securing the Future: Proposals for the Efficient and Sustainable Use of Custody in England and Wales*. London: Ministry of Justice.
6 Offender Assessment System: A computer-based risk assessment tool used in prisons and probation services in England and Wales.
7 Home Office (1990) *Crime, Justice & Protecting the Public*. London: HMSO, Cmnd 965.

Acknowledgements

We would like to thank all the prisoners who have shared their lives with us and other researchers in order to make this book possible. Thanks are also due to the prison staff and managers who make research possible, when it might not always feel in their interests to do so.

Introduction

Ben Crewe and Jamie Bennett

> To get an inside picture one must first be convicted, and then of course, anything one has to say is valueless and is treated with the gravest suspicion.[1]

How does one get a feel for prison life, for its daily texture, or for what it is really like to be imprisoned? Many of the 'classic studies', conducted during the 1950s and the two subsequent decades, make very little use of direct quotations to illustrate their insight, muffling the voice of the prisoner behind their analysis. Surprisingly few academic texts manage to convey some of the most distinctive qualities of prisons – not just their sounds and smells, which, after all, are not easy to describe on paper, but their mundane frustrations, their emotional consistency, the daily dilemmas and demands that they generate, and the combination of misery and mirth that suffuses the environment.

Prisoner writings, such as diaries and autobiographies, often do a better job of capturing the everyday culture of the prison and the interior mental universe of the incarcerated. In recent years, accounts by Erwin James and Ruth Wyner, among others, have added to a long tradition of first-hand accounts of the prisoner experience.[2] By their nature, though, these are singular experiences of prison life, and they are imperfect guides to the general experience of imprisonment (inasmuch as one can talk in such terms). As Steve Morgan suggests, they tend to be written either by 'straights' – respectable citizens thrust into a world which to them is highly alien – or 'cons' – experienced criminals, serving very long sentences or having an extensive history of short sentences.[3] Some of the more sensational 'con' autobiographies, alongside a broader canon of 'gangster-lit', have, if anything, obscured some of the truths about prison life, or, at best, presented an extremely partial picture of crime and punishment.

Arguably, then, the voices of more ordinary prisoners are under-represented in this canon. One of the main aims of this book is to expand and fill this spectrum (however incompletely), both through the range of topics it tries to cover and the inclusion within each chapter of at least two different prisoner accounts. The chapters have been designed so that they combine first-hand narrative with academic commentary. Each is divided into two sections: the first section comprises extended excerpts from interviews with prisoners,[4] while the second seeks to put the interviews in wider context, to highlight and discuss their key themes, and to note any salient issues that are missing from the interview extracts. By structuring each chapter in this way, we hope to offer richness of detail alongside a wider consideration of patterns, trends and explanations.

Our wider aims are manifold. First, we want to give value, exposure and intrinsic credibility to the inside account of the convict, whose thoughts are too often concealed or discounted, as Zeno notes in the epigraph at the start of this chapter. In doing so, we want especially to humanise prisoners, for we fear that the term 'prisoner' evokes in most people the sense of a categorically different species. As social inequalities grow, and social distance and ignorance become correspondingly greater, it is all the more likely that prisoners will be thought of only in terms of the acts they have committed rather than the lives they have led and the life experiences that provide a backdrop for their offending. As many of the testimonies in this book illustrate, violence, abuse and neglect are common in prisoners' backgrounds; recurring themes of low self-esteem, guilt and both 'respect' and 'disrespect' point to deep-rooted emotional patterns and preoccupations. Prisoners rarely talk to prison staff or to their peers about these issues, and the prison environment provides only limited opportunities to deal with them. By framing prisoners' experiences within a wider account of their lives, we want to widen the lens through which they are seen and perhaps reshape public perceptions of who prisoners are. We also hope to offer insight to staff who work with offenders and to practitioners who design the policies that affect them.

In the selection of prisoner extracts, there is likely to be some bias towards interviewees who are more than usually articulate. However, in our experience, very few prisoners struggle to depict their world and express their feelings. Even among prisoners who are deemed conventionally ineloquent, there is a clarity of expression, a directness in the use of language, and a raw descriptive quality that seems related to the extreme nature of the environment – its tendency to focus the mind on life's existential priorities and to concentrate and crystallise all manner of social and emotional phenomena, from friendship to fear.

This edited collection is preceded by books with similar aims – collaborations between academics and prisoners,[5] and exchanges between prisoners and outsiders.[6] In terms of tone, though, we have been most influenced by work by neither prisoners nor academics: in particular, the documentary films of Rex Bloomstein,[7] notably *Strangeways* (1980), *Strangeways Re-Visited* (2001), *Lifer – Living With Murder* (2003) and *Kids Behind Bars* (2005), and the oral histories of Tony Parker, particularly *The Frying Pan: A Prison and its Prisoners*.[8] Both Bloomstein and Parker manage to place their audiences inside the prison, without manipulating them into taking up moral or political positions. Academics could learn much from their style and technique. Just as his preference for dispensing with evocative musical accompaniment renders his films more rather than less evocative, Bloomstein's capacity to brave out silences and ask straightforward, humanistic questions is what makes him such an effective interviewer. Parker, too, recognised the power of silence and the need for interviewers to tolerate the discomfort that it creates.[9] The candour of his interviewees testifies to his skills as an interviewer, with his humility and 'quiet empathy' seeming to draw out their humanity and inner thoughts.[10] We hope that this volume can do something similar.

Structure of the book

Trying to capture the entirety of the prison experience is an impossible task, but we have sought to select chapters that reflect some of the most important features of imprisonment and most significant portions of the prison population. The majority of authors are academics, but also include people with professional experience working in prisons and direct experience of being imprisoned. All have spent significant periods of time 'inside', often conducting ethnographic research in order to gain an intense appreciation of prisoners' lives.

The first chapter, by Jamie Bennett, a prison governor, discusses prisoner backgrounds and biographies. Here the use of interviews is particularly helpful in revealing the multi-layered factors that shape individual life paths, including social, economic and biological factors, plus traumatic experiences. The four chapters that follow explore the inner world of prisons. Sarah Tait's chapter on custody, care and staff–prisoner relationships looks at how prisoners interact with the individuals responsible for both keeping them in secure detention and meeting most of their personal needs. Tait's work illustrates how officers who treat prisoners with respect, empathy and as people of 'equal moral worth' have a positive impact on prisoners' lives, while those who are uncaring can increase the harmfulness of the experience. In his chapter on prison culture and the prisoner society, Ben Crewe examines the ways in which prisoners interact with one another and form a social world that is both somewhat distinct from outside society but also influenced by external social developments. In particular, he illustrates how the importance of drugs in the prison's informal economy and changes in prison policies have combined to loosen social bonds between prisoners and individualise their society. The two subsequent chapters explore issues relating to prisoners' inner psychological experiences. Yvonne Jewkes discusses the impact of imprisonment on prisoners' self and social identities, how they feel in their 'inner, emotional core', and how they present themselves to others. Alison Liebling addresses the issues of vulnerability, struggling and coping, focusing on how prisoners who find imprisonment (and often life in general) most difficult try to survive it. These prisoners tend to lack the inner resources to handle their anxiety and distress, and rely considerably on prison staff to get them through their time in prison. For these prisoners, the environment in which they are imprisoned can make the difference between living and dying. Together these chapters attempt to provide a thematic exploration of some of the key social and emotional dimensions of the prisoner experience.

Prisoners have histories and relationships that pre-date their sentences and continue to exist throughout them. These are the subject of Rachel Condry's chapter. Looking at the effects of imprisonment on prisoners' families, and on prisoners' relationships with their families, this chapter documents the struggles and the (sometimes positive) changes imposed on family members as a result of a prisoner's incarceration, the practical and emotional difficulties of sustaining family relationships, and the role that family members can play in motivating and supporting desistance.

The book goes on to examine a number of groups of prisoners for whom the experience of imprisonment has some distinctive features that merit special attention. Children and young people in prison constitute one such group, as Rod Morgan's chapter outlines. Young people struggle not only with the standard pains of imprisonment but also with the 'growing pains' of maturing into young adults within the prison environment. Morgan draws out some of the problems of child detention, in particular the way that young people's futures are shaped by their institutionalisation and the dysfunctional social world in which they develop. At the opposite end of the life spectrum, Natalie Mann considers ageing prisoners, one of the fastest growing groups in prisons. These prisoners are held in institutions that are generally designed around the needs of young men, leading to a number of specific problems, which the chapter details. Women make up only around 5 per cent of the overall prison population, but imprisonment often has a particularly devastating effect on them and their families. In her chapter, Abigail Rowe goes beyond a conventional analysis of women prisoners to provide a broad portrait of the social world of women's prisons as well as some of the well-documented pains. Coretta Phillips and Rod Earle use the accounts of two racially and ethnically different prisoners in order to explore race relations, ethnic minority and foreign national prisoners. Here, they reveal the everyday tensions, adaptations and negotiations that occur as people with a diverse range of ethnic, racial and national identities are forced to co-exist in a confined space.

The final substantive chapter, by Steve Barlow and Shadd Maruna, is based around themes of rehabilitation, generativity and mutual aid. Drawing upon interviews with prisoners in Australia, the chapter appraises some of the factors that increase the chances of prisoners desisting from crime, including age, life choices and organisational policies, based around the 'pathways to reoffending' model used in prisons in England and Wales. As the chapter also notes, many prisoners want to 'give something back' while in prison, as well as after release, yet the prison environment is not always good at enabling this.

Jason Warr's Afterword provides a poignant end to the book. A former prisoner, who served twelve years in prison, Warr reflects on some of the questions that underlie this volume, comments on some recurring themes – to which one could add concerns about trust and emotional sustenance – offers some suggestions for future areas of research, and concludes with the kind of penetrating observations that we hope are characteristic of the book as a whole.

Notes

1 Zeno (1969) *Life*. London: Macmillan, p. 70.
2 James, E. (2003) *A Life Inside: A Prisoner's Notebook*. London: Atlantic; Wyner, R. (2003) *From the Inside: Dispatches from a Women's Prison*. London: Aurum Press. For a comprehensive history and analysis of prisoner writings, see Broadhead, J. (2006) *Unlocking the Prison Muse: The Inspiration and Effects of Prisoners' Writing in Britain*. Liverpool: Liverpool Academic Press.
3 Morgan, S. (1999) 'Prison lives: Critical issues in reading prisoner autobiography', *The Howard Journal*, 38(3): 328–40.
4 In most chapters, the authors have drawn upon their own interviews. Four chapters draw upon interviews conducted as part of Ben Crewe's study of HMP Wellingborough (with appropriate consent) (for further details, see Crewe (2009) *The Prisoner Society: Power, Adaptation and Social Life in an English Prison*. Oxford: OUP). In order to supply transcripts for Rod Morgan's chapter on young prisoners, both editors spent a day in a Young Offender Institution, interviewing a small number of young prisoners about their experiences.
5 For example, Carlen, P. (ed.) with Hicks, J., O'Dwyer, J., Christina, D. and Tchaikovsky, C. (1985) *Criminal Women, Autobiographical Accounts*. Cambridge: Polity Press; Padel, U. and Stevenson, P. (eds) (1988) *Insiders: Women's Experience of Prison*. London: Virago.
6 Shannon, T. and Morgan, C. (1997) *The Invisible Crying Tree*. London: Black Swan.
7 See Bennett, J. (2006) 'Undermining the simplicities: The films of Rex Bloomstein', in P. Mason (ed.) *Captured by the Media: Prison Discourse in Popular Culture*. Cullompton: Willan Publishing.
8 Parker, T. (1970) *The Frying Pan: A Prison and its Prisoners*. London: Hutchinson.
9 See Soothill, K. (ed.) (1999) *Criminal Conversations: An Anthology of the Work of Tony Parker*. London: Routledge.
10 Ward, C. (1996) 'Obituaries: Tony Parker', *The Independent*, 11 October 1996.

1 Prisoner backgrounds and biographies

Jamie Bennett

Alan was a young, white British prisoner, who always appeared happy and optimistic. He saw himself as something of a 'ladies' man' and liked to flirt with female staff. He was sanguine about his future, despite the difficulties he had experienced in life, and was an extremely likeable interviewee.

I grew up on a working-class estate. The estate was where all the bad apples went. There was a mixture of coloureds, Asians, all the ethnic minorities plus the white families. The council didn't really give two monkeys about them, get them in there quick and stop them moaning. I remember I was playing with my brother out on the street and twice a week or something there would be a burnt-out car at the end of the road and we'd always end up playing in that. All the kids on the estate would be running around just in nappies, and holes in their shoes. Other members of the family used to give my mum clothes and that for us. My mum didn't have much money to scrape together, she was always struggling. My old man was working on doors for nightclubs and pubs and just didn't give two monkeys about my mum and me and my brother; he didn't really care.

My mum and dad split up when I was three. My mum and dad didn't get on. I always resented the fact that my old man used to fill my head with, 'It's your mum's fault we split up', because I would always say, 'Why have you split up? Families are meant to be together, get your arse back here'. And he would say, 'It's your mum, she don't like me'. I always thought it was my mum, but as I got older my mum would say, 'No, it's your dad'.

Me and my dad have always had a funny relationship. I wouldn't call it a father–son relationship, more brother to brother. The amount of time I remember through my teenage years him taking me to different women's houses – it was meant to be my weekend with my dad and I'd end up sitting in some bird's house while he was giving her one. But when my mum got together with another bloke and we all ended up living in his house, I didn't like him because he weren't my dad. I got on so badly with him that I got whacked into care. He had these old LPs and I smashed them up because he told me off. He had a top-of-the-range stereo, I set fire to that just to get back at him. I hated the fact that he was trying to replace my dad. He was one of those guys, he was trying to be too nice, but in my eyes it just didn't seem right. He was always trying to fob me and my brother off with gifts and presents and I would say, 'If I want something I'll ask my dad'.

I went backwards and forwards from care to my mum, to 13. When I was 13, I met a bird from my school, I'd like to say it was my first love but I don't really know for sure because I can't really remember. One weekend she was going to stay at mine, at my old man's because I used to go there for the weekend. We got in an argument over some other girl, and I said, 'You best go', so she rang her older brother and said to him, 'Come and pick me up', so he did. I was going, 'Fuck off – see you later', me thinking at that stage that the next morning I'll ring her up and apologise, no more will be said, because the girl she was accusing me of doing something with I hadn't, so I knew I was in the right. She got in the car. An hour and a half later I got a phone call. It was her mum crying down the phone to me saying she's dead. On the way back from mine, some drunk driver pulled out in front of her brother – he had swerved to miss, and crashed into a barrier, the car caught fire. He managed to get out the car but couldn't save her. That was a shock to the system. I ended up going to her funeral, I was devastated.

By then I was already smoking weed and there was one lad in the kids' home, he was about 17 and he was into car crime, he was forever getting nicked at the kids' home. I was proper pissed off, it was two days after her funeral, and I was down. He came in and passed me a bottle of whisky. I had a few drinks with him and he said, 'Come on, we'll go out and rob some cars, I'll teach you to drive'. At that stage I was prepared to do anything because I was blaming myself for her death because I told her to fuck off. I ended up going out with him that night, robbed this car, he ended up crashing that one and then we robbed another one, got back to the kids' home about four in the morning, we had to climb back up the drainpipes. Then the police came round about ten in the morning and nicked him but I didn't get arrested. He got took to the police station because they knew straight away, he'd been seen, they knew it was him. They were saying to him, 'Who is the other guy with you?' He said, 'I don't know, there weren't no one with me', so they didn't know it was me. When he got put into prison I went to see him and he said, 'I never put you in, so do me a favour, look after my sister for me'. I didn't know what he meant, I thought he meant go around and see if she's all right. One day after school I went around to see her and she said, 'I've got no money, my brother told you to look after me'. I got back to the kids' home and there was this lad, he was always doing crime – I didn't know what, I just knew it was criminal. I said, 'I need to make money fast, how can I?' He said, 'I'm doing a factory later, come and do that with me'.

We ended up doing three factories one night and ended up with about £14,000 – this is before my fifteenth birthday. I had that much money, I didn't know what the fuck to do with it. Within the space of about six months we must have done about 40 or 50 merchant burglaries and we only got caught once, which was a shock, because I always thought the police force was a lot more use than that. Even though I was getting away with it, I thought I shouldn't be getting away with this. I had the biggest collection of trainers for a kid my age, at one stage I had about 70 pairs. I had that much money I was just chucking it away, I didn't know what to spend it on, so every time I walked into town I'd see a pair of trainers, I'd have the money on me I'd think, fuck it, I'll buy them. I remember going into town once and buying one pair of trainers and then a week later I went into town and they'd brought out a different colour. I thought, fuck it, I'll have them. If you have good trainers and good clothes, then people would look up to you. When you're wearing nice garms[1] and looking smart, the girls flock to you, the lads show you a different kind of respect. That makes you feel wanted, because when you're in a kids' home you think, 'no fucker cares about me; if they do, why am I in here?' With getting a name for yourself on the estate and people looking up to you, it makes you feel the more people that like you, the more wanted you feel.

It's like a mini-jail in those homes. It just fucks your life up. If it hadn't been for care I don't think I would have done half the shit I've done. Even though I was unruly I was never into crime. Our children's home was up by the estate and we used to call ourselves 'The Crew', and there are four of us in this jail now, that's not including me, and there is about another three or four that's in jails all over the place as well. The only one that I know of to this day that got into trouble once with us and he's managed to get out and stay clean, he's an estate agent now. The rest of us are all a menace to society. I'm not proud of the crime or anything I've done, or any of the things that hurt other people, hurt other members of my family. The way I see it, it was out of my control, because it was something that was confronted at me and I just made the wrong choice. I had two paths to take and I just took the wrong one every time, I just didn't learn from my mistakes.

David was a small, mixed-race prisoner from a deprived inner-city estate. He had a tough façade, and was highly cynical, but when he talked about his mother and grandmother, he lit up with warmth.

I was brought up on an estate in a city. It had a bad name. Even kids from other estates wouldn't go there. We didn't have much as kids, I remember that. But it's a tight-knit community. Everyone knows everyone and there used to be a youth club and everyone from the community used to go there.

My dad used to beat up my mum and he done loads of horrible things to her. Things I can't even remember. These are just things that my mum and my grandma told me, like she bought him a car and he sold it for a pint, would you believe? We went to Morecambe or somewhere one weekend. We've come back and he's totally stripped the house of everything, carpet, everything. He's never been there over the years.

My mum was a superstar. At the time when you want certain things, like the latest BMX, and she just couldn't afford it and you can't see that when you're a kid. Nine times out of ten she used to get me them things. When I look back now, I feel bad. She couldn't afford it. She used to do quite a lot with us kids, but she didn't work until later, she worked in a pub. My gran lived about five minutes from us, in the same area. I had my own bedroom there and practically every day I'd go round my gran's, and a lot of the time I'd stay round there as well. Later, when she was ill, she come to live with us.

One day my gran was babysitting and my dad kept coming round the house and banging on the door threatening to take me and one of my sisters. It scared my gran and she started to get a headache. He's drunk and he's doing circles in his car and he's got his other kids and his wife in the car as well. Gran got scared. I remember she started to complain of a headache. The headache got really bad. It turned out she was having a brain haemorrhage. My mum managed to get an ambulance and my gran went to the hospital. She was in hospital four or five months. One day she's woke up and she's turned around and she asked me who I was. She didn't even recognise me. My dad didn't give a shit about any of us. He's never been there for none of us. A couple of years after, me and my gran sat down and we spoke about it. And she says, 'Well, you know what triggered it? I was petrified that he was going to take you and your sister and I wouldn't see you again. But not only that, I was petrified for the kids in the car, when he's drinking vodka and he's driving round and he's banging on the door and all sorts.'

As I was growing up at the bottom of my street there's a junior school I went to, and next to that is the pub. Now and again when I used to go down, I'd see my dad. He seemed all right. He'd buy me a drink and stuff like that. Now and again I'd go up to see him. He used to cry his eyes out saying, 'I love you, I wish I was there for you'. But it was just false. It was just the gin talking. It was just false. He never done nothing for me. I remember once we were at my auntie's and my dad said, 'Go home, get ready and get changed, and we'll go somewhere'. Me and my sister have gone home and got changed, dressed and all the rest of it. We've gone back and that, and my cousin said, 'He's upstairs in bed asleep, pissed out of his head'. That's something that's stuck with me. There's another thing as well. I remember my brother and my cousin have gone to the shop and my dad's come walking up the road. He's seen my cousin and patted him on the head: 'How are you? Who's your little friend?' to my brother, his son. And my brother said, 'You're my dad'. He's a fucking arsehole. I hate him.

I found another father-figure in the estate. I wanted the respect he had. There ain't a man in the estate that commands more respect than him. A lot of it's fear as well. There are lot of things that I'd look at him and think, yeah, I want to be like him; like the money, the girls round them, nice clothes, them kind of things. A lot of older people in the community, like big criminals, they'd see me and they'd give me weed or they'd give me a fiver. This one man, we'd meet other people in the community, like big men, and he used to say to them, 'This is my boy, I'd do anything for him, I'd take stab wounds for him, I'd do anything for him. I love him to bits.' I remember one day we were sat there and he said, 'You know something, I love you to bits. You're my foster son.' And that always kind of stuck with me. I used to see him smoking crack, and about this time everyone around me was smoking crack. I never used to smoke it. I used to smoke weed. I couldn't smoke crack in front of him, he'd have killed me.

It was before that that I started to get into crime. I'd done the odd burglaries and breaking into cars and stuff like that, but when I was hanging around with older people I seen it's a different world, like, pimping, prostitution, crack, robberies, fraud, just everything. In the estate, the big people are either crack smokers, crack dealers, robbers, you know. There is some that work but I'd say the majority of them have got their hand in the drug case.

They respected me. A lot of them would say to me, 'You carry yourself like you're a big man, an adult'. They used to show me respect. They used to show me love. As bad as they were, evil criminals, pimps, whatever, they used to show me love. I didn't get that nowhere else really, apart from my mum.

I ended up in care because I had started to get into trouble, breaking into cars, burglaries, robberies as well. I had a best mate at school, he's serving life, as it goes. I used to stay out at night with him and go to different places, like flats and stuff like that. That's when I first started to smoke weed. Then we'd break into cars and that. I remember my mum used to come looking for me. It used to put the fear of God in me. She'd put me in the car and take me back home. I'd just climb out of the bathroom window and be off again. I just didn't want to be in the house sat watching TV, I wanted to be out there doing things. If I'd sat at home I'd be thinking, I'm missing something, I'm missing out on something, and I'd want to be out there. I just started breaking into cars. It was for lots of reasons but I did want the money so we could get the latest trainers and we wanted to smoke some weed.

Anyway I was getting arrested and what-not. My mum used to come looking for me and she'd take me back home in the car. She tried to do everything she could, bless her. One time I got arrested and through some friends in kids' homes, they're telling me stories like you can get clothing grants and stuff like that. So next time I got nicked I remember saying, 'I don't want to go back home. I want to go in a kids' home.' I didn't say anything bad like my mum's beating me, or anything. I just said, 'I don't want to go back home', and wanted to go in a kids' home. From there I went in kids' homes all over the fucking country. I went into loads of secure units. I was in and out of secure units, kids' homes and then prison.

After getting out, I started to use crack. I'd seen all them smoke it. From when I was 12, 13, everyone was smoking it. I used to be with a lot of these people smoking weed, and I said, 'Can I try that?' – tried it, and never stopped. The appeal, up until now, has been partly the buzz, and the scene, the environment. It's bad and it's horrible and it's violent. But I grew up around it. It's all I know. I just love the environment. But I hate the environment as well.

A typical day for me was sleep all day, get up about mid-afternoon, wash, change. We'd go out to work, just be driving round the ghetto, 'round the beat' we call it, robbing people, selling drugs, just wheeling and dealing kind of thing, smoking crack, going from house to house. Just moving round the beat, kind of thing. Committing crimes: robberies, cat burglaries, frauds, pimping, drug dealing. Every kind of crime there is. Committing crime and smoking crack like there's no tomorrow. The amount of money I've spent on that it's ridiculous. In a day I'd probably smoke between £500 and £600 a day, easy.

Commentary

The ways in which the public and politicians have understood prisoners' backgrounds and biographies have changed significantly in the last 60 years, reflecting broader social and political thinking. The two decades after the Second World War were shaped by the shared experiences of that long conflict and the increased social cohesion that it brought. As the post-war economic recovery took hold, most people enjoyed increasing prosperity and optimism. Against this background there was a relatively sympathetic view of prisoners, which put great store by their social situation and individual experiences. Many were seen as victims of circumstances, including poverty, social disruption and individual neglect, and the prison system was based on the idea – although not always the reality – that prisoners should be treated humanely and provided with the opportunity to rehabilitate themselves. From the late 1960s, there was an extended period of social and economic upheaval that lasted until the mid-1980s. In this era, faith in rehabilitation declined and the post-war consensus became weakened. A new orthodoxy took grip in the 1980s, characterised by a more individualistic and consumerist outlook. In social policy terms, the rise of this new way of thinking was encapsulated in Margaret Thatcher's well-known comment to *Woman's Own* magazine: 'There is no such thing as Society. There are individual men and women, and there are families.' In this environment, prisoners were no longer seen as the victims of circumstance. Instead, crime was increasingly seen as an act of personal choice and the responsibility of the individual offender. The role of prison was to protect society from these individuals by taking them off the streets and deterring them from committing further crimes. It was in this respect that Michael Howard claimed that 'prison works'. This was challenged by New Labour's pledge to be 'tough on crime, tough on the causes of crime', a shift in thinking that encapsulated their 'Third Way' philosophy. This approach attempted to mould together the two approaches, suggesting that governments should punish individuals for law-breaking, whilst also seeking to ameliorate poverty and social deprivation.

As this brief historical sketch has attempted to illustrate, the role of prisons has long been both to punish prisoners and to reform them – aims that are not easy to reconcile – but the balance between those goals varies significantly, in part according to wider discourses about society, morality and criminality.

Despite shifts in public rhetoric, criminology has attempted to present analyses of prisoners' backgrounds and histories that are more empirically driven, but also attuned to wider social forces, such as power and inequality. There are a number of factors that have emerged consistently from academic literature as being linked to criminality. The most prominent of these are biology, poverty, emotional strain and family dynamics.

The first of these, biology, has a rather undistinguished history in criminological thinking. This arises from concerns about the accuracy and reliability of biological theories of criminality, and also from the uses to which such modes of thinking have been put in oppressive states and their association with abuses such as eugenics and the persecution of religious and racial groups. Contemporary research in this area has developed in a way that is more sophisticated and sensitive than the writing of early criminologists such as Lombroso, who famously posited that some people were 'born criminal' and were physically different from those who were not. It has explored a number of factors that might be relevant to criminal behaviour, including pre-natal stress, alcohol or drug use, the effect of genetics, neurobiological factors relating to the development of the brain, and hormonal changes. In general, this research indicates that such determinants have a complex interplay with environmental factors and may predispose people to crime rather than being a direct cause on their own.[2] This context and the historical experience should be kept in mind when popular discourse veers towards such empirically and ethically dubious ideas such as identifying a 'crime gene'. While these issues are not directly discussed in the prisoner accounts above, there are certainly indications that factors such as parental abuse and alcoholism may be relevant to the experiences of Alan and David, whether through their social or biological impacts.

The link between poverty and crime is very well established. Prisoners are more likely than non-prisoners to come from socially deprived areas, and recent work mapping the council wards or postal codes where prisoners live shows that they disproportionately come from the poorest neighbourhoods. For example, Ray Houchin has shown that in Scotland a quarter of prisoners come from 50 of the 1,200 total council wards, and these wards are among the poorest.[3] These neighbourhoods and the people who live in them are not only more likely to end up in prison, they are more likely also to be the victims of crime and anti-social behaviour, and to be fearful about crime. This is most starkly illustrated in the work of Danny Dorling, whose analysis of homicide in England and Wales between 1981 and 2000 found that the poorer the neighbourhood one lived in, the more likely one was to be the victim of homicide.[4]

In recent years, one of the most cited official sources on offenders and their backgrounds has been a 2002 report by the Social Exclusion Unit, which highlighted the wide range of social disadvantage experienced by prisoners.[5] Compared to the general population, prisoners were (for example):

- thirteen times as likely to have been in care as a child;
- thirteen times as likely to have been unemployed immediately prior to imprisonment;
- ten times as likely to have been a regular truant from school;
- twenty times as likely to have been excluded from school;
- two and a half times as likely to have had a family member convicted of a criminal offence.

The report found that 80 per cent of prisoners had writing skills, 65 per cent numeracy skills and 50 per cent reading skills at or below the level of an 11-year-old child. Between 60 and 70 per cent of prisoners were using drugs before imprisonment, and over 70 per cent suffered from at least two mental disorders. The experience of imprisonment also exacerbated many forms of social exclusion, for example by disrupting housing, employment, financial security and family contact, and this could make rehabilitation more difficult.

In light of this, the experiences of Alan and David can be considered relatively typical. Both describe coming from deprived estates, with chronic unemployment and high levels of crime, as if in a state of permanent recession. For example, Alan notes that burnt-out cars were such a common feature of the landscape that they became a substitute playground. He also provides an almost Victorian imagery of children playing outside barely clothed or in threadbare shoes. What is significant is that Alan and David do not simply describe the experience of economic poverty – having little money or material goods – also they talk about social stigma and ghettoisation. For example, Alan says that his estate was 'where all the bad apples went', while David claims that his estate had a 'bad name', even among people from other estates, and was a no-go area that others would avoid. Their circumstances entail not only poverty but also social exclusion, where the ability to interact with other parts of society is inhibited or actively blocked.

The stories provided by Alan and David reveal the extent of exclusion in a way that bare figures never can. Their experience of exclusion is multi-faceted, so they both describe experiences of poor housing, disrupted schooling, entry into the care system, unemployment and exposure to drugs. Their stories indicate that these experiences are pervasive within their neighbourhoods: Alan explains that all but one of his close friends has ended up in prison; David says, 'In the estate the big people are either crack smokers, crack dealers, robbers, you know.' The accounts also illustrate the way that social exclusion is repeated across generations, with both of their fathers having patterns of disruptive, anti-social behaviour. Poverty, social exclusion, crime and imprisonment are deeply entrenched in the lived experience of people in deprived areas.

This raises questions about whether the structural disadvantages experienced by some people mean that they can be considered truly or solely responsible for their crimes. Many criminologists argue that crime and inequality are deeply intertwined. For some, criminal behaviour is a symptom of poverty and inequality, while some radical criminologists argue that the behaviours that are defined as 'criminal' and the way that crime is managed reflect a wider social system that legitimises and maintains inequality and controls the disadvantaged. However, it is interesting to note that although their backgrounds shape and in many ways limit their life chances, many prisoners accept that they are not powerless in controlling their lives. For example, Alan rejects the idea that he was unable to shape his own future: 'I had two paths to take and I just took the wrong one every time, I just didn't learn from my mistakes.' At this individual, psychological level, factors such as boredom, immaturity and low self-control may inform how choices are made. This is illustrated by the fact that both Alan and David were inducted into crime at an early age, when they found it difficult to resist peer pressure and the frisson of excitement provided by crime, in contrast to the lack of activities in their estates. Other psychological issues are more complex, such as the search for status or 'respect' from their peers and the desire for bonds of affection that are missing from their intimate family relationships. Both interviewees appear to find some sense of identity and belonging in their criminal behaviour, alerting us to the role of emotional and existential issues in offending. While there is a clear macro-level link between poverty and crime, the nature of this link and the role of individual agency mean that this relationship is more complex than is often suggested.

Emotional strain, in the form of trauma, is also related to crime, depending on the extent and frequency of traumatic events and the length of periods of stability.[6] The accounts of Alan and David reveal repeated traumatic events, including family breakdown, domestic violence, the sudden death of a girlfriend, the near death of a close relative and being taken into the care system. These events create forms of emotional vulnerability and personal instability that may then be expressed through criminal behaviour.

The role of families, and especially parents, has been widely discussed in relation to crime, particularly since increases in rates of divorce, single parenthood and female employment have altered the traditional family structure. The 1980s saw increasing criticism of 'permissive' and absentee parenting (as captured in the term 'latch-key kids'), often without consideration of the fact that economic circumstances give some people little choice about whether to work, or can make child supervision difficult. By the late 1990s, such concerns found expression within the criminal justice system in the form of parenting orders, which compelled parents to undertake training or to take action against the anti-social behaviour of their children, with the ultimate threat of imprisonment if they were unsuccessful. Absentee fathers are currently attracting significant political attention, with the possible approaches being mooted including reducing welfare payments as a punitive measure. Poor parenting is visible in both of the accounts provided here. In particular, David describes his alcoholic father's erratic and sometimes violent behaviour. These experiences can socialise children into accepting violence as a normal form of behaviour, or can diminish their capacity to exercise self-control. David and Alan also reveal more broadly how dysfunctional relationships with parents can leave children feeling emotionally neglected. Yet other parents act heroically in the face of poverty, deprivation and family breakdown. For example, David describes his mother as a 'superstar' and explains how she would care for him as a child, and try to prevent him committing crime by physically searching for him and taking him home. This is a picture of a caring and active parent facing extraordinary challenges. Despite these efforts, she was not able to stop him ending up in prison. In some circumstances, effective parenting might mean limiting, delaying or minimising offending rather than preventing it entirely.

In this respect, issues of personal and parental responsibility cannot be separated from considerations of state policies and practices. The accounts provided here raise questions about the effectiveness of housing, education, youth, employment and welfare policies. These can all either help or hinder parents in trying to cope with their role. Where the state steps in to take on parental responsibility, the care system comes into play; in the two accounts above the limitations of this are brought into particular relief. Both Alan and David not only describe negative responses to being placed in care homes, they also suggest that the care system introduced them to children who were committing more serious crimes than they were, thus providing a gateway to more serious offending. Their accounts raise questions about how effective such institutions are at addressing the complex social and psychological needs of the children they contain. Alan describes the care system as a 'mini-jail', suggesting a punitive institution, populated by those already involved in crime. David does not raise the issue so explicitly, but his account implies a continuum from children's homes to secure units to prison.

Finally, it is worth trying to explore the functions served by offending in the lives of offenders: the needs that offending meets and how this reflects upon society more generally. Both narratives illustrate the ways that crime provides material rewards that may be otherwise unavailable. Alan describes accruing thousands of pounds from commercial burglaries while still in his early teenage years. Both Alan and David explain that having money enabled them to acquire designer clothes, particularly trainers. These goods provided visible status and generated esteem both in their own eyes and in those of others. As

Alan says: 'If you have good trainers and good clothes, then people would look up to you ... the girls flock to you, the lads show you a different kind of respect'. The acquisition of particular consumer commodities confers status and standing beyond the monetary value of the goods: it conveys a sense of success and individual identity. Crime also meets a set of social needs through the relationships of loyalty, trust and affection that are built up within criminal fraternities. David's account provides a vivid example of this, outlining the way that he acquired a surrogate for his absent father in the form of an older man, who at the same time served as a kind of criminal mentor. Both Alan and David convey the general sense of belonging that they felt within their neighbourhood milieu, despite their ambivalent feelings about its temptations and conditions: 'I just love the environment. But I hate the environment as well.'

Many people consider prisoners and those involved in crime as abhorrent, anti-social, and holding values that are contrary to those of mainstream society. However, these accounts reveal that the opposite is often the case. For many prisoners, coming as they do from circumstances of poverty and social deprivation, crime provides a means through which they can pursue and realise conventional dreams of material success, the acquisition of status and emotionally enriching relationships. Crime allows people to achieve a degree of social inclusion that is otherwise unavailable to them, even if its form is fleeting and unstable. Rather than being a pure rejection of the conventional community, these accounts illustrate that crime is closely linked to the dominant values of society.

Notes

1 'Garms': garments, clothing.
2 See Savage, J. (ed.) (2009) *The Development of Persistent Criminality.* New York: Oxford University Press.
3 Houchin, R. (2005) *Social Exclusion and Imprisonment: A Report.* Glasgow: Caledonian University.
4 Dorling, D. (2005) 'Prime suspect: Murder in Britain', in P. Hillyard, C. Pantazis, S. Tombs, D. Gordon and D. Dorling (eds). *Criminal Obsessions: Why Harm Matters More than Crime.* London: Crime & Society Foundation.
5 Social Exclusion Unit (2002) *Reducing Reoffending by Ex-prisoners.* London: Social Exclusion Unit.
6 See Savage, *The Development of Persistent Criminality.*

Further reading

A recent and comprehensive overview of research on the development of criminal behaviour is contained in Joanne Savage's edited collection *The Development of Persistent Criminality* (New York: Oxford University Press, 2009). The Social Exclusion Unit's report, *Reducing Re-offending by Ex-prisoners* (London: Social Exclusion Unit, 2002) has been influential in shaping the response of prisons to social exclusion. Alternative approaches to addressing this issue, are provided in *Justice Reinvestment – A New Approach to Crime and Justice*, edited by Rob Allen and Vivian Stern (London: International Centre for Prison Studies, 2007).

Finally, Steve Hall, Simon Winlow and Craig Ancrum's *Criminal Identities and Consumer Culture: Crime, Exclusion and the New Culture of Narcissism* (Cullompton: Willan Publishing, 2009) contains some innovative ideas and spell-binding narratives based on a qualitative study of people living in a high-crime community in the north-east of England.

2 Custody, care and staff–prisoner relationships

Sarah Tait

Sharon, 20, had been in and out of custodial institutions since the age of 13. In the months leading up to her current sentence, she had started using heroin. A lively young woman who had gained enhanced status,[1] she admitted having been a difficult prisoner, saying: 'I was fighting, on a bully programme, I got caught brewing hooch,[2] I was just in loads of trouble. I just kept messing about, arguing with the staff, basically ignoring all the rules and regulations.'

Interviewer: Can you think of a time when you felt cared for by staff?

Yeah, when I was on my last sentence. I was having troubles with my dad. Because my dad was quite ill at the time, this is when I was really naughty. And, I was always in my room, and I was always kicking off[3] and going mad. And some of the staff, like Miss Long and Miss Winters, they used to come and sit in my room and like, talk to me. Miss Long would always ask me, like, what was wrong with me, ask me to talk to her about it, to get it all out of my system. She was always there for you, like, when you needed her. It's like, when you want to talk to your mum or something, and like, if your mum sees you are upset, she's always there to comfort you. And when I was upset, I'd cry my eyes out, and if I was angry, I'd sit and cuss, but she'd always sit there and carry on, she's always talking to you, because she wants to know if you're all right. I don't know why, but she did help me, but I didn't really take notice of it. Like, she's said to me she's really proud of me now, because of the way I've really changed my behaviour, and I'm not naughty now, and she's always praising me for my good behaviour now. Like, with me, I put my trust in people before I actually tell them my problems, and that was what it was like with Miss Long, I put my trust into her. Because she was always there for me. And she always stuck by her word. Like, if she said she was going to do something for you, she would have done it for you [*bangs table*]. She's a really good officer. I love Miss Lo – I'd do anything, anything for Miss Long now because, like, even though I didn't tell her all my problems, she still sat there, and talked to me, and she'd say it was all all right, and that. And if I was locked in my room,[4] she'd still come and talk to me and ask me how I'm feeling and that. And in my eyes, if someone's going to do that for you, and help you, it's give and take, really, I'll help them back as well. Because if they don't know what's up with you, they don't know what to do. So, I thought, some of the officers I didn't talk to about *anything*, but Miss Long and Miss Winters, I did, I told them how I was feeling and that, I told Miss Long all about my … about my dad, and his illness and stuff, and that's why she knew if I was upset, she knew *why* I was upset.

There's other officers like Mr Jackson, I could talk to him all day long, like, he's one of the sort of persons that you can just get on with, straight away, you know what I mean? He's always there for you. He just relates to us, I think he has, he's got a sense of humour as well. And that's what's good in most officers, if they got a sense of humour, then you can have a laugh with them. Mr Jackson, he can have a laugh, he can take things on the chin. Like I've got a mad sense of humour, and I can like, not cuss him nastily, but have a joke with him, and he can take it on his chin, whereas if I said it to one of the other staff that wasn't like Mr Jackson, I would have been nicked by it.[5] It's more fun that way, it makes you happy in yourself, you know what I'm saying, knowing that you're not always worried about what you can say, what not to say to someone, and what to say to someone.

With the staff here, on this wing, they'll come and check on you, they're out on the wing some of the time, just like mixing with us, keeping an eye on us, but they're *there*. I think it's because they've got more time over here. Like on D wing people are detoxing, so they need to see the doctor, or paperwork needs to be doing, but like you'll hardly see the officers on D wing. I saw a lot of girls upset on D wing going through their detox, they're ill, some people, it's their first time in prison, and it's new surroundings, they've been locked away. And you're locked in that one landing, you've got to shout to them. You've got to shout, 'Sir!' from the gate, and when you shout, they get aggravated themselves, because you're shouting, but we're only shouting because there's no one there. Whereas on this wing, you can just walk straight to the officers and say, 'Sir, can I talk to you, please?', or something.

Mark was a quiet, thoughtful man of 30, a father of two. His marriage was breaking down, and his wife was now living with his brother. His father had passed away recently, and also his sister, whom he described as the only person who understood him: their bond had been strengthened by growing up with an alcoholic and abusive mother. He was taking part in drug treatment for a heroin addiction, and had self-harmed several times while in custody.

Interviewer: Can you tell me about how staff responded after you had self-harmed?

They found me in my cell. They was understanding. I didn't get the impression from any members of staff that I was ... because you hear about how 'they've done it for attention' and it does belittle your feelings when you hear that, and I didn't get that impression from anybody at that time. I was taken out to outside hospital to get stitches. Yeah, if I remember rightly some of the staff were quite understanding, they were just general members of staff, you know, and perhaps not trained in those sort of things. There were no, 'Huh, what have you done this for?' Because it does happen. Because I actually self-harmed twice, and on the second occasion, how could I put it, it were more like I was being told off really, because it felt as though I were wasting their time. And one member of staff made a comment in particular that it made her look stupid, that she wasn't doing her job right, because I'm on the 2052 self-harm register, and she'd just made a comment on the file, and by me self-harming contradicted what comment she put.[6] But she hadn't spoke to me anyway so ... saying that, after that, her approach were different again. She was just letting off a bit of steam that time, she's okay with me now, like. I was taken aback by it.

I was approached by a member of staff who I used to previously work for, he was a kitchen officer, and he noticed that I was, like, possibly self-harming ... you know, from how he'd seen me before. And he approached me, and asked me if I was having any problems, and just by him doing that showed a lot of concern. Because why should he? Why did he need to ask me? He didn't really need to ask me. So he put himself forward, so that were noticing. So I opened up to him, and by me doing that it made the staff aware that I was having problems in here.

I think it was his approach really, and his mannerism, and the way he showed his concern, he was talking about me, and what was going on inside me, and asking, you know, why do I look so down, why am I not mixing with other people. It was as if he had pre-noticed me to that moment in time, it was like as if he'd been observing, you know, I picked up on that. Whereas I think a lot of staff are sort of quite ignorant to what's going on around them, you know, no disrespect, like. He was calm. Like I say, he were caring, you know, for somebody to be able to show a bit of care, it means a lot because it just doesn't happen that often, you know, for somebody in a uniform to come up to you, and to show you a bit of personal attention, and to realise that that person's been observing you, and has noticed and took time out to help you if he can do. And he did help me in various ways, arranging someone to see me from healthcare, putting me on the 2052, also speaking to the senior officer on the wing, liaising with probation, and, you know, he got the ball rolling in the areas which I needed, really.

Say you go for your medication, you're looked down upon because you're on medication for drug abuse. You get the odd comment from members of staff, 'Smackheads for treatment',[7] and things like that, you do hear it, it does go on, and like I say, if you are down with yourself, and you're not proud of your habit, it does tend to affect you, really. Especially because, then you stand back and you realise that the people who you are in care of, perhaps they're looking down on you, it does take you back a little bit. Because there has been times where I have needed to approach members of staff and because of the image that they give off, you just don't feel like you can approach them. There is a barrier there. Obviously there's a barrier there with the uniform, but you know, you can break that barrier if they are approachable. But some officers you think purposely give off that impression that they're not approachable because it makes their job easier.

Nancy was 36 years of age and a mother of two. This was her first time in prison. She was a resilient, expressive woman, proud of her creative talents and community work. She was struggling with memories of sexual abuse, and had experienced the loss of her grandmother, with whom she was extremely close, while in custody.

I didn't tell them. Because there is nobody in here I count as friends that you meet along the way. Prison is all about yourself. I can say to a girl, 'Oh, I've had a really bad day,' and I'll open my mouth to say what's wrong, and then she'll start telling me what's wrong with her! And prison officers … they're not trained for it. I can count four prison officers, and I've met quite a few, that you can actually sit down and have a real conversation with. Right? I'm talking with *compassion*. [You can tell] from the way their body language is towards you, because when you are talking to them, they will actually take that time out to *stop* what they're doing, they will tell you to sit down and even if they had to go, they will come back to you. And it's nice, because they've got so many things they're dealing with, but then they will go out of their way and then talk to you, if you ask them to get something done, it's done. Everything, the way they talk to you, they talk to you as though you're an adult, not a piece of shit, you know what I mean?

It's hard for me to put it in perspective because I'm not a person who does that 'I need to talk to you' thing. That's not me. But I know when someone is dealing with me with respect, because I'm open enough to understand it. I can give you *another* example, but it's an opposite way to the question, it's like, you've got officers that talk to you as though you're a little child and you're nothing. 'Get to your room!' 'Where are you going?!' 'Do this!' 'Go back there!' I mean when you're not behaving in a certain manner, you don't expect to get treated like that. But then compassionate officers don't do that, they will call you by your name, they'll stop and talk to you in a decent manner. I'm not a person to really come and try and cry on their shoulders ... I don't really, yeah, I can't do it, do you understand? But I mean I spoke to Miss Thompson about, you know, my nan died and that, and I spoke to her about my HDC,[8] and just look at it this way, she went *over* and out of her way for me to find out if my papers were back, yeah? And that is when you *know*.

On the day when my nan died, I phoned home, my mum told me the news of my nan, and this shriek came out, from anywhere, and an officer was actually there when it happened. She saw when I collapsed outside the phone box. She saw when my friend had to carry me up to my room, but she still didn't sort out my compassionate phone call. How compassionate is that? There was another officer in here at the time, and he shut the door, said to me, 'Oh, we'll have to get it sorted for tomorrow'. And I thought, you know what, I don't even want a compassionate phone call from you, because now my head is starting to swell, because I'm thinking, you're making me feel as though I *need* you and I'm a person like this: I don't need you, I will survive this until I get out, or I will wait until later when I've got money on my PIN[9] and I will phone who I need to phone, right? But they make you feel as though you're bothering them. Prison is degrading.

I was dealing with a lot of anger that night, very angry towards officers, and just a lot of bitterness really, because I felt alone. And really alone, because it was, that is when I felt, I felt stripped of everything. Being in the countryside. Don't even know where I am! Away from all my family. And then, no help. I felt useless. Yeah, I felt really useless, I felt like, and these people wouldn't do nothing. And what makes it worse, and I don't blame the prison for this, but I still had to get up and do a piss test.[10] Still had to keep it moving, get up in the morning at eight o'clock, keep it going. These things happen to you, but the officers just treat you like normal. I don't know, it sounds funny because you're still in prison. So maybe it's my fault for being in prison, why you get treated like this.

Commentary

The aims of imprisonment are often conceptualised as balancing custody and care. The 'custody' part of this equation receives a great deal of attention in research, prison policy, official investigations into security breaches, prison officer training, prison design and the daily routines that structure prison life. Less is known about how 'care' is understood by those living and working in prisons.

Research has identified that there are common pains of imprisonment, and that imprisonment has negative effects on prisoners during and after their incarceration. These effects are intensified by particularly harsh treatment and conditions, and affect vulnerable people most deeply.[11] Some may argue that prison should be a painful place: after all, its primary purpose is to punish offenders for wrongdoing. However, there is also the view that the punishment of imprisonment lies in the deprivation of liberty alone, and that the state has a responsibility to prevent other, foreseeable harms of imprisonment, such as disconnection from families and communities, loss of employment, and deterioration of mental and physical health. This is particularly important when we consider the demographics of those imprisoned today: the majority of prisoners have substance abuse problems, histories of poor mental health, and come from deprived socio-economic backgrounds (see Chapter 1).[12] Protecting the personal and social resources of prisoners during their incarceration, and encouraging their desire to integrate into society when released, may be critical to reducing recidivism – a primary aim of HM Prison Service and other correctional systems.

Prison officers have a significant role to play in mediating the pains and harms of imprisonment in their relationships with prisoners.[13] This role has not always been recognised, especially in early research on staff–prisoner relationships, which tended to focus on the cultural censures on staff–prisoner contact that promoted loyalty within each group. Sykes conceived of opportunities or desire to care largely as a hazard of the job and a corruption of officers' authority.[14] Many studies in the UK and the US over the last 30 years have expressed scepticism that meaningful, supportive relationships can develop when officers hold ultimate authority over prisoners. However, others suggest that the conflict between 'custody' and 'care' is now slightly less troublesome than in the past.[15] Ethnographic researchers of modern prisons have noted reduced social distance between staff and prisoners, and acknowledge that staff and prisoners share common interests in keeping the peace.[16] Spending sustained periods of time together engenders familiarity and means that officers witness prisoners' daily struggles and major life events. As the key providers and withholders of practical and emotional support, officers have the power to distribute recognition, civility and affirmation,[17] and to help prevent suicide and self-harm among prisoners.[18]

Certainly, providing and receiving care within a relationship that is characterised by such an imbalance of power presents particular challenges. Prison life constrains emotional expression, engenders powerlessness and dehumanises its inhabitants. The accounts above show that hostile and aggressive behaviour towards prisoners is prevalent, and indeed supported by the very structure of an institution that signifies offenders as outcasts of civil society. A few prisoners in my study were unwilling to accept help from officers (and perhaps unwilling to report it if they had) lest they gave officers additional power over them. However, nearly all interviewees described caring as part of the fabric of their relationships with staff. Some described care as an isolated experience, set against ongoing games and power plays, hostility and antagonism with officers.

Still others found it hard to pick just one caring interaction to describe: for them, caring was unexceptional. Against the backdrop of dehumanising treatment, care took on a significance that some prisoners acknowledged they would take for granted on the outside.

In general, care responds to need, or pain, producing subjective improvement in the well-being of the person who is cared for.[19] Prisoners identified several common needs that were mitigated, or intensified, by the actions of an officer. The first was uncertainty and lack of control over their living conditions, their future (like Nancy's difficulty in securing her HDC), their health (such as receiving help for drug withdrawal), and their family (as Sharon describes with respect to her father's illness). The second type of need was related to feelings of isolation. Following the officer's indifference to her grandmother's death, Nancy describes feeling more alone than ever. In addition to loneliness, some prisoners felt that they were losing their sense of self in the absence of relationships with other people. Third, officers could moderate the feelings of worthlessness that life in prison engendered. Prisoners' lower status was reinforced everywhere by rules, gates, security practices such as cell searches and mandatory drug testing, and behaviour reports. Coming into prison, particularly for first-time prisoners, was characterised as disorientating and shaming, intensified by strip-searching, the removal of possessions, and the allocation of prison-issue clothing. It also signified failure – to stay off drugs, to stay out of trouble, to support their family – and a stripping back of identity. Mark's and Nancy's narratives both convey a resigned sense that they might 'deserve' poor treatment or indifference because they are in prison.

There was striking similarity in the structure of prisoners' narratives of care and uncare, regardless of gender, age and institutional history. The experience of care by prison officers was characterised by three distinct components: relating across staff-prisoner boundaries, finding a pathway to care, and disclosure/response.

Caring officers treated prisoners as if they were of equal moral worth. They spoke to prisoners with respect, and empathised with prisoners' situations. Prisoners experienced caring officers as 'on a level' with them (despite large social gaps that existed, in terms of age or background). The sociability of caring officers was important. To prisoners, 'mixing in', 'having a laugh', and interacting with prisoners in a familiar and easy manner demonstrated that an officer viewed prisoners as of equal worth as human beings. Caring officers came out of staff spaces and entered prisoner spaces, playing pool and hanging out in association rooms. Sharon's account illustrates the meaning of sociability and availability, which was perhaps particularly important to younger prisoners. Prisoners could identify by their body language officers who were uncomfortable among them, perceiving this to be indicative of a sense of superiority. They described uncaring officers as flaunting or emphasising their power and status, and creating barriers to interaction: they were 'stiff' and 'aggressive'; they stood with their arms crossed, and slammed cell door flaps shut. They shouted often, and responded to prisoners in curt and sometimes hostile ways that discouraged further interaction. They showed a lack of respect by talking about prisoners within earshot of others, by mocking them, or referring to prisoners as 'junkies' or 'nonces'.[20] Their words and demeanour served as a continual reminder of a prisoner's status as *prisoner*. By contrast, caring officers were described as confident and unruffled in their interactions with prisoners. Jokes, banter, and conversation about football or last night's television were social levellers and brought some lightness to the day. Using prisoners' nicknames or first names were important signifiers of officers' recognition of their humanity.

Prisoners observed that caring officers demonstrated the same professional approach and sociability all the time and with everybody, and their consistency gave prisoners faith that their manner was genuine and a reflection of their true nature. By contrast, uncaring officers were described as 'two-faced'. Being subject to discipline was not incompatible with receiving care, depending on the manner in which it was administered. Officers who enforced the rules suddenly, without explanation, with hostility, uniformly, or without flexibility, were experienced as unfair and uncaring: prisoners felt that they were being treated as one of a number, without regard for their individual needs or circumstances.

Beyond an appreciation for their professional demeanour, prisoners described a spontaneous recognition of commonality with some officers, as Sharon describes in her relationship with Mr Jackson. This ranged from 'just getting on with them', 'feeling comfortable' with them, liking them, and sharing a sense of humour, to deeper connections ('he gets me') and even friendship. Some found this connection with staff who had ties to their home communities, or whom they had known over many years of imprisonment. They also built relationships with officers they knew from prison workplaces, healthcare, or even segregation units. On these smaller units, prisoners had had the opportunity to spend time with officers and in a different role – as a worker, as a sick person, as 'disruptive' – which brought their individuality to the fore. Prisoners who took on roles of responsibility within the prison, such as cleaners and Listeners,[21] also had the opportunity to get to know officers on a more equal footing.

Respectful, sociable relationships based on a recognition of shared humanity and a prisoner's individuality were experienced as caring in themselves and alleviated (to some degree) the threats to personhood which inhered in the prison as a punishing institution. Sharon calls this 'feeling happy in herself'. However, problems could require the specific intervention of an officer. Prisoners in distress described considerable apprehension about exposing their vulnerability in approaching an officer for help. Thus, they identified officers they could trust through careful observation and trial and error. They actively avoided officers they had witnessed or experienced ignoring requests for help, who routinely told prisoners to 'go away' or to 'fuck off', or who publicly humiliated those in need. Prisoners were conscious not to overload any particular staff member if possible, knowing that reliable officers could become burned out.

Thus it was more common for prisoners to disclose their distress to an officer who approached them. A meaningful approach by an officer signified that the prisoner and his or her distress had been noticed and conveyed genuine interest in the prisoner's well-being. Being noticed meant that an officer had recognised a change in behaviour or mood and was drawing on their knowledge of the prisoner as a person, as Mark describes. Caring officers made time to come and talk to the prisoner, pulling them to one side, or coming into their cell to offer the prisoner some privacy and sense of control in the interaction. They were, in effect, bracketing the forthcoming interaction, signalling a departure from typical officer–prisoner modes of social exchange, permitting the disclosure of distress.

Disclosure elicited two distinct but related forms of response: taking action and being present. Caring officers used their power to improve prisoners' situations, from ensuring standard entitlements, such as clean clothes, to providing information on issues of pay, visits, and home leave. Beyond these basic provisions, prisoners spoke of actions that officers had taken to give them a little extra comfort, security, or emotional space, which were tailored to the individual and surpassed prisoner expectations, such as using the office phone for an emergency phone call, lending a book, or delaying a feared move to another prison. Seemingly small actions, like making a cup of tea for a prisoner who had just lost his father, held great meaning. Whether these tasks fell within or outside the official remit of their job, these officers were viewed as 'going out of their way' for prisoners. They were observed to respond always and immediately, whether they took action straight away, or stopped, listened, made a note, and followed it up later. Their consistency and timeliness created trust in their response. Over time, prisoners became more likely to approach these officers, giving prisoners a sense of safety, predictability, order and control over their environment, and going some way towards alleviating the powerlessness and frustration of prison life.

In addition to taking action, caring officers were present with prisoners in both the physical and affective sense of the term. They sat down with people, which was highly significant on wings where officers were busy and responsible for observing large groups. Caring officers were experienced as always 'there for you' as well as fully 'there' during a particular interaction. They stayed present through the expression of overwhelming emotion, as Sharon describes in her account. They 'really listened' and were non-judgemental. These officers did not try to 'fix' the problem and prescribe a course of action; rather, they empathised with the prisoner's feelings, asking questions to further their understanding. Caring officers explained things if needed, and they reassured prisoners about the future and provided encouragement. Prisoners felt that they had been heard, that someone was on their side, that they were not alone in their problems and feelings, and that there was some hope for the future.

By contrast, prisoners felt that uncaring officers expressed little empathy or compassion for their distress. Drug users were particularly susceptible to this form of indifference; distress over broken relationships, physical aches and chills, and emotional flooding following withdrawal were dismissed as their 'own fault'. As Mark describes, several who had self-harmed had been told that they had done it for attention and sympathy, and were blamed for inflicting pain upon themselves. Uncaring officers took disruptive behaviours at face value, which could escalate conflict, while those identified as caring investigated and addressed underlying causes of distress, often quickly diffusing volatile situations with an expression of concern.

Consistently helping prisoners with practical things built trust and prompted disclosure of more personal problems. Sharon's trust in Miss Long was predicated on her consistent responsiveness to requests for practical help. Equally, due to the heavy institutional dependence of prisoners on officers, beyond empathy, prisoners nearly always required some practical intervention. Listening without taking action could undermine faith in the extent of an officer's understanding and commitment to help. Caring officers provided the right balance of presence and action that was directed by individual prisoners' needs. In summary, care incorporated values, practices and attitudes. The values of respect, interest, and responsiveness to the person were communicated through the practices of civility, sociability, bracketing, and offering practical help. Underscored by all prisoners was the assertion that caring officers expressed a more intangible, yet detectable, 'caring attitude'. This attitude was experienced as genuine desire to help and to understand the prisoner's world-view. For prisoners, 'uncare' meant being treated with indifference, being treated as of lower status and moral worth, and being treated unfairly. Caring interactions could not ameliorate all problems and distress experienced by prisoners, but could mitigate feelings of powerlessness, isolation and worthlessness engendered by the prison environment. Care created security, or basic trust in the environment, laying the foundation for improved mood and well-being. Those who had attempted suicide or who had suicidal thoughts saw caring officers as a lifeline: 'that there is something worth carrying on for'. Prisoners who felt cared for expressed a desire to cooperate with staff in order to give something back. A few prisoners who experienced care from officers as well as wider institutional support for health and mental health needs, housing and employment, described renewed hope for their future upon release. By contrast, uncaring interactions intensified feelings of powerlessness and isolation and prompted low mood, hostility and depressive rumination. They could precipitate violence towards staff, and fuel hopelessness.

There were some important variations in the experience and effects of care from staff. Prisoners' degree of distress affected their care-seeking behaviour, their perceptions of officers' caring behaviour, and the impact of being cared for.[22] Highly distressed prisoners, like Mark, reported a greater need for care and required more evidence of officers' personal commitment to them before perceiving them as caring. Care could temporarily lift their mood, but longer-term effects were rarely evident. Further, highly distressed prisoners found it more difficult to approach an officer for help. It was not until an officer observed his self-harm that Mark received intervention. His account of being called a 'smackhead' is illustrative of how uncaring behaviour could compound this group's existing feelings of low self-worth. Highly distressed prisoners were receiving care from a limited number of officers (or specialist care workers) with whom they had built up trust. They found it difficult to generalise care from one officer to officers as a group, but were likely to generalise uncare from one officer to officers as a group. The pervasive hopelessness of these prisoners was frustrating to staff, who felt powerless to help them. These exchanges could become hostile and threatening, as distressed prisoners perceived their efforts to elicit care to be thwarted, and were highly attuned to signs of disrespect and unfairness. Later in his interview, Mark recounted how he had assaulted an officer who had shouted at him while on the phone to his family.

By contrast, 'coping' prisoners, like Sharon, were more likely to develop good relationships with officers. They benefited more deeply from these relationships, integrating reassurance and affirmation from officers into their self-concept. Sharon took on board the positive regard and encouragement offered by staff, and credited much of her personal change to their efforts. Coping prisoners were also willing to continue to approach officers for help, even after being 'fobbed off'. As Nancy describes, those with more resilience were defiant in the face of officer indifference, and chose to ignore these officers in the future.

Some gender differences were noted in the emphasis on different aspects of care. Men focused on officers' sociability, and their willingness to bridge the institutional power imbalance. Affective presence was the most commonly mentioned feature of care for women, which included references to being really listened to and disclosing personal histories. As Sharon describes, notions of patience featured strongly throughout, with several women noting that caring officers 'didn't make you feel like you had to rush', or 'will sit and talk to you for *time*'. Further, in a wider survey of prisoners in both jails, women were more likely than men to agree that they felt cared for.

Gender norms may form part of the explanation for these differences.[23] Women may have been better at, or more comfortable with, describing the content of a caring interaction and thus revealing their vulnerability in the interview setting, as Sharon does in her account. Men tended to summarise an officer's response as 'listening' and move on. Mark does not dwell on what he shared with the officer who approached him. Men did describe the benefit of processing their emotions within the context of a caring interaction, in particular with non-discipline staff like psychiatric personnel and counsellors, rather than with officers. Nearly all the men interviewed stressed that they trusted no one in their lives, while most women reported being able to trust family members and close friends. Men were used to relying on themselves to solve their problems and saw emotional interdependence as a personal failing (many cited their partner as their 'biggest weakness'). Women may be more likely to reveal their vulnerability to others, to be more emotionally expressive, and to prioritise relationships and thus more likely to initiate, accept and engage in caring interactions (and to discuss these with an interviewer). Further, given women's systemic lack of social power in relation to men, women may be less likely to contest feelings of powerlessness in relation to officers. Of course, there was variation among women: several women with long institutional histories scorned other women's expression of distress, arguing that it made prison life harder for others. Like Nancy, some women were highly sensitive to signs of disrespect in their interactions with officers, as many men were.

Gendered differences in the accounts of caring interactions could also reflect differences in need. The proportion of highly distressed prisoners at the women's prison was nearly double that of the men's. Although distress levels were high in both prisons, women were more likely to have thoughts of suicide, feel depressed, feel unable to handle their emotions, experience major feelings of distress, have problems sleeping and feel unable to relax. Although the proportion of prisoners in each prison with drug problems was about the same, the level of psychiatric vulnerability among women was particularly great, and prolific self-harm was the most pressing issue facing staff and managers at the women's prison (see Chapter 9). Women reported greater feelings of worthlessness, and appreciated when officers provided reassurance, positive affirmation and encouragement.

Caring for women was validated by institutional values (a sign in the reception area stated, 'We care for prisoners'). Many officers explicitly stated that care was a priority for women because of their histories of abuse, high levels of mental illness, and the pain of being separated from children. Most (though not all) officers saw women in prison as 'victims' rather than 'offenders', and thus more deserving and in need of care. However, a minority of staff felt powerless in the face of extreme vulnerability, and described self-harming as a form of manipulation. This justified punitive responses, such as withholding support.

At both prisons, the composition of staff on each wing determined 'how caring' it felt to prisoners. A minority of staff at each prison were highly confident in their caring role, and a larger group offered support as part of their professional duty. Others, however, felt that caring was in direct conflict with their security and control duties, and their form of care was experienced by prisoners as yet more control (for example, saying 'no' was 'for their own good'). Wings with high numbers of these controlling and authoritarian officers were difficult not only for prisoners but for other officers who wanted to integrate their caring responsibilities with other demands of the job. Caring officers could burn out from being isolated in this way, and often sought assignment to smaller, specialised units where they received peer and institutional support for care work.

Other structural differences between the two prisons shaped the availability and form of care. At the women's prison, informal conversations between officers and prisoners were more common due to smaller wings and more time out of cell. Women reported forming close relationships with other prisoners, and may have felt less need for sociable contact with officers. As a larger establishment, with men either at work or education or locked in their cells, social exchange with officers at the men's prison may have taken on more meaning. Expressions of vulnerability were more likely to occur at the edges of the prison, such as in the education department and drug treatment programmes. At both sites, wing size and function were important: large wings and detoxification units were too busy to allow most officers time to engage with prisoners, as Sharon describes (although exceptional officers were noted).

While care from prison officers played an important, though varied, role in the experience of imprisonment for the men and women interviewed, attention to this aspect of staff–prisoner relationships has generally been limited to efforts to reduce self-harm and suicide. Emphasis in officer training is placed on security and procedure, and the focus on reducing recidivism through programming undervalues the daily interactions that can protect and build prisoners' personal resources, improve cooperation between prisoners and staff, and offer hope for the future. Care is a vital part of staff–prisoner relationships that can mediate the pains of imprisonment for an increasingly vulnerable prison population.

Notes

1 The Incentives and Earned Privileges scheme assigns prisoners to three regime levels: enhanced, standard and basic, based on recorded behaviour, which specify entitlements with regard to time out of cell, visits, property, etc.
2 'Hooch': alcohol.
3 'Kicking off': shouting, fighting, or destroying property.
4 Due to being denied association.
5 'Nicked': given a disciplinary warning or punishment.
6 The F2052SH risk of self-harm policy required officers to record their observations of prisoners who self-harmed. It has since been replaced with the ACCT (Assessment, Care in Custody and Teamwork) care-planning system.
7 'Smackhead': heroin addict or user.
8 'HDC': Home Detention Curfew. This scheme allows prisoners to be released with an electronic tag to serve the remainder of their sentence in the community.
9 'PIN': Personal Information Number, used to keep track of phone credit and to provide phone access to approved phone numbers.
10 'Piss test': a urine test for drug use, a requirement for those living on 'drug-free' wings.
11 For a review, see Liebling, A. and Maruna, S. (2004) *The Effects of Imprisonment.* Cullompton: Willan Publishing.
12 Prison Reform Trust (June 2008) *Bromley Briefings: Prison Factfile.* Online at: http:// www.prisonreformtrust.org.uk/temp/FactfilespPROOFspJUNE08small.pdf.
13 This chapter is based on interviews with 20 women and 21 men in two contrasting local jails, holding prisoners on remand and with short sentences. The focus of the interviews was to elicit a description of a time when prisoners felt an officer had been caring towards them, and when they felt an officer had been uncaring.
14 Sykes, G. M. (1956) 'The corruption of authority and rehabilitation', *Social Forces,* 34(3): 257–62.
15 Liebling, A., Price, D. and Shefer, G. (2011) *The Prison Officer,* 2nd edn. Cullompton: Willan Publishing.
16 Sparks, R., Bottoms, A. E. and Hay, W. (1996) *Prisons and the Problem of Order.* Oxford: Clarendon Press; Crawley, E. (2004) *Doing Prison Work: The Public and Private Lives of Prison Officers.* Cullompton: Willan Publishing.
17 Liebling, A. (2004) *Prisons and their Moral Performance: A Study of Values, Quality and Prison Life.* Oxford: Clarendon Press, p. 252.
18 Harvey, J. (2007) *Young Men in Prison.* Cullompton: Willan Publishing.
19 Mayeroff, M. (1990 [1971]) *On Caring.* New York: Harper Perennial; Held, V. (2006) *The Ethics of Care: Personal, Political, and Global.* Oxford: Oxford University Press.
20 'Nonces': derogatory term for sex offenders.
21 'Listeners': prisoners trained by the Samaritans to offer peer support.
22 Each interviewee completed the General Health Questionnaire, a well-validated short screening tool for anxiety and depression. From the spread of scores, I identified a 'high distress' group and a 'low/moderate distress', or 'coping', group. Note that as

distress levels for prisoners are generally higher than in the community, those who were classified as 'coping' here were experiencing 'threshold' levels of distress for intervention when compared to community samples.

23 See Gilligan, C. (1982) *In a Different Voice: Psychological Theory and Women's Development*. London: Harvard University Press.

Further reading

For more on staff-prisoner relationships, see Alison Liebling (2004) *Prisons and their Moral Performance* (Oxford: Clarendon Press, 2004). Further reading on the role of prison staff in supporting prisoners' well-being in prison includes Joel Harvey's book, *Young Men in Prison* (Cullompton: Willan Publishing, 2007), and Greg Dear's edited collection, *Preventing Suicide and Other Self-harm in Prison* (London: Macmillan, 2006).

3 Prison culture and the prisoner society

Ben Crewe

Stephen was an intelligent, softly spoken prisoner, serving a long sentence on the prison's wing for life-sentence prisoners and 'long-termers'. He described his upbringing as 'pretty good', and said that he had done well at school until he 'went off the rails a bit' as a teenager: 'I made one mistake, basically, and got arrested. Then it's been downhill from there.' He had quite an 'old-school' view of staff, based on his experiences in prison in the 1980s, and he was torn between trying to comply with the regime and seeking to subvert it. He was extremely polite and interested in my research and he was one of the most candid and articulate men I interviewed.

> People do their sentences in different ways. I can't knock the people who do their sentences in the block,[1] people who kick off. But it's just not the way I want to do my time. I don't want to spend a day in jail longer than necessary. I try and avoid doing anything that's going to keep me in. I don't want to give them or the system the excuse to keep me in longer. That's the reason I don't misbehave. Because I see that as a loss, a defeat, to do an hour longer. I'm always polite. The first thing they put down about me is polite and compliant. Two important words. Because I've learnt in the last few years that a weapon that staff can use against you is that they'll smile and talk, call you by your first name and things, and then they'll go in the office and kill you off on your file – write something bad about you. I even think about who I walk round on exercise with, and what I have on the walls of my cell, things like that. In the old days, they could fuck you up with their fists. Now they can fuck you up with their pen. The power of the pen is really mighty in prison nowadays. Psychologists have taken over prisons in the last ten years. They write the reports on you. If a psychologist says you've addressed your offending behaviour, then that gets you out. If a psychologist says the opposite, that keeps you in.
>
> I don't have a lot of contact with staff. On my wing, they try to be quite approachable. [But] I just can't relate to them. I'd never be the one who goes to them and says, 'What did you do at the weekend?' When I

was young, if an inmate was seen talking to staff, very often they'd be in trouble from the other inmates. Now, you see them playing pool and table tennis together, and all that. People would get a slap for doing that years ago. You can often have little victories over officers, without them even realising, in conversations. Like little head games, you know. One [officer] is a Liverpool fan, and I used to take the piss terribly and he never used to realise I was doing that to him: 'Oh, did you used to wear a scarf to the match?' And he doesn't even realise that we're taking the piss. That's the best way to do it. Because if you let them know that you're taking the piss, then they can always win. They can always win because we're in prison.

On my wing, it runs itself. They don't need to control anything. Because we all want a quiet life. We all want to get out. So everyone behaves themselves because of that. It keeps you under control: getting into getting out. Most of the time, people have got it in their head, 'I'm going home in a few weeks, I'm not interested.' I've heard people say that, when this noisy guy moved on [the wing], people said, 'Look, I'll just put up with it. I'll put my headphones on. I'll turn my telly up louder. I don't want to get involved.' Whereas ten years ago, when they were first sentenced, they'd have been in there smashing the guy up. That's the difference.

A lot more than ever, [my loyalties are] to myself and to my kids. People are quick to jump up and say, 'Let's do this, let's do that', but a lot of those guys are doing short sentences. The ones who seem to be the vocal ones, who cause trouble, are the ones doing mid-range sentences, five–six years. The ones doing bigger sentences seem to be more controlled. They'll go to a certain point, speak up to a certain level, and then walk away, cos, y'know, we've got too much to lose.

I think people in any environment are drawn into little groups, aren't they? And in prison it's just the same. In some prisons, it's done out of necessity, fear of violence. Personally I try and spread myself around quite a bit. I sort of say hello to a lot of people. But there are perhaps four or five people, one or two in particular, that I would call mates. A lot of the Asian guys, Muslim guys, I've noticed, their time revolves around their religion. It's part of how they do their time. They pray a lot, they spend a lot of time talking about their religion and following that lifestyle. The black guys seem to sort of spread around a bit, but the Muslim community, religion is the main thing that gets them through their sentence. That's their way of dealing with it.

Drugs do play a big part in it. You can have a senior, heavy, armed-robber type character who'll be hanging around with a house burglar simply because they both take smack. Whereas in the old days you wouldn't get that. People were drawn to each other because of what they were in for. Now, to an extent it's still to do with what you're in for, but the drugs have had a big influence on that. There's tension between the smackheads and everybody [else]. Because nobody trusts them. If something goes missing, people know that they're the ones. They're usually in debt.

The [drug] dealers attract a lot of people – there's this expression, 'powder power'. They kind of get an attitude when they've got their drugs, they kind of become something different to the day before when they didn't have their stuff to sell. People try to be friends with you when you're a drug dealer, but they're not being friends with you, they're being friends with your *drugs*, it's not genuine. I've had a weakness for substance abuse: drink and whatever else. In my last prison, I was under a lot of pressure. I just started using [heroin] as an escape thing. And it quickly took hold, you know. It takes away all your worries. It takes you out of the prison system. It's the best prison drug. It could have been invented for prison.

One thing that's come into prison in the last 10, 15 years, that I've noticed, and that's politeness. People are polite to each other. People get offended if people aren't polite. That didn't used to be the case. You had to put on an aggressive image. People used to walk down the landing and deliberately knock people out of the way. Now people are 'Excuse me, sorry' – politeness has come into prison. If you've got a senior, heavy millionaire drug dealer on the wing, he will be polite and have polite conversation with a house burglar, whereas outside, he wouldn't be seen dead talking to that person. But those people are still looked at as the senior people on the wing. Money has a lot to do with it. If you've got money, and you carry yourself in that way that [shows] you're a sensible person, then people will respect you no matter what your racial background or whatever. You gain respect from people. To a certain extent, physical presence [matters]. You know, how someone looks, how violent they might appear to be. Intelligence has a lot to do with it as well. If you're clever, it doesn't matter how much money you've got, people will still want to know your opinion.

I don't know about leaders, but there are people who people would always want to say hello to. Not because they're the hardest person on the wing, or the richest. But just because some people have got something about them, haven't they? People are kind of drawn to them, even in this sort of society. In more violent prisons, obviously the more violent person rises to the top, whether they're likeable or not. If someone can bash you, you have to give them – even if it's fake – a bit of respect, y'know. But in these more mellow places like our wing, you respect people for different reasons.

Politeness, sometimes it's taken for weakness. Sometimes you have to kind of toughen up your conversation. I enjoy talking about politics and the world and all that, but you couldn't go in certain people's cells and sit down and talk about that. You have to be adaptable. Prison's taught me how to be adaptable. You've got to live around the same people for a number of years, possibly, so you can't just blank someone because they're black or Asian or because they support Arsenal and you support Chelsea. You have to adapt.

The golden rules would be: never go and argue against an inmate with an officer. Even if you agree that the member of staff's right, never actually say it. Not grassing, on your mates or on anybody. Stealing from other inmates. That used to be a big, big one. But now, because of all the smack,[2] that's what's changed things a lot in prison – drugs. Most people would never steal off each other or grass each other up, but now that's just commonplace, grassing and cooperating with staff. In here, the ultimate penalty for breaking most of them rules is a violent outcome. Outside [prison], if I borrow ten quid off a debt company, the worst they can do is take me to court. In here, things get sorted out more with violence than they would outside. Outside I would imagine violence takes a while to come [i.e.] in a dispute with your neighbour outside. In here, you have to always have it in mind that … if you tread on someone's foot in a paper shop outside, they're not likely to come up to your room later and beat the shit out of you, whereas here it can happen that way.

Ewan was a career criminal in his twenties serving a short sentence for theft. He was relatively unusual, in that drugs played little role in his life outside prison and were not related to his crime. He hated prison – 'it ain't no life' – but considered it an 'occupational hazard', and although he had 'tried to change along the way' he made no claims that he was likely to go straight upon release: 'It's hard to say for definite that I'll keep out of it.'

You've always got to stand up for your friends in here. If one of them gets into trouble, then I'd get involved as well. Any trouble against them is trouble with me as well. I wouldn't stand and watch them get into a fight, and just stand by and watch. Same goes for them. If anyone tries anything with me, they'll stand by me. That's what friends are for. You stick with that set of people. But there's only a certain amount of people that you can really class as mates here. There's a lot of people I like on the wing, but I wouldn't class them as friends. You've got associates that you get on with, but then you've got your true friends. On the wing, I've got three people who I class as friends, and then the rest I talk to and try and have a laugh with. I don't associate with bullies. I can't stand bullies. I won't associate with them. They don't get a lot of respect. I have respect in my own way. I've got my certain group of people I hang out with, and I stick to that group.

On every wing, you've got about 15 people who – they're just private people. And then the others are just normal. I'd say you've got about ten people who are not exactly bullies, but they like to intimidate people. You've got half of the wing or two-thirds of the wing who are normal, then you've got the top tier of people, about ten. If you're a fucking nonce,[3] then you're not going to last five minutes. No one likes that kind of person. And the reason why nonces are totally disliked – everyone's either got a girlfriend, a mother, a sister, a child, or anything. If anything happened to any of my loved ones then I'd be out to kill the person, know what I mean? Certain crimes will always have a certain stigma in jail. It's like – an armed robber sees himself as a better criminal than the rest. Being in for theft [like me], that's a low-tier crime, it's neither here nor there. It's not going to earn me respect. And to be honest, I don't really want to earn respect off my crime. My crimes are wrong, I know they're wrong. But it's just something that I do, to begin with because I got a buzz from it, and now, because I have money off it.

There's a lot of nasty bastards in jail. They didn't get put in here for nothing. You've got the thieves, and you've got drug takers and drug dealers and all that lot. [Then] you've got people who murder people just for the sake of it. There's people in here what I would class as bad people. I'm a criminal, but I don't see myself as a bad person.

You might be all thieves, but you don't thieve off one another. Grassing on each other is not done. Whatever someone else is doing is *their* business. It's like going to the authorities on the out. You just don't do it. That's for straight-heads to do. Grassing is probably the biggest evil you can do in the criminal world. It's just not done. You shouldn't borrow something and not be able to pay it back. As soon as you've borrowed something if you've got no intention of paying it back, that's trouble. People getting bullied, I disapprove of that, but if they're not willing to stand up for themselves, then it's their own [fault]. Not that bullying's right, I don't abide by that at all. But if they ain't strong enough to stand up to it, then they've got to live with getting out of the occupation they've got into. As soon as you've got a weakness, you're going to get someone coming down on you like a ton of bricks. It's a very unforgiving place.

You have to hide your feelings from everyone. You don't open yourself up. You don't want someone's pity. They've all got their problems as well. I don't want to be sitting listening to their problems day in, day out. And I don't want them to feel that they're sitting there listening to my problems. If I've got something that's upset me or something, that's what the family's for. So I keep that to myself. Anything that's a weakness, you keep that to yourself. You can't really express yourself like you can out there. It's a cold place. There's no women here, so you can't show affection. You have to be kind of stone-faced. You only really show half of your emotions and feelings while your inside. There's no one I'd really want to show warmth to. I've got mates in here, good mates. But at the end of the day you still don't show warmth to your mates. I just lock up any feelings that would get me feeling sad or down, I just lock them away. As soon as I get sent down, they're locked away. Deep down. You just don't think about it. You switch off to it. You just forget about the outside world. If you keep on thinking about what's going on out there, what you could be doing and all that, that just sends you ... you know what I mean?

TV's all right, but it's mind-numbing. It's easier with the telly, because there's [normally] a film on or a TV programme that you can get into. But have you ever sat there watching telly for 12, 18 hours? It's fairly mind-numbing. The only reason they put tellies in was to placate people. It's just a weapon against us. It's a stick and a carrot. It's a carrot to make us get on with normal life, but it's a stick that they can beat us with. Because if we do something wrong then they'll take it away. No one wants to lose their telly. I don't like watching telly all day, but if I didn't have it, I'd be pissed off, because it's another way of getting out of here. It's an escape out of it.

Commentary

As Gresham Sykes noted,[4] as soon as prisoners interact with each other, however partially or tentatively, they create a social system of relationships, norms and hierarchies. Terms such as 'prison social life' and 'the prisoner society' refer to these kinds of features: the patterns of friendship and rivalry between prisoners, their informal 'value system', and the distinctions that they make between each other. In short, they describe the 'unofficial' world of the prison that exists alongside (and as a response to) the prison's official rules and formal roles.

It is not surprising that there is a hierarchy of status and stigma within the prisoner community. As Ewan suggests, and as prison researchers have consistently noted, prisoners judge and classify each other in terms of crimes, morality, dangerousness and a range of other factors, and they often express fear or disgust about the people with whom they are forced to co-exist. It is easier to identify prisoners who are stigmatised than those who are admired. Men convicted of sexual offences generate the highest levels of contempt and hostility, and generally they have to be segregated from other prisoners for their own safety. 'Mainstream' prisoners commonly argue that the damage caused by sex offenders is far graver and more lasting than 'ordinary' crimes. As Ewan suggests, many prisoners associate such offences with harms against their loved ones, and a large proportion have themselves experienced sexual abuse. Prisoners who inform on or steal from their peers are also abhorred, for breaching the 'inmate code' that demands mutual loyalty (see below). As

Ewan declares, 'You might all be thieves, but you don't thieve off each other.' Prisoners who are weak, immature, unintelligent or mentally ill are derided, and these men may be mocked, exploited or ostracised, although they can generally survive within the mainstream prisoner world.

Within the mass of prisoners who make up the bulk of this population, further distinctions are complex, and there are various different forms of power and status. As Stephen suggests, characteristics such as intelligence, maturity and stoicism are respected in themselves. Carrying a credible threat of violence ('physical presence') helps to protect a prisoner from being exploited (placing him 'above the line'). However, unrestrained aggression and arbitrary violence are not admired and they carry the risk of provoking retaliation or institutional punishment. Some crimes attract more esteem than others, for example those involving high levels of risk, organisation or reward. However, while organised criminals and drug dealers tend to look down upon 'petty criminals' – domestic burglars, thieves and low-level fraudsters – these low-level offenders often condemn more serious criminals for disregarding human life. It is important to be respected enough to ensure some level of safety and autonomy, but most prisoners – like Ewan – are content to be relatively inconspicuous, both to other prisoners and to staff. On most prison wings, a handful of men carry social reputations that give them more power than the majority, but this power tends to be limited to particular social groups. There are few visible leaders or men who have the capacity to 'run' a wing.

Drugs shape the prisoner society in a number of ways.[5] As Stephen suggests, they provide a means of alleviating stress and psychologically 'escaping' the environment, and therefore find a ready market in prison. Prisoners who deal drugs within prison are able to accumulate a considerable amount of power by taking advantage of this demand. The power that they wield is not exactly the same as 'respect', in that many prisoners dislike men who sell drugs, associate with them only in order to obtain drugs, or defer to them out of fear rather than admiration. However, these forms of 'respect' are often conflated in prison, in that many prisoners admire people precisely because they are powerful or feared by others.

Drug users in prison generate the opposite sentiments. They are disliked in part because of a widespread aversion to the acts that drug addicts engage in outside prison: in particular, exploitation of family members and petty theft. Many prisoners have been direct victims of such offences or are ashamed of having committed them at some stage in their own past. Heroin is considered an especially 'dirty' drug in terms of its effects on personal health and morality. Within the prison, drug users breach a number of norms that make collective living more manageable. Their moods are volatile and unpredictable, they scavenge for goods that they can trade for drugs and sometimes steal from other prisoners, and they are considered untrustworthy, manipulative and generally unreliable. The debts that they build up create friction or lead them to inform on their creditors to staff. Drug use can therefore undermine the status of men who might otherwise be respected.

As Stephen notes, drugs also shape the nature of prisoner social relationships in bringing together prisoners with quite different criminal histories. Imprisonment itself is to some degree a leveller. Men who would not associate with each other outside prison are forced to interact, and sometimes develop friendships, as a result of sharing space over long periods of time. In this respect, an interesting aspect of prison culture is the tone of tense courtesy that Stephen highlights. Collective living requires prisoners to be tolerant of each other – in Stephen's words, to become 'adaptable'. As well as needing to exercise patience and stoicism in relation to the institution, prisoners have to find ways of enduring the views and habits of multiple neighbours in what is a highly compressed living environment. Early scholars of imprisonment proposed that this was precisely the purpose of the 'inmate code' that appeared to exist in all prisons regardless of their location or population. They argued that this value system – which consisted of informal rules such as 'don't exploit other prisoners' and 'show fortitude' – arose as a response to the intrinsic 'pains of imprisonment' and helped to make prison life collectively more manageable.[6] If prisoners shared their resources, were resilient in the face of irritations and frustrations, showed mutual respect and loyalty, and so on, they could alleviate deprivations in goods and services, reduce interpersonal tensions, and generally recoup some of the loss in status that imprisonment entailed. When Ewan declares his contempt for bullying, advises against any display of weakness, and recommends that a prisoner should not borrow goods that he can not repay, his views can be seen in this light. Of course, these norms and attitudes are not exclusive to the prison. The 'inmate code' is really a modified or intensified version of various values that exist in criminal and street cultures outside prison.[7] It is also worth noting that the code represents a set of ideals rather than a description of how prisoners actually behave.

Some aspects of the prisoner code seem to be remarkably consistent across time and space, in particular, the decree that a prisoner should not inform or 'grass' on his or her peers. Many prisoners agree with Ewan that grassing represents a fundamental breach of the code among law-breakers – it is 'just not done' if you make a living from crime, not least because so many prisoners are convicted because someone has informed on them. Other prisoners dismiss the notion that there is any such code of honour, but promote a value system that says you should 'do your own time', that is, not meddle in someone else's business unless it affects you directly. Some prisoners believe that grassing and getting involved are acceptable in certain circumstances, for example if a prisoner is being bullied or is in danger from serious violence.

Stephen states that one of the 'golden rules' is that a prisoner should never side with an officer above another prisoner, but it is also worth noting his comment that it has become much more acceptable for prisoners to socialise in friendly ways with prison staff. The inmate code responds to shifts in prison culture and policies, and informal rules prohibiting such relations have softened in recent years as staff attitudes have become less authoritarian. Since prison officers have considerable power through the discretion they wield and the reports to which they contribute, it has also become advantageous for prisoners to get on well with them. Prisoners like Stephen with 'old-school' attitudes tend to retain a suspicion of 'the system' and may seek out 'little victories' over officers even while being superficially polite to them. Such victories help prisoners to maintain a sense of control over their lives in an environment where they are largely powerless.

Another important component of the inmate code is the injunction against showing weakness and vulnerability. Again, it has been argued that this reflects some inherent characteristics of the prison. Prisoners recognise that their problems are rarely worse or more pressing than anyone else's, and that there is limited patience for emotional off-loading. Like Ewan, they often link the emotional coldness of prison life with the absence of women. In an environment where reputations stick and it is hard to escape victimisation, they fear that emotional expression will leave them open to being derided or victimised. As Stephen comments, even being kind or polite can be interpreted as signs of weakness. And although, in adult men's prisons,[8] outright bullying breaches the value system, prisoners who 'allow' themselves to be bullied receive little sympathy. Like Ewan, many prisoners claim that imprisonment suppresses some emotions as well as prohibiting them from being expressed. Negative feelings are difficult to manage, not least because problems and sources of stress (such as relationships with people outside, guilt about past acts, anxieties about court cases or parole hearings) are often beyond one's control. It may be easier to stifle these feelings entirely than add to the burdens of confinement by allowing them to fester. Prisoners forced to endure this culture over many years describe losing touch altogether with some emotions and fear that they will never regain the capacity for warmth, trust and intimacy.

Many accounts of men's prisons describe this culture as 'macho' or 'hyper-masculine'.[9] In part, these terms refer to the culture of emotional indifference and self-hardening described above. They also denote aggression, homophobia and misogyny, and an environment where all hints of femininity are reviled. A common argument is that by removing from men conventional markers of masculinity such as work and heterosexual relationships, imprisonment encourages men to engage in compensatory acts that exaggerate traditional masculine traits. Whether 'hyper-masculine' is an accurate description of the culture of men's prisons is somewhat questionable. Imprisonment creates a complex culture in which women are objectified and denigrated in the prison's public world, but are sentimentalised and sometimes revered by prisoners in private.[10] Many prisoners talk openly with each other about how much they miss their partners and children (and this is evidenced daily in prison visiting rooms, where emotional expression is culturally acceptable). It is also simplistic to suggest that prisons are places that are relentlessly or randomly violent. During months of fieldwork, a visitor or researcher might not see a single fight or assault. To some degree, this is because such acts occur in backstage areas, where they are less likely to be observed. It also reflects the fact that, most of the time, violence is present more in terms of threat than action. Stephen makes an astute sociological point when he compares the role of violence within the prisoner community and in the outside world. In the absence of alternative channels for conflict resolution and rule enforcement, violence becomes the ultimate regulator and is a constant possibility. Nonetheless, warmth, humour and kindness and are all features of prison life, alongside fear, tension and aggression.

Like the prisoner value system, social relationships help prisoners to cope with their confinement. Friendships provide some degree of protection from loneliness, material scarcity, and – as Stephen notes – violence. At the same time, it is difficult in prison to develop trust and establish close friendships from scratch. Thus, imprisonment encourages prisoners to develop social ties while also limiting the forms that they can take. Most prisoners consider the environment distorted, transient and inauthentic. It is hard to evaluate another prisoner's character when one knows so little about his or her past behaviour; the prison offers limited opportunities to observe someone's moral conduct and trustworthiness or gauge their future behaviour; and there may be more to lose than gain in opening up to other people. For these reasons, prisoners tend to form close relationships with few other people. Both Stephen and Ewan distinguish between the kinds of 'mates' or 'true friends' that can be relied upon and the larger number of 'associates' with whom they merely socialise. The former are normally men that a prisoner already knows from his home town, either directly or indirectly. They may be associates from a previous sentence, whose reliability has already been assessed. Even these friendships are often circumscribed, involving forms of material and social support but little emotional intimacy. Some prisoners serving long sentences report having had no meaningful friendships for decades.

The degree to which prisoners are willing to 'stand up' for their friends depends on a number of factors. Stephen claims that prisoners on shorter sentences tend to be more vocal and disorderly because they have less to lose if they get into trouble. Men on parole and indeterminate sentences are generally less inclined to make sacrifices on behalf of other prisoners if they might jeopardise their release date by doing so. The stage of a prisoner's sentence is also relevant: as release approaches, loyalties to members of the outside world tend to become more powerful relative to those inside the prison.[11] It becomes less tempting to 'get involved' in prison trade or confront other prisoners about minor issues. But some prisoners are more concerned than others about reputation, and some claim that they would stick up for their friends regardless of the risks this might entail. If prisoners who mix with other men from their home town appear disloyal, they risk losing credibility when they return to their communities outside. Information can flow with remarkable speed between the prison and the outside world.

Overall, prison social life is cellular but somewhat fluid. Some prisoners are loners, preferring to 'get their heads down' with few ties or obligations. The majority of prisoners operate within small cliques while mixing more widely in workshops and education classes. Loyalties often extend beyond immediate cliques, forming around religion and ethnicity, for example. Prisoners from different ethnic and racial groups generally get on reasonably well (see Chapter 10). Many prisoners come from mixed-race communities where they socialise in ethnically mixed groups, and do the same in prison. There is certainly not the kind of interracial gang-based antagonism that characterises some prisons in North America.[12] Nonetheless, there is a considerable degree of underground racism, and as Islam has become a more prominent feature of the prisoner social world, there are growing signs of tension between some prisoner groups.

If one accepts that the prisoner world is determined in part by the deficits, frustrations and demands of prison life, then it follows that prisons can influence the character of this inner society through their policies, practices and cultures. As Stephen comments, 'in more violent prisons ... the more violent person rises to the top', whereas you 'respect people for different reasons' when the environment is more relaxed. Prisons with more authoritarian cultures are more likely to generate an anti-institutional culture among prisoners. In such prisons, the taboo on talking to officers and informing on other prisoners is likely to be particularly powerful. Most prisoners concur with Stephen that the strength of the inmate code has diminished in recent years, and this partly reflects the gradual humanisation of prison life. Prisons that are less depriving are also less likely to force prisoners to try to lessen their frustrations by exploiting or banding together with each other. In the UK, the incentives and earned privileges scheme, which provides televisions and extra visits (among other things) in return for positive behaviour, has a significant impact on prisoners' conduct and compliance. As Ewan maintains, these privileges normalise and improve the experience of imprisonment somewhat, but they also serve as control mechanisms – 'a stick and a carrot' – because they can always be removed. The policy splinters prisoners' interests and encourages them to focus on personal rather than collective aims. It makes it less necessary for prisoners to turn to each other to make their imprisonment more bearable, reducing the amount of power that any one prisoner can accumulate. New forms of psychological power have similar effects. Prisoners on parole and indeterminate sentences are particularly preoccupied by the reports that assess their 'risk', evaluate their behaviour, and ultimately determine whether they progress through the prison system. As Stephen says, in the contemporary prison, it is these reports rather than physical coercion that are most likely to 'fuck you up' and 'kill you off'. As a result, among long term prisoners, psychologists as well as officers have become objects of resentment and hostility.

This represents a significant shift in prison culture and social life. Psychological power induces in prisoners a particular form of compliance and self-regulation (see Chapter 9). As Stephen suggests, it becomes important to think about all aspects of personal conduct: who one socialises with, how one's cell is decorated, and so on. The focus of judgement is not just obedience and conformity to rules, but engagement with the regime and all-round behaviour.

In this respect, the prisoner social world is shaped by two opposing forces. Most of the long-standing and virtually inherent pains and frustrations of imprisonment impel prisoners to identify with each other's predicament, form friendships, and involve themselves in trade. But new sentence conditions, privilege schemes and the grip of psychological power serve to 'individualise' prisoners, pushing them to restrict their loyalties and limit their involvement in the social world. How these forces weigh upon prisoners, and how prisoners weigh them up, depends upon a range of factors, including sentence length, family circumstances, personal needs, masculine identity, etc. Like Ewan and Stephen, prisoners differ along a number of lines, and it makes little sense to talk about 'prison culture' or the 'prisoner experience' without some appreciation of these differences.

Notes

1 'The block': the prison's segregation unit.
2 'Smack': heroin.
3 A 'nonce': a sex offender (derogatory).
4 Sykes, G. (1958) *The Society of Captives: A Study of a Maximum-Security Prison.* Princeton, NJ: Princeton University Press.
5 Politicians and members of the public often wonder how drugs can get into a secure environment such as a prison. Practitioners acknowledge that members of staff are often responsible for smuggling in drugs and other illicit goods (such as mobile phones) in return for money. Prisoners show considerable ingenuity in finding ways of importing drugs themselves, through visits, over prison walls and fences, through the mail, and by 'plugging' drugs in their bodies when they enter prison from the courts. It might be possible to impede these methods, but to do so would require significant resources and would come at great human cost. For example, one could stem the flow of drugs considerably by preventing prisoners from having any direct contact with their visitors, but this would be deeply dehumanising, and would have implications for the prison's legitimacy and stability.
6 Sykes, G. and Messinger, S. (1960) 'The inmate social system', in R. A. Cloward *et al.* (eds) *Theoretical Studies in the Social Organization of the Prison.* New York: Social Science Research Council, pp. 5–19.
7 See Irwin, J. and Cressey, D. (1962) 'Thieves, convicts and the inmate culture', *Social Problems*, 10: 142–55.
8 It is also important to recognise that the value system varies between prisons. In Young Offender Institutions, bullying is both more common and more culturally acceptable than in prisons for adult men. In women's prisons, there are fewer constraints on emotional expression and on the formation of close relations with officers (see Chapter 9). Prison-based therapeutic communities make a concerted effort to invert conventional prison norms, encouraging prisoners to display their vulnerabilities in the interests of therapy, and promoting 'informing' as a way of challenging self-destructive behaviour.
9 See, for example, Sim, J. (1994) 'Tougher than the rest? Men in prison', in T. Newburn and E. Stanko (eds) *Just Boys Doing Business.* London: Routledge.
10 Crewe, B. (2006) 'Male prisoners' orientations towards female officers in an English prison', *Punishment and Society*, 8(4): 395–421.
11 See Wheeler, S. (1961) 'Socialization in correctional communities', *American Sociological Review*, 26: 697–712.

12 For the classic account of inter-ethnic hostility and gang violence in an American prison, see Jacobs, J. (1977) *Stateville: The Penitentiary in Mass Society*. Chicago: University of Chicago Press.

Further reading

For a classic account of prison social life and culture, Gresham Sykes's *The Society of Captives* (Princeton, NJ: Princeton University Press, 1958) is essential reading. For a more recent study, see Ben Crewe's *The Prisoner Society: Power, Adaptation, and Social Life in an English Prison* (Oxford: Oxford University Press, 2009).

4   Identity and adaptation in prison

Yvonne Jewkes

George was a shy, intelligent prisoner, who had served over 20 years in prison, as part of a life sentence for murder. He repeatedly described his upbringing as 'dysfunctional'. Finding himself in care and discovering alcohol on top of his emotional and psychological troubles was 'a bit of a potent combination'. At the time of his interview, he was anticipating a final move to a Category D (open) prison and reflected on his plans for the future.

> I think I've got an identity that is on hold until I get out. It's difficult for me to know, beyond more than general terms, what my life's gonna be like out there, how people are gonna respond to me ... will I be treated as an adult or will I be treated as an ex-con? I'd like to think that I'd be treated as an adult who's trying to sort of put some plans into action ... it's only a small thing really, I suppose, but I find it difficult sometimes going down to the office and sort of asking to be given a razor, and asking to be given a bar of soap, or queuing up to be given my tobacco or a Mars bar on a Friday, rather than going in and making a purchase. It's little sort of dependencies, all the time, which I suppose, if you thought too deeply about them, could undermine you in a way. But it's just part and parcel. It's the way the prison is taking responsibility away from you, and then on the other hand they're always telling you to take responsibility for your life. But they don't give you anything. Like there was a job for 'education cleaner' advertised the other week, and the notice said, 'We see this as a very responsible job', and basically all you're doing is pushing a broom up and down the corridor, so that's the level of responsibility you're given.
>
> I wanna try and put myself into social situations where I can make friends. I mean if I did go to college, or university, obviously there are people there, I'm bound to make friends there, but I'm interested in reading and social history and stuff; maybe there are some sort of discussion groups or meetings and all that sort of thing, so I'll have a look around and see what sort of social arenas there are for me to sort of get involved in and see if I can try and make friends that way. It's a question of gaining confidence, really, I think. I mean, my experiences of my two town visits,

I did feel very dislocated from what was going on around me, more of an observer than a participant, particularly the first time, but obviously I'll have to get over that. The first time I went out, I didn't feel as if I had any right to be out there, it was a weird feeling, very strange. The second time, it was more sort of curiosity about what was going on around me, but I didn't feel connected with it in any way. It's very fast, nobody seems to have much time for anybody else ... I found shop assistants very rude [*laughs*] ... it did seem very impersonal, but then I was dislocated from it, so perhaps that was me being impersonal.

But, I think ... how can I put it ... prisons are an impersonal place anyway, they're quite superficial, the friendships and alliances, very superficial, and usually very instrumental. Whereas outside there's more opportunity to get to know people in depth ... the sort of people who you'd want to know. I mean, the impression I've got over the years is that a lot of the friendships and alliances [in prison] are based on either drug use or the part of the country you come from, or even what football team you support, things like that. It's a question of having to get along with people because you're in the same confined space. It's more sort of expediency than anything else. I mean, you can get to know people and you can get to like them, but you know at the back of your mind, even in a subconscious way, that you're gonna be transferred, you're never gonna see them again, so there's not much point in investing too much emotional energy in a friendship that ain't gonna last. Even when you get out, you can't really arrange to sort of carry on a friendship because you wouldn't be allowed to really, it would be frowned upon [as a life-sentence prisoner].

I think it's a reasonable guess, perhaps a reasonable assumption, that for those who get visits, for friends and family, you can let your guard drop and express yourself when you're on a visit, and I mean, when I've been over on visits a few times and at the end of the visit, there's a lot of cuddling and goodbyes and it is quite an emotional time for people. And I think people save it up, if you can save emotions up. But I think that's where they truly express those natural human feelings. I feel very diminished as a human being at the moment ... over the years, I've become emotionally stunted ... I do [have emotions] but it's a very narrow range, I think [*laughs*] ... I dunno if perseverance is an emotion ... if determination and frustration ... erm, hope, if that's an emotion ... but other things, I don't know. It's difficult. But I haven't had visits for years, you see, this is it for me. I get the occasional visit from a chap who was my probation officer; I'd count him as a friend, because now he comes to visit me as a friend, but I only get about two or three visits a year. You can literally go for months without touching a human being, and it's just something you get used to.

I think it's the length of time, just the length of time, it can wear you down. I mean, there are other people who've done longer than me [and] seem to be on top of the world, but we're all different. Maybe they get visits every month from a loving wife and a few bouncy children ... so that gives them a sense of belonging and a sense of worth, a huge part of their identity. I mean, I've had to sort of construct a worth and identity out of the past and the circumstances here [but] it's all geared towards getting out. One reason I want this move so much to a Cat-D is it's gonna get me out of this rut and present me with new challenges and I'll be able to gauge a lot better where I am as a person, what I've gotta do, what I am gonna do, cos at the moment I don't feel as if there's any context to my existence; it's just marking time, and I have been for four years, five years, just marking time. I remember at the start of my sentence, on a Friday night I'd think, oh, I'd be out with my mates now, I'd be doing this, I'd be going there; but after a while that feeling fades, and you begin to sort of forget what's gone before.

There aren't many sort of social niceties and social graces in this type of world. It's very sort of up-front and in-your-face ... but it's artificial, it's not real. I mean, that was brought home to me very forcibly on my days out. As soon as we stepped outside the gate, Officer X became Bob X. It was like a shedding of a skin, cos almost immediately, just driving out of the car park, he was saying, 'Oh, that fucking officer, he don't half want help', and he'd never say that in the prison, and he'd tell me about his wife and his army days and, you know what I mean, that would never happen in here. As soon as we got out there, totally different.

Doug had been in five prisons and described himself as 'a thief through and through'. He was tall, wiry and extremely candid both about himself and about the prisoner subculture.

I don't get private cash and at the moment I don't have a job, so I'm not making any wages, you've got to juggle things to keep yourself in, not a lavish lifestyle but, you know. You can get by on what you're provided with, you don't have to pay to play pool or whatever, but I'm a heavy smoker, I like to dabble ... Say I've got £15 on my canteen, I need £7 worth of burn to get by,[1] some Rizlas, shower gel, toothpaste, and then you've got a couple of quid to play with at the end, and just say you've got draw and I've got two phone cards,[2] I can buy two spliffs off you, cut it up and make it into three, give two away, get two phone cards back and I've got a spliff for myself. It's just investing, it works with everyone. There are a whole load of things ... It's just jailcraft. If you do enough time in jail everybody learns about it, you know about phone cards as well, don't you? Everybody gets to find out [the scams] once you've done long enough in jail. It's not like somebody turns around and says, 'How long've you been doing jail? Eight months? It's about time you learnt how to do this.'

[Prison] takes a grip on everybody. I don't accept that people can become institutionalised to the degree where they'd rather be in jail than out there, that's bullshit, unless you've done life and you've got nothing to go out to. Doing three years, three and a half, I can switch between, I get locked up, it don't bother me, I get back out and I'm straight again, I can just chop and change. Normally when you get banged up, most people, [for the] first couple of weeks are, 'fucking hell', all wounded and that. I get locked up, for the first night, [I think] not fucking jail again, what a stupid fucking move, and then the next day, [I'm] straight back on it because I realise that you've got to hold your shit together otherwise it sends you mad. So, when you first get there, first couple of weeks you're grafting like mad to get all your little luxuries and that, because when you land you've got no radio, no phone cards, you've got fuck all, you've just got an empty pad, prison shampoo and a toothbrush. So first things first, you want some toiletries, you go around, 'How are you doing, you remember me from last year? Yes, I just landed this morning, you got any shampoo? Nice one, I'll give it you back when I've got myself together.'

You do change in jail … It makes you more suspicious of people. I don't give a fuck what anybody says, you're always looking out for the next bit of trouble. You step on people's toes quite often, like on my wing you've got 70 people, something like that. Ninety per cent of us are predatory kind of people. You just get on with things as you can, if you can find someone you connect with, you run with them. It's really no different from being out there apart from you've got to keep your guard up a little bit because everybody who is in here will take advantage if they can.

Charlie was from London. Although initially he had done well at school, he had a sense of fatalism about the path he had chosen in life, saying that there was always violence in the house. He described his mother's side as 'quite a violent family, all drinkin', thievin' and things like that', and he blamed his entry into criminality on the fact that he had an older brother who 'was always fighting'. He had got involved with football hooliganism and stealing and had received his first sentence aged 16 for 'bashin' someone up'. At the time of the interview, he was serving a long fixed sentence.

You've gotta be level-headed in prison, so you're still growin' but it's like there's two different worlds. Everything in prison is the same today as it will be tomorrow and will be next week. Outside, everything changes from day to day, and coming away [to prison] you're kind of stuck in a time warp, you're doing the same thing day in, day out. Everybody else outside: they grow away from you, or you grow away from them, or you can't catch up to them, it's strange.

I ended up going back to [X prison], and it was a case of, 'Right, we're going back into a B-cat now, so we gotta start being violent, we gotta get back to this bravado again'. When you turn up in a new prison, for someone like me, you have to have a bit of an appearance: if you look like a nutter, or you act like a nutter, or you got a reputation as a nutter, people will leave you alone, and I didn't really wanna get into any problems and it was like, 'I don't know this completely different side of England to where I used to do my bird'.[3] And I basically just pumped myself back up again, walked into the prison, and was like 'right, I'm ready to have a chat with anyone who wants to have a tear-up'.[4]

I won't let anybody bully me, take any liberties with me, or mug me off, I won't have none of that, but as far as respect goes ... I mean I get on with everybody on my wing, they all know who I am because I'm still a little bit loud ... I'm a character. I suppose it's by the way you carry yourself, I mean, I walk round and people see me and they all mainly assume I'm confident of what I'm doing, er, which is not necessarily the case; I might look that way, but there's a lot of things that I don't feel comfortable with. Confidence is down for me, it's a brash exterior.

There's nobody in 'ere that I know from outside, so I don't have to put on that front. When I'm at home, everybody thinks I'm a nut, a complete nutcase, lunatic, and you kind of embroil yourself in that role. When you come to prison, if there's people there that you know, you carry on with that role, but if there's not anybody 'ere that you know, you can do what you wanna do and feel how you wanna feel ... If I went home tomorrow afternoon and somebody knocked on my door and started screamin', I would have to knock 'em out, because that's what everybody would expect me to do, and it's what I would expect people to expect me to do. In 'ere, if somebody starts screamin' and shoutin' I can say, 'no problem', I can walk away, because no one doesn't know me any different, and I don't like hittin' people. I've got to the stage now where it's a road to destruction for me, and I want off that, and by being in 'ere, this way, I've learnt a lot about meself where I've realised that life outside is a falsehood. There's so much, so much bullshit goes on in these places. Everybody in this prison [claims they're] a millionaire, they've all got huge, big, flash cars, big yachts and big houses, and they've got nuffink ... everything in 'ere is exaggerated to make you look good.

Kyle said that he used to be a 'jack-the-lad' but described a pivotal moment when he had looked at a photo of his partner and baby on his cell wall and decided, 'Enough is enough, I don't belong here.' He said that he had turned his back on crime and described his main aim now as gaining control of his destiny and providing for his family.

The majority of men – I won't speak for all men – are pigs, for want of a better word, they're just too self-obsessed. You try and tell another bloke about your feelings, nine times out of ten, especially with some of these in here, they'll laugh at you, or they won't laugh in your face, they'll wait until your back is turned. You tell a woman that, they seem to be on the same sort of understanding. I've been accused before of having too much femininity in me, but I find that a good thing … it's like gay men, they get on better with women. Even though I'm not gay myself, it's because they're in touch more with their feminine side.

This time, I'll get out and I know for a fact I'm not coming back in because I've had enough. This ain't my idea of fun … My idea of having a good time now is getting out, finding a decent job, getting a decent enough lifestyle that I care for me, my missus and the baby, and focusing all my energy that I've got – I've always had lots of energy – rather than using it for a negative purpose, using it for positive by concentrating my efforts on my family and fuck the rest of the world, I don't care what's happening out there … I want to earn the money for my family. Call it male chauvinistic or whatever, but I think it's the male's job to provide for his family.

If someone was to try and break my emotions out there you can walk away, get away from them. In here, there is no escape, so either you vent your emotions out or you hold back and you're just a walking time bomb. When my missus divorced me I was a proper walking time bomb, and then four months later my uncle died, and two months later my grandma died, and I'd managed to keep that all in. Brother died was just the last straw, and someone said something to me and I ended up leathering him and got nicked, all because I'd kept my emotions close to my chest and wouldn't let no one near me. Even my co-d[efendant] was saying, 'You need to talk about this'. There is not a lot of support really in prison [for people] like myself, emotional people who find it difficult to hold their emotions close to their chest and not being able to speak to certain inmates about what's going on in your head. I write it all down on paper and send it to my missus, that's the only way I can deal with it while I'm in here.

When you come to jail, the strong survive, the weak get bullied. It's a fact, they always will, so when you come to jail everyone has to put on a front because otherwise either someone is going to start trying to bully you and you'll end up scrapping all the fucking time, so you have to put on a front … It's just men, isn't it, macho bullshit. It's like Joe, out there he's a good bloke, family man, top geezer. In here he has to put on a little bit of front to save face, if you want to call it that. I know that, he knows that, people that know him know that.

People try and jump on the pool table. If you say, 'Next', and some guy comes along and says, 'Hold on, I'm next', and you say, 'Hold on, you weren't here, you fucked off and now you're back and trying to claim your go again', then that's it, the chest comes out, the neck gets put forward, and one of you has got to back down. If not, you're scrapping, and over

> a game of pool, it's just not fucking worth it, so one eventually gives in. I don't think a lot of people, even me, sometimes I don't even realise I'm doing it, it's just subconsciously you do it, your mind switches, you've got part of your brain that's designated for when you come to prison and it just turns on.

Commentary

All four prisoners quoted above appear to be experienced prisoners ('old lags' even) who have spent many years inside. A common theme in the sociological prison literature is therefore absent from their narratives: the brutality and dehumanisation of the reception process. Commonly described – after Goffman[5] – as a 'mortification of self', or likened to being fed into an administrative machine, the shock of entering such an austere and depersonalised environment, together with the sudden and enforced separation from family and friends, can result in severe trauma. Withstanding 'entry shock' is, then, the first of many psychological assaults that the new inmate has to face, and attempts at suicide and self-harm, and the onset of self-destructive psychiatric disorders, are most prevalent in the initial phase of confinement. But for prisoners like George, Doug, Charlie and Kyle, any initial problems with adapting to confinement are long forgotten and coping strategies are largely pragmatic. Their no-nonsense attitudes to life in custody are evident in the identities they present to others, and they all reveal in their interviews aspects of the processes of identity management in which they are almost constantly engaged. It is not necessarily that the identities adopted in prison are false; they may be a version (at times exaggerated, at other times downplayed) of the personalities they manifest outside prison or in private, and most prison scholarship of the last 20 years shares the view that prisoners import with them into custody the diverse personas, experiences, belief systems and moral standpoints that they exhibit on the outside.

Nonetheless, prison sociologists also emphasise that the experience of confinement unites prisoners, to some degree, in a shared experience of, and response to, pain and deprivation, one adaptation to which is the suspension of elements of their pre-prison identities. It is common in the prison literature to find quotes from prisoners expressing such sentiments as, 'I left my identity at reception and I'll pick it up on my way out,' or describing their identity as being 'on hold' until they are released, as George does here. Jewkes[6] draws on a study of identity transformation in an American maximum security prison by Schmid and Jones[7] to argue that in order to acculturate to their new environment, prisoners suspend their pre-institution identities and temporarily construct an inauthentic identity that masks the true self. Put simply, 'identity' constitutes outward presentation, the image one wishes to project to others, while 'self' might best be conceptualised as the inner, emotional 'core'; a place of retreat where the public façade can be put aside and one can 'be oneself'.

This distinction is usually conceptualised by prison researchers (again, following Goffman) as 'backstage' and 'frontstage'. On the whole, the social aspect of one's identity will be presented frontstage in engagement with others. Backstage is where one's basic, personal ontological security system is restored, and where the tensions associated with sustaining the particular bodily, gestural and verbal codes that are demanded in this setting are diffused. Imprisonment may involve disruption of the equilibrium between the two spheres, resulting in further damage to the individual's sense of well-being. If forced to share a cell with one or more other inmates, the prisoner may be continually in an enforced state of 'frontstage' with little opportunity to restore his sense of self. If locked up on his own for prolonged periods, however, he may suffer equally in his inability to engage in frontstage activity. In prison, the boundaries between frontstage/backstage and personal/social identities may not be clear-cut, and the pressure for conformity and compliance may undermine the prisoner's personal and social identities, preventing both from functioning as they would in other circumstances. Interestingly, George's narrative suggests that prison officers also adopt frontstage and backstage identities. Acclimatised to wearing a mask while on duty, staff may be relieved to let it go when they leave the prison gates, even if escorting a prisoner on an outside visit. The transformation of Officer X to Bob X is described by George as the 'shedding of a skin'.

The requirement to hold one's emotions close to one's chest, as Doug describes, is understandable in the hyper-masculine and frequently violent prison culture that all the interviewees discuss. One of the most significant factors in the increase in interpersonal violence right across the prison population is the drugs culture that is evident in all British prisons (see Chapter 3). Another partial explanation may be the role of the popular press who give a high profile to criminal cases involving certain kinds of offences, encouraging other prisoners to place themselves in the role of vigilantes on behalf of society at large.

Hegemonic masculinity in prisons, then, is clearly as bound up with aggression and violence as it is on the outside. That is not to say that the most violent men (in respect to their crimes or to their behaviour in prison) are the most powerful inside; indeed the volatile offender is more likely to be marginalised than respected. Nevertheless, a certain degree of controlled aggression, as noted by Kyle, is considered desirable in order to survive the psychological and physical rigours of imprisonment, and even looking and acting 'like a nutter' (as Charlie does) will fend off most unwanted attention. The necessity of establishing a no-nonsense, tough reputation in prison is well documented in personal accounts of life inside and Kyle's account of the posturing and scrapping that can accompany a game of pool illustrates why all forms of association can be seen as potential flash-points. Such physical jostling for positions of power and status are common among groups of males in many environments, but it is perhaps especially visible in prisons because they are such blatantly status-depriving environments and therefore create a particularly acute need for indices of relative status.

Of course, even after a tough façade has been established, it has to be maintained and this in itself can be a great source of pressure. Some prisoners go to extraordinary lengths to accommodate an image of themselves that conforms to a hegemonic masculine ideal, but find that their manly self-portraits crumble or are gratefully relinquished during conversations with researchers. In this light, Kyle's confession that he has a feminine side – which, on the surface, seems rather brave – might only have been expressed to an 'outsider'. Nevertheless, he qualifies his admission by going on to describe the importance of putting on a 'front', 'saving face', and adopting aggressive body language when required. However, this is not borne out by everyone. For some, putting on a front and maintaining it over a long period of time simply may be beyond their impression management skills, and they will be forced to withdraw literally and emotionally into their private self.[8] Even George's view that prisoners save their emotions up for visits from loved ones, times that represent the only occasions when inmates can 'truly express those natural human feelings' and let their guard down, may not be a universal experience. As someone who gets very few visits, George might underestimate the emotional constraints that inhibit many prisoners when they see family members. Some prisoners are careful not to offload their emotions onto visitors and feel compelled to present a front even with their closest loved ones: 'You have to put on a mask to your family. Sometimes it would be easier not to have visits. You have to get in a right good mood, whether you feel like it or not.'[9]

More common, however, are references to the mask that must be worn on a day-to-day basis when frontstage on the prison wings. The imperative to put on an acceptable front in a macho environment, while at the same time being true to one's self, can be debilitating. George's poignant observation that he feels diminished as a human being and has become emotionally stunted is echoed in many prison ethnographies. It also suggests that a long prison sentence may contribute to a sense of arrested development. Time has many complex and contradictory facets for the long-term or life-sentence prisoner who may find himself living his life along two different trajectories. In one sense, he has 'too much' time and the copious references to 'doing time', 'killing time' and (as George describes) 'marking time' that underpin sociological prison research indicate the amorphous, monotonous, endless nature of temporality in prison just as effectively as the term given to a prison sentence in popular discourse: a 'stretch'. But while prison inmates must find ways of passing significant amounts of unstructured time trapped in a stultifying, regressive present, they must simultaneously cope with a sense of their lives being foreshortened, of having time stolen from them. In these circumstances, it is not unusual for the passage of time to blunt their awareness of their growing maturity or give them a sense of existing in the 'wrong' time, of being of a different generation from their peers, or still thinking of themselves as the same age at which they first entered custody. As Charlie says, there is a sense of there being two different worlds, with everyone on the outside moving at a different pace while he is stuck in a 'time warp', unable to catch up. This phenomenon is alternatively described in the academic literature as a state of 'cold storage' or 'deep freeze'. These terms are suggestive not only of the suspension of time but of life lived one step removed, as it were. The cruelty of this kind of life-course is illustrated by Kyle, who states that after his wife divorced him, and then his uncle and grandmother died in quick succession, he was a 'walking time bomb'.

Feelings of arrested development may be augmented by an enforced state of infantilisation, illustrated by George's desire to be treated as an adult when he is released back into society. For him, this would be an antidote to the requirement in prison to ask permission for everything, even a new bar of soap. Prison sociologists have highlighted that it is not just that one has to ask officers' permission for virtually anything one wishes to do that contributes to a sense of diminished responsibility, but that dependency is further enforced by the manner in which permission must be sought; one has to ask 'correctly' in order to avoid conflict with staff. The irony and sarcasm that underpin George's comment that pushing a broom up and down the corridor is described as a position of responsibility also echoes numerous academic studies that have argued that prison labour is monotonous, exploitative, demeaning and inappropriately waged.

To some extent, the assaults on one's sense of self described here are alleviated by association with others and, for most prisoners, the desire for self-insulation from the stark realities of incarceration is superseded by the need for human contact. There is relatively little research data available concerning emotional and sexual relationships in prison and George's moving observation that 'you can literally go for months without touching a human being' highlights one of the classic 'pains of imprisonment'; the deprivation of heterosexual relationships. But while the majority of prisoners might feel ambivalent towards their fellow inmates (expressions of differentiation from others are common in prison scholarship), they spend too much time in the presence of others to avoid all interaction. Kyle's comments are interesting in this respect: he wishes to distance himself from the 'self-obsessed pigs' that surround him and he is proud to admit to having a 'feminine side', but at the same time he appears to be both sociable and willing, when necessary, to conform to the norms of the hyper-masculine milieu.

Few prisoners claim to have friends inside, however. It is simply rarely possible to put your trust in another individual in a society as unpredictable and volatile as the prison. If he is lucky, a prisoner may find one or more companions inside with whom he can 'be himself', although the terms used by George to describe relationships in prison ('impersonal', 'superficial', 'instrumental', based on 'expediency') indicate how difficult it is to forge 'real' friendships in that environment. The pointlessness of trying to maintain contact with fellow prisoners is highlighted in a classic 1972 study by Cohen and Taylor[10] who observe that even the closest relationship can be perilous insofar as it is inevitably cut short when one individual is moved on to another prison or comes to the end of his sentence. As George says, 'you're gonna be transferred, you're never gonna see them again, so there's not much point in investing too much emotional energy in a friendship that ain't gonna last'. George's further comment, 'Even when you get out, you can't really arrange to ... carry on a friendship because you wouldn't be allowed to really, it would be frowned upon,' underplays the reality for many ex-prisoners for whom it is a condition of their release on licence that they do not fraternise with known offenders.

As the narratives above describe, and as the prison literature endorses, while there is little evidence of the universal inmate solidarity that early studies describe, there nonetheless exist social networks consisting of many and varied subcultures, whose affiliations may be based upon shared nationality or regional identity; religion or faith; football teams; the culture of the gym; drugs use; gambling; shared music or education interests; or contraband trading. Doug's description of 'jailcraft' – which might include brewing hooch, dealing in drugs or (before the introduction of PIN phones) manipulating phone cards so that they permit more calls than their face value – not only constitutes an important coping strategy and earns him extra money, but may also enhance his social standing among the rest of the prison community. 'Jailcraft' is one aspect of a phenomenon known to prison researchers as 'prisonisation',[11] a term used to indicate the process of socialisation or assimilation that takes place when the prisoner enters an institution. Like institutionalisation, prisonisation may involve the acceptance of inferior roles and a large degree of passivity in relation to the formal structures of the institution. But unlike institutionalisation, it also indicates a positive willingness to accept the values of the prison culture and is a rather more proactive survival strategy by which inmates learn how to 'play the system' and use the proliferation of underground economies, and the existence of subcultural gangs and hierarchies, to their advantage. According to prison scholars, these illegitimate activities, far from grinding down the inmate, actually provide him with the status and power necessary to ameliorate his sense of social rejection and loss of status (certainly more successfully than those who exaggerate their wealth – often referred to as 'plastic gangsters' – as described by Charlie). All these behaviours represent attempts to flaunt oneself symbolically – a kind of psychological one-upmanship.[12] But more importantly, such roles work to sustain and nurture the personal, interior, psychological self. For these reasons, Doug may be correct in suggesting that prisonisation is a more common adaptation to confinement than institutionalisation. A career criminal and self-confessed 'thief through and through', his inference seems to be that if he doesn't take advantage of others, they will take advantage of him.

Given the fragility and volatility of relationships in prison, many prisoners may look forward to forming more 'normal' bonds with people on release. However, George's expressed hope that he will make friends and have a social life when he is back in the community seem tempered slightly by his experiences of the outside world when taken on escorted visits in preparation for release. His sense of dislocation is illustrated by his disappointment at experiencing the rudeness of shop assistants and by his impression of a fast-moving, speeded-up world. Such sentiments are typical among those granted leave from prison. For example, Jewkes found that no amount of watching television or reading newspapers can prepare the long-term inmate for release back into an ever-changing social environment. One of her interviewees said that after 11 years inside, it took him four months to pluck up courage to catch a bus, because he simply no longer knew how to: 'I knew they didn't have conductors any more, because I've seen it on telly, but I didn't know what to do, how you were supposed to pay. I felt like a Martian ... the world moves at a million miles an hour. It's terrifying and anyone who tells you different is lying.'[13]

It is little wonder that many prisoners regard the prison world as an artificial construction requiring a false identity to be adopted, which can be discarded on release. For others, far from being a 'false' identity, the presentation of self within prison will be a familiar, if exaggerated, version of the social identity developed prior to entering prison. Charlie's self-analysis of his 'inside'/'outside' personas indicate the complexities of maintaining a 'hard man' image when a situation calls for it. He refers to his 'brash exterior' and reputation as a nutter, yet also indicates that these identities are resources primarily drawn upon when he arrives at a new prison or when he encounters someone he knows from his home town in prison. For individuals who import into prison the values, norms and behaviours of tough, hyper-masculine environments outside, imprisonment may come as something of a respite. One of Jewkes' respondents described a similar pattern: 'It's on the outside that you have to be a hard man ... On the outside you have to put up a front, defend yourself. You're on the front line. But in here you don't have to be like that ... To be honest it's a relief to be in here and to be able to let the mask drop.' That the real mask may be worn outside prison is also underlined by Charlie's statement that 'I've realised that life outside is a falsehood'.

The illegal socio-economic system that Doug dabbles in allows individuals like him to buy and sell drugs and other commodities that ameliorate another classic pain of imprisonment: the deprivation of goods and services. Those who are involved in contraband economies are arguably deflecting attempts to socialise them through formal channels and are instead constructing their identities around notions of resistance and counter-culture, demonstrating that there may be an inverse correlation between prisonisation and socialisation. Much of the academic prison literature conceptualises imprisonment as a U-shaped curve.[14] That is, individuals enter custody for the first time with an outsider's perception of what it will be like (often based on exaggerated representations from television and movies) and many suffer from a kind of trauma known as 'entry shock' as they are forcibly removed from their familiar (and familial) surroundings and processed through a prison's reception and induction units. Attempts at suicide and self-harm, and the onset of self-destructive psychiatric disorders, are most prevalent in this initial phase of confinement – (as Doug puts it, 'Normally when you get banged up, most people [for the] first couple of weeks are "fucking hell", all wounded and that'.) For newly admitted inmates, then, there is a need to learn from others the rules of the prison (both formal and informal) and assimilate into the culture as quickly as possible. By the middle of their sentence, many inmates (Doug being a prime example) will have come to adopt an insider's perspective on the prison world, but the more prisonised they become, the less conventionally socialised they may be. Many prisoners are continuously involved in the business of making plans, trading goods with other prisoners, devising ways of 'getting one over' on a fellow prisoner or member of staff, playing 'mind-games' or keeping abreast of new legislation that might affect them. Thus, in spite of the Prison Service's own attempts to shape socialisation processes, prison inmates assert a strong degree of agency in deciding exactly how far they are prepared to be socialised. However, with the prospect of release, most prisoners will revert to an outsider's view in the final months of their sentence. By way of illustration, Kyle wants to state publicly that he has respect for prison officers and police officers (something that would be surprising to hear from an individual at the 'bottom' of the U-shaped curve, in the middle of their sentence) and he spends much of his time planning his future life with his young family. Meanwhile, George looks forward to building his confidence and perhaps registering at college or university. Despite having no family to return to and expressing some trepidation about being released after over two decades in custody, his sense of optimism is palpable.

Notes

1 'Burn': tobacco.
2 'Draw': cannabis.
3 Doing 'bird': serving a sentence.
4 A 'tear-up': a fight.
5 Goffman, E. (1961) 'On the characteristics of total institutions: The inmate world', in D. Cressey (ed.) *The Prison: Studies in Institutional Organisation and Change*. New York: Holt, Rinehart & Winston.
6 Jewkes, Y. (2002) *Captive Audience: Media, Masculinity and Power in Prisons*. Cullompton: Willan Publishing.
7 Schmid, T. and Jones, R. (1991) 'Suspended identity: Identity transformation in a maximum security prison', *Symbolic Interaction*, 14(4): 415–32.
8 Cohen, S. and Taylor, L. (1972) *Psychological Survival: The Experience of Long-Term Imprisonment*. Harmondsworth: Penguin.
9 Prisoner, cited in Jewkes, *Captive Audience*.
10 Cohen and Taylor, *Psychological Survival*.
11 Clemmer, D. (1958) *The Prison Community* (2nd edn.) New York: Holt, Rinehart & Winston.
12 Cohen and Taylor, *Psychological Survival*.
13 Jewkes, *Captive Audience*.
14 Wheeler, S. (1961) 'Socialisation in correctional communities', *American Sociological Review*, 26(5): 697–712.

Further reading

For a classic account of life-sentence prisoners that describes many of the themes highlighted in this chapter, including identity, (sub)cultures and adaptation to life in custody, see Stanley Cohen and Laurie Taylor's *Psychological Survival: The Experience of Long-Term Imprisonment* (Harmondsworth: Penguin, 1972). For a more recent study, which focuses on the impact of television and other media in prisons, but which has much to say about identity, self and masculinity, see Yvonne Jewkes, *Captive Audience: Media, Masculinity and Power in Prisons* (Cullompton: Willan Publishing, 2002).

5 Vulnerability, struggling and coping in prison

Alison Liebling

Adam was a 20-year-old from Essex interviewed in a Young Offender Institution as part of a study of suicides and attempted suicide in prison. He had made a serious suicide attempt on a Sunday evening a few months before the interview, and was still located in the prison's healthcare centre. Things 'just got on top of' him and he 'couldn't take it no more'. He 'couldn't be certain' that he 'wouldn't do it again'. He was serving a three-and-a-half-year sentence for robbery. It was his third sentence. He was involved in group work and individual therapy at the time of his interview. He struggled to cope with other prisoners but was able to form dependent relationships with therapeutically inclined staff. His relationship with his family was fragile.

> I thought the sentence was a bit long. My barrister said I should have got less. I was transferred here [a prison with a therapeutic facility] from Hollesley Bay because I was having problems there. I had problems with alcohol and with my family and with myself. He told me about this place and I said I wanted to go here. They said yes.
>
> There were problems at home before I started offending. It goes back quite a long way, really. My dad went away for a while, so he must have been doing something wrong, for someone to come round and take him away.
>
> I was out for a whole year before this, but then I started drinking really heavily. It was family trouble and pressures. I was using drink as an escape route, to forget about problems. I used to get on really well with one of my uncles, I don't even know where he is now. They got divorced. I used to do plumbing with him. If they'd stayed around, I'd probably still be doing that now.
>
> Yes, I get visits still. Well, not really. I sent them a VO[1] but I've had some excuse. It's rubbish. I've had a lot of difficulty getting them up here, they're always making excuses. They are just making me sit and wait. I'm not sending them VOs any more. The last visit was awful. They just wanted to talk about this lovely holiday they'd just been on. I was really pissed off.

The first time I went in they said, 'Don't worry, you can come home', and everything and then first day I got out, my old man said, 'Fuck off, you're not coming back in this house'. I went over to my mate's. I was on probation, but he left the profession. He didn't do his job properly.

I don't really think about anyone from the outside. I've got more support in here. I don't really keep up with what's going on outside. I can't be bothered. I don't have friends in here, no. Some of the staff, maybe.

I don't think they thought much about my transfer here. I find the groups helpful but it's hard to express yourself when there's that many parts to it. If you find out why you are in a mess, it makes you mad. I just couldn't handle it. My dad used to batter me, with bamboo sticks and with his fists. At that point I would have smashed him over the head with a chair. I suppose I am working on it. I mean, before, when I've been in other prisons, I was determined to get out and blow them away. I am still not sure I want to stay in contact when I get out. I might change my mind later on.

Since I first went into prison I've been living rough really. I'm going out to a probation hostel. I had a job before I was supposed to leave school. I used to truant all the time. I hated it.

I don't know how I get on with my mum. Not good. I used to love my mum really a lot. But now she's making excuses, going off somewhere or whatever. She gave me some money to find somewhere else to live and I spent it on drink.

I'm not sure I am coping in here. I'm dodgy really. I'm getting under pressure in here at the moment, from other lads. I am very tense. I am seeing the psychologist but I have not seen her for quite a few weeks. Outside I was drinking myself senseless. It became a habit. I used to thieve all the time. I didn't pay for the hostel I was in, spent the money on drink. They threw me out. One felt sorry for me and found me somewhere else, and I burgled his house. There was nothing left of it. I came back and stripped the whole lot, carpets, everything. When I first came in I couldn't cope with being sober.

I'm not a violent person. I'm against violence, but if I ever did have a fight, I might kill someone. I've got a very bad temper. I haven't been happy since I was about 15. I think the booze has damaged my brain cells. I get ratty. In here sometimes I just lie in bed. I think about the past a lot. I don't think about the future very much. At the moment I'm a bit weary, because of whatever ... I can't sleep.

I was serious, yes. I tied the end of a sheet. I didn't even know what knot to tie, so that it doesn't matter if you pull it, you can't get it off, you have to cut it. I tied it onto the bed and dropped myself – bang – and I expected to be dead. I definitely was serious. I know a few what's done it. It's tension, pressure, you can't handle life and what's going on in here, worry, addictions. I only thought about it for five minutes, not long. I just made up my mind and off you go, let's get on with it. It had occurred to me before, yes, once or twice. I had so much going on, it just all got on top of me. I just couldn't take it any more. I was going out of my head. Will I do it again? I don't know really. I can't really say. I can't be certain that I won't do it again.

I was scared to talk to anyone. They didn't really want to help me, or understand. Some officers are like that. It's led me into here so it must have helped me, in the end, but that wasn't part of the plan.

I'd like to work with the mentally handicapped. I'm learning about that. In here I'd like to be an inmate counsellor. I tell them to take it easy and slowly, don't rush things. I tell them about my problems to make them talk. I had a really long chat with a lad yesterday. They should train us.

This place is not an easy ride. It's very up and down. You sit and think so much. It's less that I'm bored than that I'm worried. About myself, whether I can cope. Most of the time I'm two'd up with this geezer who gets on my nerves. It takes some nerve to sit in a cell for hours on end with just him. I get edgy. Time goes quicker when I'm working. Night times are bad. I listen to the radio sometimes.

The staff are brilliant up here. The psychiatrist especially. She's great, doesn't treat you like dirt or anything, She works really hard. The hospital staff work hard too. It's only when, at this time of year, when a lot of the staff are on leave, and you're waiting to get something out, and groups are cancelled, it's very hard to be here then. I must admit, I've never had staff go on at me. They do try and help and work with you. I think now I'm going to walk out of here better. This place is great from that point of view. It helps you to talk about yourself and understand. You get really involved. You find out you're responsible for some things. They've trusted me and changed my security rating.

Ruth had been in prison for 14 months. She was interviewed as part of an evaluation of new suicide prevention procedures in several prisons, including new first-night arrangements for women undergoing drug detoxification. She was 32, and had never been in prison before. She had a daughter and quite a good relationship with the rest of her family. She had been terrified on entering prison for the first time, and had faced her own problems with addiction. Her sentence was three and a half years. She did not know whether her remand time counted, but hoped she might be out on tagging before too long. She worked in the kitchen. She was also a Samaritan-trained Listener.

I had problems with drink and drugs before I came in. Before I came to prison, I'd gone onto prescribed medication to come off the heroin and I found that a lot harder. They gave me Subutex to start with, because I didn't want to go on methadone. It is really good. It stopped the craving and then I think I was lost with time. I didn't know what to do with myself. I didn't have a lot of help.

This was all before I committed the crime ... I just turned to drinking on the medication. I didn't really know what I was doing. When I look back it was horrible. I felt isolated really. When you're on the drugs, you'll go round to people's houses, you're mixing with people. When I came off, I had to stay away from them, so it was a lot harder and I felt ...it sounds silly, but I felt lonely because when you're with these people ... they're not your friends but you're still with them and you're doing things with them. So, it's done me a favour really coming to jail. I hate to say it, but it has, it's done me good. I think it's either that or you end up dead.

You get so bad ... how can I explain it ... when you're on the drugs, you want to come off them, but there's not really a lot of support because you can go to these counsellors but they're always giving you prescribed medication, so always have a script on you ... you're going onto something else and there's another addiction there, so... I found it really hard to come off the prescribed medication. It was only when I came in here that they reduced me. They still put me on the detox wing. They put me on medication to cut down what I'd been taking, and they said it's just as bad really because I was detoxing off that. I came off it quite soon, within about four weeks. That's when they wanted to get me off the wing and get me working. I felt a lot better. When they come in, I don't think staff realise ... because it is a drug thing, when you're coming in here, they've got to face up to all their problems in one go and it's an awful lot, you know, because when you're on drugs, you don't feel anything and you're not really thinking properly. So, when you're coming in here, you're thinking an awful lot and then they get depressed, don't they?

I didn't think I was going to be locked up as much when I first came in. You're locked up a lot. And not a lot of people ... the officers come and sit with you for about five minutes. Of course, you're ever so tearful and upset so you're not really listening to what they're telling you, and that's it then, they go and you've just got to follow everybody else so... I know we're in prison, but girls need to be told what's happening – what they can do, what they can't do. I suppose the staff haven't got time, have they? But, it is a hard situation, Some of them are still in shock that they've come into prison.

I was surprised by the other girls – how helpful they were. They were quite supportive because I was always a bit, like, thinking of bullying and the things you hear from other people, it's quite scary.

Life outside was horrible, really. When I look back, at the time, I thought it was all right. I was just carrying on. I was getting up drinking every day and I think I was just lost. My daughter was staying at my mum's quite a lot, so I wasn't at home and my house was just going downhill. I'd been to counselling, I think about six months before I came to jail, and then I told them I was on the medication and that I was drinking a lot. He said he couldn't help me because he was a drugs counsellor and he'd have to put me on to AA or something. Because I'd got on with him and he knew my problems, I felt let down then. I felt like I could talk to him, so when he put me off like that, I just thought, no, so I didn't bother after that.

My mum and dad ... I hid a lot of it away from them, so they didn't know what I was going through. I'd argued with my brother about it because he was really ashamed by my drugs. I felt really ... that I'd let him down. I didn't know what I was doing half the time. When I think back, I can't really remember. The six months building up until I committed the crime, I can't remember a lot about it ... I remember the way I was acting: it was quite loud and aggressive. So, I must have felt angry. When you're on drugs ... you're numb. You don't think of anything at all; you don't think of your problems, so coming off of them, I had to deal with everything. I had to get up in the morning, take my daughter to school, and in the end, I had to tell my parents and they took it really hard. They didn't know at all. I hid it quite well because I was working as well. They were devastated. We've talked a lot since and sorted an awful lot out. They were scared at first because they thought I might do something stupid because the way I'd been acting and the way I was feeling, but I've come a long way. I'm very pleased.

I was really scared when I came in. I thought I was having a heart attack because I was shaking, I was crying, really scared. You're like in a line, because you're all coming off the bus and the next one it's like, well, you're just a number really. You're just in and out, aren't you? And they're trying to get you in as quick as possible. I didn't know about the Listening scheme. I didn't even know that you could talk to people. I was so scared, I was just waiting to be told what I could do and what I couldn't do, so I just waited until the officer came in, in the morning. There was only one woman officer and the two that strip-search you – they're just chatting as if you're not there. I just felt that they were ... I know that we'd just come in but I think they should explain a bit more ... you know, you've got to follow them into the bit where you get strip-searched and they tell you what to do, you take your clothes off and it's degrading. Then we get dressed and we get left again, so you don't get told a lot of information. It was scary. They just asked me questions, you know: my age, what drugs I was taking and things like that, and that was it; just questions. I think you're scared about what to say, because you don't know what to expect or what they're going to do, if you do say you are feeling suicidal so... my uncle had hung himself in a prison a few years ago so I was ... My auntie was phoning up quite a lot, so I think she was scared. I was worried they might put me somewhere else, you know, separate me or something. I kept saying to my auntie, 'I'll be all right. Don't say anything', sort of thing.

I just wanted to go home. It was horrible. The feelings ... it's fear. At the time, I didn't know what it was because I was shaking and my stomach was going and everything and I just couldn't sleep. My mind just worked overtime because you're thinking of your family and everything, and what's going to happen. Of course, I wasn't sentenced either so I didn't know how long I was going to be here ... I felt ... I wouldn't say suicidal, I just felt like I didn't want to be here. It was hard. After about three days, I felt all right. Once I knew my surroundings and where I was going, I felt a bit better then.

I didn't cope very well with the first 24 hours. I didn't feel I could talk to staff. I suppose there are certain times of the day when you come into the jail – if it's evening, I suppose they rush you through because you've got to be locked up. But then you are just left there, aren't you? Maybe, if they could come and just have a little chat to reassure you that it's going to be all right and then come in the morning, I think that would be all right. You're thinking, oh my God, what's going to happen? And you don't know if any of the girls are going to bully you or if you're going to get picked on. There is a lot of bullying. I think it's more for tobacco. It's really bad.

It's really hard because they don't seem to know what to do for the detoxing, or how to treat them. I know they're prisoners, but the way they're feeling is absolutely terrible. I know ... a lot of them say ... you get told it's self-inflicted as well, but the way they're feeling is terrible and I don't think anybody knows. The officers don't seem to understand how they're feeling. They need a lot of care.

The best way of coping is getting a job, working hard, doing as much as you can with your time instead of sitting around. In here, I've done Listening. I put in an application. I heard about it with the posters. A friend of mine used to do it before she left and she enjoyed it so I put my name forward. I had a letter through to say to attend a meeting and interview. They don't actually tell you if you're in until ... you have the interview and then a few training sessions, then another interview and then they tell you. So, you're thinking, oh my God, have I got in or not? It's the Samaritans that come in. They're good. We've asked for extra training on self-harming, because I don't think anything prepares anyone for going into a room and seeing what they see sometimes, so I think we need more training in that. There's only three of us at the moment. We had a problem this year. They just keep getting shipped out,[2] or they come to the end of their sentence. So by the time they train people, they get moved.

I've noticed when Listening, I feel so sorry for them because in a way ... it has helped me and luckily I've got back with my family and the support's there, but for other people, they seem to ... wind them up, and create more problems. They have got an awful lot of problems.

Two Listeners would go down there [a remand wing] and stay overnight and we'd take it in turns then as well, so it would help us if it was too busy, and we'd stay on, you know, the next day ... one of us would stay on duty. So, it did help a lot of the girls, but I think they find it hard now because we're only on until ten o'clock because there's only three of us. I feel guilty. Because I've [been] doing it for quite a while, I want to, like ... for example, last night I went out Listening and I'd finished and there was one more girl and I thought, you know, I don't like to say no. I'd rather go and see her, just in case, because you don't know what's going to happen. I don't think I'd be able to sleep if I hadn't gone there ...

There's been quite a lot of problems with girls that have rung bells, asked for Listeners and they've been waiting three hours, and I don't know why because we've been sat on the wing. All the Listeners spoke to each other and we can't understand why it's taking so long. They need to come and get us. It loses their trust as well because they've been sat thinking for those three hours. By the time you get over there, they're quite upset and then they're angry as well.

I've got one Listener, she's been telling me that she's had problems with officers, saying that they've been turning round saying there are no Listeners on duty. I think you get half that are for it and half that are against it. So, some don't mind and appreciate what you're doing and then you get the others that think it's disgusting that an inmate's going to see another inmate. I suppose because they think that we are criminals and we shouldn't be doing it. But we're doing it because we care, and we know what the other girls are going through. We want to help them and support them, but they don't like that. They think that we should be locked up continuously and punished.

They talk to you. You can have a conversation and they do seem to care. I think ... they like to see that you're getting on well and I suppose if you work hard, they can see that. There's a bit of respect on both sides. If you're a good prisoner, then they treat you okay, but ... I've heard some officers say things about inmates that are disgusting and the inmate's heard that as well and I think that's really cruel. I think to speak to an officer, if I was really upset, I'd find it hard. I'd rather go to a friend in here. I suppose if they were a bit more approachable because they've still got that ... to me, they come across that they still have that bit of power over us, you know. Some are brilliant. There's a couple of young ones where my friends, when they've been really upset, they've gone to the officer and they've really helped them. And then you get others that are too busy and don't want to know ... well, they say they're too busy...

We get a couple that they just won't call a Listener out. They've got to trust you. You want them to call you out, but you don't want to force them to call you out, because they might think that we're being nosey or something. It is upsetting, especially if they are self-harming. There's one girl especially that does it and she's really, really bad, but she won't call Listeners out. She feels she can't talk. I think sometimes it's comfort, as well, if somebody else is sat there.

It's hard being away from my daughter, now I'm straight and I've sorted everything out and I know what I want, it's really hard because you just want to go out. You think, I've done my time. I want to go home. Visits ... I don't have many. I don't really like the Visiting Room with my daughter coming in because she's coming up to eleven now. I've just my town visits. I've had one, so I'm due another one this week, so I can go out, which is easier because I'm out all day with them then. They're once a month.

I think the courses have helped. I've been on quite a lot. I've done as much as I can: Assertiveness, Drug Awareness, Enhanced Thinking Skills. They've helped me. When I look back, I could never say no. I've always wanted to help everybody. I was always helping other people and just letting myself go. So I would like to be a bit more assertive, I think. There's CARATS[3] and they can put you on this drug awareness course and that did help me, but some girls aren't going to sit in a classroom and talk about what it does to you, the effects it has and everything. Some girls can't write and read, so they're not going to go to the class ... some it helps and some it doesn't. Maybe counselling would be a bit more ... somebody that they could talk to about their problems because that's what's coming out of them when they're detoxing, their emotions are coming back ... It could maybe break down their problems and see ones that aren't big and ones that are and break them down and put them in order.

I had to meet my victim. She asked if she could come up and meet me. And I didn't really want to at the time. I was really nervous about it, but my officer on the wing, I asked if she would come with me to support me, and she did. That was really good. She came up to the prison and it worked out really good so I was glad I done it. It was scary. I wanted to do it because of the guilt I was feeling, but I didn't want to face her because it's frightening to know that somebody doesn't like you because of what you've done. But once I let her talk and listened, it was good and she felt a lot better as well, so it did work out well and the officer was just really supportive. She is my Personal Officer now. There's four different officers that come on the wing and we can go to any one of them so ... luckily, she was on that day so she came along. Probation sorted it out. I was glad that the woman saw me as a human being and that I wasn't this horrible, nasty person that had robbed her, basically. And the officer ... some of the questions I wanted to ask, I'd forgotten, so the officer was there and she sort of gave me the idea again and she was brilliant.

People commit suicide in prison because they just can't ... they can't cope with being locked up and the feeling of being isolated. They think the officers are against them. Some people think that they don't care, and that they're not being looked after properly, so it's really hard for them. They just can't cope. They can't see the end either. They think that's it, that's their life, and they do want to die.

The single thing that would make a difference is I think actually for the officers to be more caring, you know, listen; take that bit of time just to care; maybe there might be something that they're able to do. If they can't get a job, maybe there's something else. I know we're inmates and we do get told that enough times and we're here because of what we've done. We know that. On the day that we've been in that court room and we've been sentenced, we know that we are coming to prison to serve a time. So, maybe the officers could be a bit more understanding.

Commentary

Adam and Ruth both struggled with aspects of imprisonment, and with aspects of their emotional lives, before and during the sentence. Ruth had been an addict, but she had a good detoxification experience in an improving prison, and outside support. She also had a daughter. She had more developed internal resources and a more sustaining external environment: a handful of supportive staff, good friends in the prison, and a meaningful job. Adam was younger, and barely coming to terms with his turbulent early life. He was ambivalent – wanting support and connection – but ready to reject it when people let him down, as he expected. He was full of anger, and felt at the mercy of uncontrollable impulses. He could not always bring the best out in staff, as they triggered his early experiences of carelessness and abuse. He was afraid of other prisoners. His chances of finding his way into a supportive environment and staying there were slim. He had landed in a therapeutic environment as a result of his serious suicide attempt. But even here, there were gaps in the supply of 'care'. Both wanted to help others in similar predicaments – but Ruth found her way into an institutionally organised Listener scheme. She flourished in this role. Her interview said as much about others and their experiences as it did about her own. She was other-oriented, even when she was in distress. Adam was more confused, and had much undigested experience and feeling to work through. He was extremely vulnerable. He felt let down by the probation service (where he experienced further losses in continuity) and lost contact with an uncle who had given him work when this uncle divorced. His family life was fractured and unstable as well as violent. His school life was unhappy.

In prison, he was very aware of his inability to cope, and was not confident that there were people around who could help him or might want to listen to him. Like many vulnerable prisoners, psychologically wounded in the past, he struggled to identify and communicate his complex feelings. In interview, prisoners would sometimes jump at words offered: 'lethargic' – 'yes, that's the right word'; or 'angry' – 'maybe I am angry'. They needed time, and collaboration, to find the right words. Adam's prison file, on the other hand, was littered with negative labels for his experience: 'inadequate', 'attention-seeking' and 'immature'. He showed many of the symptoms of depression. He was not at all oriented towards the future and seemed devoid of hope. Prisoners at risk of suicide in the study from which this interview is drawn showed a general lack of inner resources. They were less able to occupy themselves when alone in their cells for long periods of time, were susceptible to feelings of anxiety and self-doubt, and thought little about the future. Despite the material improvement in his circumstances following his attempt, Adam had intended to die and was not being strategic. There was a glimmer of hope in his motivation to help others, and in the trust that had been extended to him.

Ruth, on the other hand, had a different relationship with drugs, and with her internal self. Despite using drugs to dull pain, she found she could handle her feelings, with assistance, once she received help with detoxification. She had since done every course on offer, and received quite a lot of support as a first-time, slightly older prisoner. She behaved in a way that was easy to manage in prison, and (in a reversal of some widespread assumptions about women in prison) experienced her anxiety internally rather than acting it out. She had many advantages, including a family who supported her and worried about her.

Both Adam and Ruth found some staff who were supportive and others who were indifferent or hostile. The officers were unaware that they could make the difference between a survivable environment and a non-survivable one. They mattered far more than they realised. They expressed antagonistic views at times, which impacted negatively on individuals, and on the environment and what was possible in it. Prison officers act as gatekeepers and facilitators. If they did not support a Listener scheme, it failed. The attitudes, values, expressed ideologies and working practices of prison officers were critical. There is a randomness to prisoners' encounters with officers. Where they come across helpful and supportive staff, the trajectory of their lives alters. Ruth was helped to face a meeting with her victim, and where she faltered, her 'brilliant' personal officer helped to prod her memory. This was prison officer work at its best.[4]

Both found life in prison better in some respects than life in the community, for a period at least. This is not an argument for prison, but an indication of how difficult prisoners' lives can be prior to imprisonment, and how little support is available in the community. Both Adam and Ruth also found or expected life in prison to be frightening and dangerous. How tragic, therefore, that it was in any way preferred to life outside.

Ruth described a prison under transformation – as part of the pilot for the new suicide prevention strategy, this prison was one of six to receive significant investment and headquarters support in order to improve its reception and first-night facilities. The strategy (where well implemented) also led to a better culture, to improved safety, and to higher levels of care for prisoners in distress. This had a significant impact on suicide rates.[5]

Research shows that suicides and suicide attempts in prison arise as a result of a combination of individual 'imported' vulnerability and the strains and deprivations of the prison environment.[6] Imported vulnerability can include drug addiction, family breakdown, prior abuse, and frequent offending, and takes the form of an inability to manage prison life, peers, staff and inactivity and isolation well. All prisoners show some vulnerability, but some find prison life excruciating and beyond their endurance. Prisons vary significantly in the extent to which they expose these kinds of vulnerabilities. One study has shown, for example, that highly vulnerable individuals do well (that is, they show much less distress) when they are in establishments with predictable, active and supportive regimes.[7] Dedicated detoxification facilities, well-run first-night centres, and Listener schemes make a significant impact on the experience of entry into custody: a period of extreme risk. In this study, prisoners reporting high vulnerability but low distress were more likely to be employed in prison and much less likely to be locked up for more than six hours during the day. They were less likely to report that association was frequently cancelled (a symptom of a well-run prison with cooperative staff). They were more likely to be on the enhanced level of privileges, to be doing an offending behaviour course, to be receiving visits, and to be close to home. Regime activities, supportive and approachable staff, family contact and closeness to home were protective.

Regarding unsuccessful suicide attempts and self-harm as 'manipulative' is dangerous and disparaging. Studies show that the urge to live is always present alongside the urge to die (Sylvia Plath described her many suicide attempts as a kind of gamble with life, offering a feeling of renewal, if survived). Research also shows that those who self-harm have a much multiplied chance of dying by suicide in the future. Responses to attempts should always include a sensitive discussion of 'why did this happen?' rather than an interrogation on what it was intended to achieve. Self-harm is often a 'cry of pain' rather than (as so often stated) a 'cry for help'. Suicide is a continuum along which one first step requires exploration and support. This is particularly the case where the state has taken on the role of corrective authority and depriver of liberty, and the form the punishment takes is experienced as beyond endurance.

It is significant that even in long, exploratory interviews it often took some time for prisoners to open up and find words to describe their experience. Many of the young prisoners interviewed in the first study had speech difficulties, struggled to articulate their experience, and took time to build up trust with the interviewer. They were used to giving short answers to questions. Some expressed surprise when they realised that this was 'just an interview' intended to be accepting and validating, and without constraints. Individuals sometimes used shorthand ('I was bored') when more complex feelings were indicated ('Yes, I get visits still, well, not really'). It was noticeable that interviewees were more able to describe 'why people in general might attempt suicide in prison' at the end of a long interview than they could articulate their own feelings at the beginning. This need for trust, time and validation is relevant to suicide prevention efforts in general as well as for methods of and approaches to risk assessment. Adam describes 'being trusted' as a turning point in his experience. It is paradoxical but significant that the professional group most able to express appropriate responses to prisoners undergoing suicidal crises were the prison chaplaincy ('we could all do with more sitting where they sit') whereas medical staff could sometimes be dismissive and judgemental.[8] For prisoners who have 'never been properly heard in all their lives', empathetic listening could save lives.

The single most important difference between a prison that felt survivable and one that did not was a feeling of safety. This was associated with good staff–prisoner relationships, decent relationships with other prisoners, and with the approachability of staff. Approachable staff provided reassurance and predictability. Prisons differed significantly in the extent to which they felt safe, and as in communities, this was not directly related to the risk of violence and assault but to a kind of 'trust in the environment'. The evaluation in which the second interview took place showed that prisons could significantly improve their levels of safety, thereby reducing levels of distress by active engagement, the support of specialist staff, providing an active regime, and by 'dynamic' and relational approaches to security and order.[9] 'Feeling unsafe' included feelings of uncertainty, powerlessness, frustration and distress, as well as the desire to harm oneself. Relationships, safety and fairness were experienced as a form of care in prison. Indifference, on the other hand, was experienced as an injustice, and a harm.

Specialist support (for example, mental health in-reach) was significant in increasing staff confidence and expertise, as well as providing direct care to prisoners. Dedicated detoxification facilities made an impact on the experience of coming into custody, as Ruth describes. Coming into custody with a drug problem, or while withdrawing from drugs, was described as a frightening experience. Prisoners often spend a few nights in police custody with no medication, and describe feeling 'shipwrecked' when they arrive in prison. Coming into prison was, at the same time, described as a relief for some drug users, who could escape the chaos of their life outside, and access food, medical care and a place to sleep. Prisoners withdrawing from drugs often experience overwhelming emotions, and often have difficult or non-existent relationships with family and friends. As access to their emotions returns, they realise the damage they have done to their relationships, often with guilt and shame. Their isolation is intensified by the realisation that friendships that had revolved around their drug use are now meaningless, as Ruth describes above. Prison staff often feel ill equipped to deal with the symptoms of addiction, and the strong emotions that surface. These complex aspects of the work of prison officers (bordering on the therapeutic and psychiatric) are seriously underestimated.

While there is no single profile of the 'prison suicide', suicide attempts in prison are often the culmination of a process, beginning outside and influenced to a considerable extent by the nature and quality of the prison environment. Prisoners differ in their abilities to cope with, or generate solutions to, the problems of this environment. The way prisoners use time varies significantly, and is linked to lifestyles outside prison, as well as to the future prospects of offenders, whose coping behaviours are often negative. Supportive environments expose less of this imported vulnerability, whereas harsh or indifferent environments, isolation, inactivity and lack of contact with outside relationships can bring about feelings of hopelessness. The principles of good prison regimes, first outlined by Ian Dunbar in *A Sense of Direction* – relationships, individualism and activity – are also the principles of good suicide prevention practice.[10]

Zamble and Porporino argued in *Coping, Behaviour and Adaptation in Prison Inmates* that offenders often pass the time rather than *use* it, often resort to alcohol and drugs as a way of dealing with difficulties, and tend to deal with life in an unplanned and impulsive or reactive manner.[11] Studies of suicide attempts in prison show that this is especially the case with those who are vulnerable and at risk. These prisoners often return to prison quickly between sentences, showing evidence of poor coping in the community as well as in prison. They respond positively to interventions that teach emotion management techniques as well as practical and thinking skills. Mood can affect the ability to call on coping strategies. In prison, problems are more difficult to resolve, as the range of options is limited. Staff play an especially critical role in mediating or ameliorating this environment for the vulnerable. Other prisoners can also be of help, whether via formal Listener schemes, other organised groups, or individually. A 'guide to getting free', produced by the Prison-Ashram project (now the Prison Phoenix Trust) called *We're All Doing Time*, advocates and instructs yoga and meditation techniques, helping prisoners to do their time as 'prison monks', using the experience to learn lessons about 'the vastness inside', and to make real change, rather than endure it 'as convicts'.[12] A series of conferences known as the 'Lincoln Conferences' (hosted by the Bishop of Lincoln) during the 1990s likewise advocated humanity, respect and kindness towards prisoners, in the interests of a better life for all. This model, of gentle reorientation, support and guidance, suggests a rather different policy agenda from that derived from the neo-liberal, responsibilisation, cognitive-behavioural model that has become fashionable since then.

Prisoners are often vulnerable and troubled, and feel in need of help with their emotional lives as well as with their offending, to which this emotional turbulence may be linked. Their relationships are often fragile and their hold on stability precarious. Seeing such offenders as simply 'posing a risk' misrepresents that nature of their experience and inhibits our understanding of both the effects of imprisonment and the causes of crime.

Notes

1 'VO': Visiting order.
2 'Shipped out': moved to another prison.
3 'CARAT': drug-related Counselling, Assessment, Referral, Advice and Throughcare System.
4 See further, Liebling, A., Price, D. and Shefer, G. (2011) *The Prison Officer*, 2nd edn. Cullompton: Willan Publishing; Liebling, A. and Tait, S. (2006) 'Improving staff–prisoner relationships', in G. E. Dear (ed.) *Preventing Suicide and Other Self-Harm in Prison*. London: Palgrave Macmillan, pp. 103–17; and Tait, S. (2008) 'Care and the prison officer: Beyond "turnkeys" and "care bears" ', *Prison Service Journal*, 180: 3–11.
5 Liebling, A. (2008) 'Why prison staff culture matters', in J. M. Byrne, D. Hummer and F. S. Taxman (eds) *The Culture of Prison Violence*. Boston, MA: Allyn and Bacon, pp. 105–22.
6 Liebling, A. (2006) 'The role of the prison environment in prisoner suicide and prisoner distress', in G. E. Dear (ed.) *Preventing Suicide and Other Self-Harm in Prison*. London: Palgrave Macmillan, pp. 16–28.
7 Liebling, A., Durie, L., Stiles, A. and Tait, S. (2005) 'Revisiting prison suicide: The role of fairness and distress', in A. Liebling and S. Maruna (eds) *The Effects of Imprisonment*. Cullompton: Willan Publishing, pp. 209–31.
8 See further Liebling, A. (1992) *Suicides in Prison*. London: Routledge.
9 Liebling *et al*., 'Revisiting prison suicide'.
10 Dunbar, I. (1985) *A Sense of Direction*. London: HMSO.
11 Zamble, E. and Porporino, F. J. (1988) *Coping, Behaviour and Adaptation in Prison Inmates*. Secaucus, NJ: Springer-Verlag.
12 Lozoff, B. (1985) *We're All Doing Time: A Guide for Getting Free*. Durham: Hanuman Foundation.

Further reading

For a detailed account of prisoners' experiences of suicides and suicide attempts in prison, see Alison Liebling, *Suicides in Prison* (London: Routledge, 1992). For a review of more recent studies, see Liebling's, 'Suicide and its prevention', in Yvonne Jewkes (ed.) *Handbook on Prisons* (Cullompton: Willan Publishing, 2006); and on the themes of safety, fairness, trust and relationships and their role in prisoner well-being, see Liebling's (assisted by Helen Arnold), *Prisons and their Moral Performance: A Study of Values, Quality, and Prison Life* (Oxford: Oxford University Press, 2004). See also Alison Liebling and Shadd Maruna (eds) *The Effects of Imprisonment* (Cullompton: Willan Publishing, 2005) and works on coping and life in prison by Hans Toch.

6   Prisoners and their families

Rachel Condry

Jeremiah was a young, black British prisoner, from a notorious area of a large city in north-west England. He had been involved with gangs in his early years, and had already served one fairly long sentence, but he was determined to go straight on release, having recently become a father: 'When she told me she was pregnant, that's when everything changed for me.' He was large and very muscular, but his demeanour was relaxed.

> I had a very good upbringing, my father and mother was there, brothers and sisters. Back in them days money weren't … it weren't the best of things, we were living in a council house, my parents were working people. Mum was always a big factor in my life, she's always shown me love, she's always been there. I've always been shown love, so it's not like I had grown up with no love. I'd say it was by choice I went into gang life.
>
> Well, when I come out of jail I met my missus and we were courting and obviously from courting, a little child come, but I left her out there pregnant and it's only since I come in jail that my child was born. Leading up to before I met my girl I was still doing the same thing, but she kind of calmed me down, because she said, 'You know what, you don't have to do all them kind of things', so she's got a big influence on me now. She can't stop me doing them because she's not there with me 24/7, but she can speak to me, you get me? I wouldn't say certain things to a man because I'd feel weak, but my girl – I'd say I'd more trust my girl.
>
> When she told me she was pregnant, that's when everything changed for me. When I come out of prison and she told me she was pregnant and she said she wanted the child and all that, you know, it changed me. I said to myself, you're going to be a father, you know, analysed my view and how I'm living my life. And I'm saying to myself, I'm going to gradually come out of this kind of life, because I don't want my son growing up having to witness certain things. So my son is a big influence on me, changing me, walking away from that lifestyle. When I get out, I'm subject to lifer conditions, it's a recall thing, so unless I change myself now I'm going to lose everything I've got, I'm going to come back to prison, I'm going to

stay in prison for a long time, so I analyse that myself and say, you know what, the best thing for me right now is I need to get out.

So I'd say my influence right now is my child, because he's been born since I've been in, and he hasn't really known his father. It's been very hard for me, because the first time I seen him was on a visit, the first time I held my son was on a visit, instead of me being at the hospital. I've never really done nothing for him, I've never really given him a bath, I've never took him to the park, I've never cooked him a meal, so it's hard. That four and a half years, it's been a struggle, because certain jails have been like 300, 400 miles from home, and my girlfriend's coming up on the train on her own with a child.

It's easy to fall into bad lives in prison, it's easy … you know, to get into bad lives, like move with the wrong crowd, get into mischief, so with me knowing that I've got my child out there, from that early stage in my sentence I said to myself, you need to get your head down, you need to complete what you need to complete, stay adjudication-free, get on with everyone and try and get out as early as possible so that you can be there for your son. So I'd say that's the line that I took since I've been in prison, I think I've done well on this sentence in the fact that I've … to date I've addressed everything that I'm supposed address, and I'm coming to the end of my sentence. Since I've been inside I've never had a fight with no one, I don't come across angry to inmates around the prison.

I draw my strength from me first of all, and then from outside. Family members – it's mainly like my mum and my girl and my child, that's the main people. They're the main people in my life right now, them three people. And it's them people that I contact more than anyone, and my sister occasionally.

I don't get visits as often as I would like because of the distance. My girl drives, but she's only just learnt. It's hard on her, so I don't really like to put an added pressure on her, you understand, because she works from Monday to Friday, so obviously she can't come through the week. Weekends, she's an active member of the church, so she goes to church Saturday, but I don't really look to put no pressure on her. She does come up, but I don't put that added pressure on her.

Well, they say absence makes the heart grow fonder, so I'd say the distance and the time that we've been separated has made us stronger. I think because we've had time to think, both of us, I think it made us stronger as a couple. I've never been dependent on her. Not at all. I don't put pressure on her to send me money, I don't put pressure on her to do nothing, I've always fended for myself, understand what I'm saying to you, if it's criminally – or if it's me to go out there now and get a job.

I do feel guilty because I've left her out there, I've left her out there to struggle. I know the struggle that she's gone through, you understand what

I'm saying to you, standing at the bus stop with my son late at night, and I phone her and she's crying and it's cold and she's waiting for the bus to come home, or guilty in the sense where she has to travel all over the country to see me with my child. So I feel guilty in that sense, that I've left her to defend for herself with a young child when she was young herself.

It's hard to be a husband and a father, because at the end of the day you're not there every day to see the ups and downs, but because of how I used to treat her, this is why she's waiting for me, that made her see me for what I was, so that alone has made her think, you know what, even though he was up to this and that, then was then, and now is now. She's put that trust in me.

Prison weren't set out to be easy, was it? I'd say the hardest time in prison is when you initially wake up and you see the same bars and the same door, and you can't even do what you need to do, you've not got that freedom. The best part of the day is when I can get on the phone to my family, when I've got my units [phone credits], or I get a letter from my loved ones. I'd say that's the best part for me when I phone and I speak to my family. Not to say that I'm down in between, you understand, but I feel better when I can speak to people that I know.

There's the frustration of not being able to do things that you want to do. If you get on the phone and you hear that a loved one's passed away or a certain member of the family's going through a difficult time, you're stuck in here and the frustration that you can't even help them. It makes me feel like less of a man that my child and my wife, they have to fend for themselves right now and I don't think I'm being there to support her, so that makes me feel less of a man, that I'm not there to support and take responsibility for what I created.

I anticipate my freedom, I can't wait to get out. I don't think I've got too many fears at this moment, because I've got a good family background, a strong relationship, I've got a healthy child, I'm healthy, my girlfriend's healthy. I've got a job offer, so no real fears or concerns as such, but just to know within myself that I need to change and implement a lot of things in my life where I've gone wrong before.

Luke was a white British prisoner in his late thirties, who had spent much of his adult life in prison, mainly for petty offences. As a child, his father's disciplinary methods had included whipping him until his legs bled. He had also been traumatised by the brutality of the juvenile detention system which he had entered as a 16-year-old. He had left school aged 15, and had worked in the family business, but his relationships with his family had become strained due to his drug addiction: 'I got addicted to hard drugs and it destroyed me, really.' He was determined to repair his relationships and reform himself while inside: 'I came to prison and made a decision to keep away from drugs and pull myself back together.' He had a history of self-harm and found prison extremely hard.

My name's Luke. I'm from quite a good background. My father owns a dry cleaning business. And I came from a happy home. I have two brothers and a sister. Quite a settled early childhood. And one of my first memories was running around in the house and coming down the stairs and my parents having cocktail parties. I remember sitting on the bottom of the stairs eating melons and fruit and that from the cocktail party. And then quite abruptly my parents' marriage fell in trouble. And my parents went through a divorce. And I moved with one of my parents to another town, where he owned another cleaning business. And we went from living in a great big house, in quite an affluent area, to living in a council flat in the middle of a council estate. So it was like chalk and cheese, really, the change. And I went to school there. From about the age of 10 to about 15. Didn't like school at all. I feel that I was never nurtured to do something that entertained me, to keep my interest, at school. And basically I failed at school, although I'm not stupid. Left school at 15. Didn't like it, just stopped going. So any excuse I could, I'd rather work in my dad's business. So at 15 years old, basically, I could run a cleaning business.

My dad was very Victorian in his principles. He was in the army. He was prisoner of war for four years. He came out of there very distressed, and it had a psychological impact on him over there, what he had seen and the way he was forced to live. I always remember my mum saying he was in a bad way when he came back. But he survived – he was very lucky. And then he got all these businesses. But my father, he was a showman in his business. And he liked to be involved around running those shops. So my relationship with my dad was close but not close, if you understand.

When I was 16 I got into trouble a couple of times and they sent me to a detention centre. Which was an experience in itself. It was quite a brutal regime. This was about 1981, 1982, something like that. I think I had my seventeenth birthday while I was in there. And that was not good. It didn't teach me anything. As much as to say, my father, when he used to discipline me, he used to lock me in – we had a big warehouse with one of his shops, and he'd lock me in there, and the whip used to arrive, what you whip horses with. And he'd whip you to pieces with it. And when he used to whip me I used to go out and do the same thing again. Just purely for the fact that he'd whipped me with that. I didn't like it. My brothers and sisters, they got it as well. My dad loved us and that, yeah. But to discipline us, he was very – like I said, he was very Victorian in his principles.

I could be in contact with a lot of people outside. But I'm restricted to my family. For personal reasons. Because – er – I got addicted to hard drugs and it destroyed me, really. Heroin and crack. I've always been involved in drugs. Not as in selling drugs, but as in taking drugs. Always. From when I was very, very young. I started sniffing glue, as I mentioned, then moved on to cannabis, and – I've always smoked cannabis all my life. But I've stopped now. I don't take any drugs at the moment. From my personal choice.

I'd choose not to have the people who are involved in drugs come and visit me. Because I don't want drugs around me. Because I feel my life's better without drugs. And my life will continue to be better the more I distance myself from the drugs geographically. And I'm away from that scene and the people who are involved in it. Whereas now I just have my family come and see me. Because it's important to me to secure my family ties again. Especially with my mum, and my sister.

When I was bad on drugs I don't suppose I was very nice as a person and it did affect my relationship with my family. And that is very important to me. Unfortunately my brother died. He was drunk, and took some drugs while he was drunk, and he choked on his vomit, asphyxiated. And he died nearly three years ago now. He was 35. And it was a big blow to our family. And at the time when he died I was on drugs as well. Heavy drugs. And it affected our family deeply. And as my mum is getting on a bit now, I didn't want to let my mum see me like that. So when I got this prison sentence, back in 2001, I came to prison and made a decision to keep away from drugs and pull myself back together. Which I have done.

My mum comes and sees me, my sister, and my uncle. And they think I'm doing great. My family send me some money. Only £10 a week. But that's all I asked for. And occasionally they'll give me a pair of trainers, or whatever, so that I can keep my self-respect. I am dependent on people outside. Well, put it this way – I earn, in the prison, now, if I just stick to what I get from the prison, I get £7.50 a week. I pay a pound for my television, per week, and a newspaper I buy on a Sunday, which is 50 pence or something. So I pay £1.50 off that. So that's six quid. Now out of that six quid, you're supposed to buy tobacco, if you smoke, your toiletries, save to buy anything out of the catalogue you want if you don't have things sent in, it's just – you know, a pair of trainers is like 40, 50 quid. You can't manage. Unless you get money from outside, you're living an existence in prison that's not very nice. You should be able to work in prison and earn your keep, you know what I mean? Even if you had – you can't tell me that a prison couldn't set up a scheme where we are working within a prison, earning decent money, doing anything? There must be packing jobs and that, contracts a prison can take on.

I have a son. He's five. Lovely, lovely little boy. I haven't seen him for over two years. I wouldn't bring him to a prison. It's not right. I was in prison when my son was born. And I come out of prison after a year, and he was one. I did see him when he was very young, but obviously he wouldn't understand where he was, or anything. But the age he is now, he would straight away. So I can't have him here. When he was very young he did see me, when he was a baby, and that. I had a really, really good, loving relationship with his mother. Lovely girl. Beautiful woman. But women want you there, and you're not there. So we had our troubles, anyway. The relationship survived a three-and-a-half-year prison sentence. I was away for 18 months. The baby was a year when I came out. I stayed with her. I thought right, that's it, I'll go and get a job, which I did. I got a job in London and I done all the right things. It still wasn't enough. So we ended up splitting up.

I still stayed in contact with her, still visited, still went to see my boy and everything. But I think people move on. So my girlfriend's in a relationship with someone else. When I first got this prison sentence, she started to write to me, and she was upset and crying on the phone. And I'd been through it before. So I said to her, 'Look, I'm going to be away for four years. I'll be very lucky if I get parole.' I've said to her, 'Get on with your life', basically. You can't sustain a relationship in prison.

It's as hard for them out there, as it is for us in here. If you are in love with someone, and you are in a proper loving relationship with someone, and one of those partners goes to prison, it's a terrible thing. The heartache is terrible. It just does you in. And the conditions for visiting, and things like that, in prison, are hard. Terrible. It's just a recipe for destruction. If you come to prison with a loving relationship it's terrible.

When I was in prison, in 1999, my relationship went wrong. I cut my wrists. Which, when I look back now, I can't believe I done it. But I was clinically depressed. Very ill. And I, um, found prison a very, very lonely, horrible place. If you're clinically depressed, you're mentally ill. And I found it a terrible place to be. No one's got the time, you know, or anything to help, really. And I don't think, when someone is as ill as I was, they should be in prison. When I cut my wrists I was very disturbed. But now, I'd be a million miles from doing anything like that. It was just, you know, I went through a really terrible patch in prison from when my relationship failed. And it was a bad time for me.

The main thing that will cause big, big problems in prison, is relationships outside. I mean visits in prisons, they're terrible. Because no matter what – you see, drugs comes into it here. Because the reason a lot of conditions are bad on visits is because of drugs. As soon as you put a suggestion forwards – 'can't do that because people will smuggle drugs in'. You cannot sustain a proper relationship. Prison broke my relationship down. I know we put ourselves in here, and this and that. But at the end of the day when you're here you've still got to try and hold things together. Visiting conditions for kids – terrible! They've got a little box a quarter of the size of this classroom. And a few toys in. Terrible. If you've got a wife and kids, I mean I've got a five-year-old boy. I just wouldn't bring him to this prison. I don't want my boy in a nick.[1] It's dirty out there in the visiting room. I saw them wheeling out a plastic high chair to put a kid in. It was filthy. I wouldn't put my kid in that for a million quid.

Being kept away from my loved ones has got to be the hardest thing about prison. In prison, you get no love, no affection, nothing. You'll be lucky if you can glimpse an hour on a visit *if* you've got a girl who's going to come all the way up here. And then it's just a tease, isn't it? It just does your head in. I switch off, me. Because there's nothing else you can do. I mean for four years – no one's ever cuddled me for four years. By the time I get out I wouldn't have had anyone cuddle me – my mum kisses my cheek on a visit when she comes to see me, and that – but I mean no proper, like, love and affection like when I was in a relationship. It drives me nuts when I see them on a visit. I just want her to go home. It punishes me. The biggest punishment is being taken away from my loved ones.

On my first day out, I'll go and see my mum. My main objective – my mum now is quite old and she's been through a lot with us kids. And it's time to put something back in. You know. Like a money-box really, innit? You can't take anything out if you don't put something in. So for me it's time to put something in, really. Not only me, but for everyone around me, it's about how they suffer as well. Because it's not just the prisoners who are being sentenced, it's the people around you who love you: they do it with you.

Commentary

There are some significant gaps in our knowledge about prisoners and their families. Most research has been conducted with supporting family members who are reached through visitors' centres and few studies take the network of an individual prisoner's kin and friendship connections as their starting point. It can be difficult to reach families through prisoners. Prisoners might be reluctant to share information about their families – they might want to keep their relatives as separate as possible from prison life, to protect them from identification and association with the prison, or to avoid revealing their own vulnerabilities.

It is impossible to be certain how many people are affected by the imprisonment of a loved one each year; we can assume that many of the current 85,000 prison population in England and Wales have connections to family and that there are at least some hundreds of thousands of adults currently affected. In addition, it has been estimated that around 160,000 children in England and Wales experience the imprisonment of a parent every year[2] – while in the US, it may be as many as two million.[3]

Prisoners' families are drawn within the reach of the criminal justice system and must manage a range of difficulties, yet their needs are demonstrably absent from the focus of criminal justice – they are at best perceived as contributing to a prisoner's welfare or rehabilitation, often just constructed as posing a threat to prison security that needs to be managed, and rarely seen as having their own support needs (other than by a number of poorly funded voluntary organisations). No statutory agency has responsibility for the needs of prisoners' families.

Most research on prisoners' families has focused on female partners of male prisoners or on the children of prisoners. Members of a prisoner's birth family – parents, grandparents, siblings or uncles and aunts – are often absent, but may be important in the lives of prisoners, as both Jeremiah and Luke describe. The impact of imprisonment on relatives can also be gendered – Jeremiah describes his mother, his 'girl' and his sister as his closest supporters and a number of studies have shown that it is often female relatives who provide this primary support to prisoners. This might include shopping for items of clothing, sending in money, visiting, writing letters, and liaising with legal or other professionals. This can be time-consuming and can place a significant financial burden on relatives with low incomes. Luke explains how difficult it is for prisoners to survive on prison wages and how they are often financially dependent on relatives as a result.

Jeremiah and Luke have been remarkably candid and their accounts of the impact of prison on their kin relationships parallel the findings of research on prisoners' families. Imprisonment can affect relationships in a number of different ways. Some relationships do not survive the strain, as Luke describes; others are said to be strengthened in the face of separation and adversity, as Jeremiah's description suggests. Certainly relationships need to be transformed or reconfigured in particular ways to cope with the changes wrought by imprisonment, which include loneliness and the pain of separation, a lack of sexual intimacy, a redistribution of responsibilities, and a raft of new worries about the welfare of loved ones on both sides of the prison gate.

Prisoners' families experience a range of practical and emotional difficulties. In addition to the financial burden that might be imposed by the loss of a family income or by the costs of supporting a prisoner, there is the burden of having to negotiate the criminal justice process and the maze of prison visiting. Relatives can be drawn into each stage of the criminal justice process and it is not just prison that has an impact. They might have their house searched, or be questioned by the police, they might attend court, and have a role to play on a prisoner's release. Families often describe a lack of information about prison visiting and about the prisoner's welfare. There could be serious concerns about a prisoner's drug use, mental health issues, risk of violent assault, or risk of self-harm or suicide, all significant issues in both the male and female prison population. Luke had to contend with some of these problems and he describes how, during an earlier prison sentence, he had suffered from depression and had cut his wrists after his relationship broke down, and how he was addicted to heroin and crack cocaine when he began his current sentence.

Some studies have found that for prisoners, one of the most difficult aspects of imprisonment is their separation from family and friends.[4] As Luke says, 'The biggest punishment is being taken away from my loved ones'. Luke describes this pain as too much to bear, although he says he does not allow his five-year-old son to visit him. It can be difficult for prisoners for whom relationships have ended to retain contact with their children, as doing so requires a great deal more effort and goodwill from ex-partners than it would outside prison.

Although Luke has kept contact with other relatives, some prisoners choose to cut off all contact with people outside prison as they find it too difficult to manage kin relationships at the same time as their prison sentence – this is sometimes known as 'hard-timing'.

Being estranged from children and 'missing out' on years of their childhood is often of prime importance to female and male prisoners. The former are more likely to be primary carers of children prior to imprisonment and their children are much more likely to be taken into state care. Both Jeremiah and Luke powerfully describe their preoccupation with this estrangement and while their solutions are quite different – Jeremiah is focusing on release and being reunited with his son, while Luke has ceased to have contact – they similarly share the pain of not being able to take responsibility for their sons or share in their upbringing. Research has found that children of prisoners face specific difficulties with psychological effects stemming from the separation from a parent, possible home or school moves, poverty and deprivation, social exclusion in its various forms, and potential long-term consequences affecting their future outlook.[5]

Relatives on the outside might also experience a sense of loss or grief, particularly if a sentence is long term or if the offence was serious. It can be difficult for relatives of serious offenders to come to terms with the offence itself, particularly if it was sexual or violent, and relatives might have to contend with stigma, shame and blame. Again, this can be gendered as mothers and wives within the family are perceived to be guardians of family morality and somehow more culpable for the actions of their kin.[6]

Contact between prisoners and their families is subject to constant regulation. This contact can include prison visiting, exchanging letters, telephone calls (often prohibitively expensive), and sometimes (where eligible and deemed appropriate) temporary release for home leave. A number of changes in prison policy in recent years (in response to concerns about security and risk management within prisons and prison policy) have made contact more difficult and restricted, and rates of prison visiting have actually decreased.[7]

Visiting prisons can be time-consuming, stressful and expensive. Prisons are often located a long way from an offender's family home – Jeremiah describes a 300 or 400 mile journey – and might be poorly served by public transport. Prisons have complex rules about items that can be taken or sent in for a prisoner and it can be difficult to navigate the regulations on visiting day. There may be long periods of waiting – even more difficult if children are visiting – and visitors know that they will be subject to searches, might encounter drug detection dogs, and can potentially be asked to submit to more intimate searches. Prisons are particularly concerned about the possibility of drugs being brought in by visitors, but many relatives report finding the pervasive sense of suspicion profoundly uncomfortable. Visitors' centres at prisons can help relatives to navigate some of the complexities of prison visiting and may provide children's play areas and refreshments but they are unevenly distributed and vary in how well they are resourced and the quality of the help they can provide.

If prisoners' families feel they have been unfairly treated, it is difficult for them to challenge or resist prison regimes. There may be formal routes of complaint, but relatives express concern about creating additional difficulties for the prisoner or jeopardising future visits. There have been some legal challenges mounted by relatives of prisoners and by organisations that support them (for example, challenging the legality of prisoners being charged more than five times the public payphone rate for telephone calls), but this is a route taken by a small minority of prisoners' families. Families often feel powerless and unable to resist the rules and regulations of the prison system. Additionally, they are often lacking in 'social capital' and the resources needed to facilitate formal resistance or protest.

The exclusion and marginalisation of prisoners' families has led to claims that some of the punishment meted out to the offender is experienced vicariously by the offender's family. Research from the US has looked at the impact of imprisonment on families of prisoners and on communities (and how this impact is unevenly distributed, having a particular impact upon low-income African-American communities) and describes how families of prisoners experience the 'collateral consequences' of punishment.[8] This is taken from the military euphemism of 'collateral damage', which refers to the deaths of civilians or other indirect or unintended consequences of warfare. These consequences of imprisonment might similarly be construed as unavoidable in the pursuit of the higher aim of the punishment of offenders, or part of the necessary pains of imprisonment. However, the notion of extending punishment to those who are legally innocent is problematic and does not take account of the wide range of social, emotional, economic and health consequences that can flow from the imprisonment of a family member.

However, prisoners' families are not a homogeneous population and the effects of imprisonment are contingent on a range of factors, one of the most important of which is the state of a relationship or a family's circumstances before a prison sentence. For some, a prison sentence might bring relief or a breathing space to try to resolve pre-existing problems. One US study of female partners visiting male prisoners in San Quentin prison demonstrates this powerfully.[9] The women in this study were said to assume the status of 'quasi-inmates' as they came under the rules and discipline of the prison and as the boundary between home and prison became blurred. However, collateral consequences co-existed with positive functions that enabled the women to sustain and shape relationships in ways that would not have been possible on the 'outside'. Prison played 'convoluted and counterintuitive' roles in their lives, becoming a resource for the women who were able to use incarceration as a tool to reframe and manage their relationships. The author warns against taking an oversimplified and one-sided view of the impact of prison on the lives of prisoners' families and highlights the need to question whether imprisonment mitigates or alters the conditions in which families live before imprisonment. It is difficult to disentangle the impact of penal policy from the impact of poverty, social disadvantage and concomitant problems.

The experience of prisoners' families might also vary according to their previous experience and exposure to the criminal justice system. Some relatives might have first-hand experience as offenders or may have had other relatives or friends in prison. They might also come from communities where prison is 'normalised' and interaction with the criminal justice system is less stigmatised. A body of research from the US has shown how the massive expansion of imprisonment has drawn in more and more families and that the distribution of incarceration is inextricably linked with ethnicity and poverty.[10] As a result, patterns of incarceration are unevenly distributed and have a powerful impact on particular communities. Some impoverished neighbourhoods have very high rates of incarceration which are associated with a range of different problems such as instability and high crime rates. However, the exact ways in which imprisonment has an impact at the level of the community are complex and again are difficult to disentangle from the range of problems that blight poor communities in the US in an era of diminished social welfare. We might also note that trends and patterns in the UK differ from those in the US (the source of most sociological literature on prisoners' families). Although there are continuities in the growth of the prison population and the unequal impact on low-income black populations, there are a number of important differences in the scale of the rise of imprisonment and its impact on geographically bounded communities.

One might expect prisoners' families to have a more central role in criminal justice policy given the body of research evidence, which stretches back for decades, showing the importance of a supportive family to a prisoner's well-being and to how a prisoner fares on release. Studies have repeatedly found an association between supportive families and more successful resettlement, rehabilitation and desistance from crime.[11] This association is also recognised in Home Office and other official reports, although it is not clear exactly how this works. Do families provide financial support? A place to live or employment opportunities? Moral support and a reason to desist? Reduced opportunities to offend if time is spent with family rather than with peers? Or do these factors work in combination? Jeremiah describes how his determination to keep out of trouble in prison and not reoffend on release is driven by his commitment to his son and his strong desire to fulfil his responsibilities as a father and a husband.

The association between family support and desistance can lead to high expectations being placed on families to support prisoners financially and emotionally and there is sometimes an implication that families share in the responsibility for a prisoner's resettlement. They may also be expected to 'police' an offender who is released from prison with specific restrictions. Even though supportive families can have an important role in reducing recidivism, it is important to question what it is right or reasonable to expect from family members, many of whom will be wives or mothers, and many of whom will be receiving little (if any) support themselves. The role of families in desistance needs further exploration and we must not lose sight of relatives' own needs and the range of difficulties they face throughout the criminal justice process and beyond.

Notes

1 'Nick': prison.
2 Prison Reform Trust (July 2010) *Bromley Briefings: Prison Factfile*.
3 Mazza, K. (2002) 'And the world fell apart: The children of incarcerated fathers', *Families in Society*, 83(5/6).
4 For further discussion see Mills, A. (2005) 'Great expectations? A review of the role of prisoners' families', *Selected Papers from the British Society of Criminology Conference*, 2004; and Codd, H. (2008) *In the Shadow of the Prison: Families, Imprisonment and Criminal Justice.* Cullompton: Willan Publishing, p. 24.
5 Murray, J. (2007) 'The cycle of punishment: Social exclusion of prisoners and their children', *Criminology and Criminal Justice*, 7(1): 55–81.
6 Condry, R. (2006) 'Stigmatised women: Relatives of serious offenders and the broader impact of crime', in F. Heidensohn (ed.), *Gender and Justice: New Concepts and Approaches.* Cullompton: Willan Publishing.
7 Brooks-Gordon, B. and Bainham, A. (2004) 'Prisoners' families and regulation of contact', *Journal of Social Welfare and Law*, 26(3): 263–80.
8 For a review of the use of this term see Comfort, M. (2007) 'Punishment beyond the legal offender', *Annual Review of Law and Social Science.*
9 Comfort, M. (2007) *Doing Time Together: Love and Family in the Shadow of the Prison.* Chicago: University of Chicago Press.
10 For example, see Pettit, B. and Western, B. (2004) 'Mass imprisonment and the life course: Race and class inequality in U.S. incarceration', *American Sociological Review*, 69: 151–69.
11 See Mills, A. and Codd, H. (2008) 'Prisoners' families and offender management: Mobilizing social capital', *Probation Journal*, 55(9): 9–24.

Further reading

The best study of prisoners' families in the US is Megan Comfort's book *Doing Time: Love and Family in the Shadow of the Prison* (University of Chicago Press, 2007); see also Megan Comfort 'Punishment beyond the legal offender', *Annual Review of Law and Social Science*, (2007, 3). For prisoners' families in the UK see Helen Codd. *In the Shadow of the Prison: Families, Imprisonment and Criminal Justice* (Cullompton: Willan Publishing, 2008) and the website of the organisation Action for Prisoners' Families (http://www.prisonersfamilies.org.uk/). For the multitude of difficulties faced by the relatives of those who commit serious offences see Rachel Condry *Families Shamed: The Consequences of Crime for Relatives of Serious Offenders* (Cullompton: Willan Publishing, 2007).

7 Children and young people in custody

Rod Morgan

Jack – a white, British prisoner – had been through the custodial revolving door several times since the age of 12. Now 21, he was serving a two-year sentence for robbery, to which had been recently added a further six months for setting fire to his cell while in prison. He was bright and engaging, but distressingly resigned to a hopeless future.

I grew up with my parents until I was ten years old. And then I went through the local authority care systems and through various children's homes, foster placements all up and down the country. I started getting into trouble from when I was about 12. And then one day I decided that it would be funny to set fire to my room while I was in it. From then on I was remanded into a secure children's home. I think it's prepared me to come into YOIs [Young Offender Institutions] as well. I mean, I know it's the wrong word to use, but I probably would call me 'institutionalised'. I've been here that many times. You get so used to one thing and it just becomes the norm, becomes easier to be in here than it does out there. Time seems to go quicker in here than it does out there.

I didn't have the love and support of family and stuff. I suppose I've become numb to feelings and emotions and stuff like that, and I do think I missed out on a lot of years, but obviously, I had to be locked up, for my good and for other people's good. I don't think it's good to be locked up so young. I mean, they can lock someone up from when they're ten, and I don't think it's good for anybody. I was very scared. It's intimidating, very intimidating. I was bricking it when I first went in. I mean, for the first, I think, four or five days I didn't come out my room. Ten to 16 was the age range. There was a lot of bullying that used to go on. I mean, there's bullying everywhere, but it was really bad in them, sort of, young years.

Last time [I was released] I slept on the streets. I managed to get myself in a hostel after, I think, about eight or nine days. And from there I just started getting into trouble. It was just a bad environment for me to be in, really.

I've had three visits now in the past month and a half, but before that I haven't had a visit for two years. I speak to my little sister, and it's up and down with my mum at the minute. It always has been, ever since I went into care. I get visits from my girlfriend. I've been with her now for four years, but near enough three of them years I've been locked up. It's hard, very hard. There's always that uncertainty of whether she can be cheating while you're in jail. Everyone thinks a girl's cheating.

I've got a two-year sentence, but I've also got an extra six months for setting fire to a cell. I went through a rather bad patch. I put on an old t-shirt and set myself on fire. I can't remember exactly why I did it. I've been diagnosed now with two personality disorders. I'm on anti-depressants, but they keep me calm and placid most of the time. But ... I just think it's been a never-ending cycle and to be honest with you, prison ... they say, 'Oh, we're here to rehabilitate you', but nine times out of ten, they don't ... they won't even try. They just keep you locked up for as long as possible and then just let you out when they've got to let you out.

Track Works – that's a pretty good course. I'm not allowed on it cos I'm a 'high risk'. I wouldn't be allowed the saws that they use and stuff like that. I live completely off prison wages. I don't get any money sent in and ... I mean, it's not a lot ... it's seven pound a week. I think it's a load of shit.

I've had problems with drugs and alcohol. Last time I was on cocaine, a lot of cocaine, smoking a hell of a lot of weed. One of the reasons why I went into care was drugs. I found drugs in my mum's house and I took some and smoked a bit of weed. I think I was about seven. And I used to run away a lot as well and hang around with the homeless community. That's where I had a lot of drugs. I wouldn't say I've ever been addicted to heroin or crack cocaine, but I have dabbled in it.

I've got nothing to go out to. I mean, I have applied for housing and stuff like that. I've more or less found myself a job. It's not a paid job. It's working at a church, but now they're arguing that I wouldn't be able to go to it on ROTL[1] cos you're not allowed to go to a place of worship.

There are quite a few members of staff that I really get on with. They're the ones who treat you like you're a human being and not just a wage packet. Some of them actually care what happens. Some of them don't, but some of them do. Most of them don't want to call you by your first name. They can be really arrogant, nasty, but then there's some of them that are brilliant.

They say that they're going to look after vulnerable prisoners, but they don't. I mean, I was speaking to a prisoner today, he's not all there in the head. He was in tears with me but the staff were just talking to him like he's a piece of shit. They say everybody should live in a comfortable environment, safe and comfortable, free from fear of bullying and threats and intimidation, but they don't give a rat's arse, really.

I feel safe, but I don't think it's a safe environment for some people. As I said, with the kid that I was speaking to, he's very down, depressed. The officers won't keep an eye on him. And I've seen his cell bell be on for, like, 15, 20 minutes before it's answered. And then there's other people that are getting bullied openly in front of officers and it's not safe. There's a lot of violence goes on in the showers. There's a lot of violence. Could be about anything – just need someone to give someone a wrong look or whatever ... could be over debts, gambling debts, debts for burn,[2] or it can just be over where you're from or they think you're a nonce,[3] or whatever.

I think the first couple of months is always a sketchy one, no matter what establishment you go to, even if you've been there before. But I think once you get used to it and once people know that you're not going to be pushed about, then things become completely different. I'm with people that I know, I feel comfortable with, but also, really, I've got nothing out there. It's not as if I've got a family to go back to, so basically this is my empire, this is where I'm comfortable at.

I believe that everyone's got the capacity to stab you in your back. I don't fully trust anybody. It's just the way I've always been. I've grown up not to trust anybody. Cos at the end of the day, if you can't trust your mum and dad, who can you trust? People do miss family and stuff, but I've never had that so I don't know what I'm missing, if you know what I mean.

It's going to be an uphill struggle and I don't have 100 per cent confidence in myself staying out of trouble because I've had no help whatsoever. I'm having to do everything myself. I've got an adult literacy and an adult numeracy thing here, which is nothing, really. It's just a piece of paper ... it's a certificate. I've been in and out for a long time now. It's going to be hard for me to change my way of thinking and getting used to life out there again.

Ben was a 20-year-old white British prisoner, serving a sentence of over three years – his first – for street robbery and false imprisonment.

I lost my older brother a couple of years ago. I started going off the rails a bit then, with drink and drugs and started going stupid. He were the only person that used to calm me down when I were younger. My drinking got stupid. I were drinking all the time. And split up with my girlfriend over drink and then started doing stupid stuff like robbing people all the time to make money for drink. I've been with her on and off for about three years ... off at the minute. I've got a little lad with her who's going to be three in October. She didn't want to wait for me, sort of thing. She's writ to me a couple of times but I think it's nearly a year since last time she wrote. She was meant to visit me at one time and she refused to bring the little lad with her cos she seems to think it's the wrong place to bring a lad to come and see his dad. Obviously, I can kind of see where she's coming from, but I still want to see my son. It's enough of a punishment not being able to spend as much time as you can with him ... it tears me apart. Not being able to see him. I hate it.

It's hard for my mum to come and visit because she doesn't drive and it's hard for her to get a lift over. I phone my mum a lot. My mum and dad, they realise how much more help and support I do actually need. I respect them a lot more for stuff that they were put through with me. Like doing stupid shit – selling my mum's stuff, you know, basically robbing my own house when I needed some money, and my mum's, like, not kicked me out. I respect them a lot more that they've not turned their back on me.

[It's the] First time I've ever been in jail. I were scared, definitely. I were on B wing but I got kicked off there first week, for fighting. Someone tried to say that they were going to take my burn and that, so I thought, right, fuck that, I'll swing him. Started fighting and then I got moved. A lot of them know that when it comes to it, if I've got a problem with someone then I don't really give a fuck, sort of thing. I'll pull a shank on someone in front of the screws.[4] I have it in my pad, just for the simple fact if someone comes in my pad to try to take my shit I'll take it to their face. If someone nicks a bit of your burn or something, you've got to, at least, give them a bit of a beating or someone's going to come up in your pad tomorrow and take everything that you've got.

There's all types of different wars going on in here at the minute. There's like, all people from Nottingham and London, trying to say who owns the jail. I'd say about two or three month ago, every single day at least one person [was] getting stabbed up, but it's calmed down a lot now. You get used to it. It's like if wars are going on in your street, you don't move from the area, you just cope with it.

None of them [officers] respect you. No, they look at you like you're something they've just stood in, sort of thing. Basically they try treating you like you're not a person. It's like they're not bothered about you at all. They don't try and help you or nothing. There's only a couple of them that do. I'd say there's two of them on my Unit that I get on with, like, decent screws.

I miss seeing [cars]. You know, I used to see them every day if they passed me and that. I don't even like them that much. It's just, like ... yeah ... miss standing out in the rain and stuff as well, like, just being able to stand there getting wet when it's warm, stuff like that. Miss stuff like that.

I think I've changed myself a lot. Before when I used to be out, I used always to be about drinking and fighting and doing stuff like that … but I realise there's a lot more to life now than doing stuff like that. I want to make a go for my life, to have a good life for me and my lad and settle down. I've just realised what's important to me. I've managed to stop drugs and that, so I can't see how drinking's going to be much more of a problem.

I moved onto a course called Track Works. It's for railway engineers. I'm hoping to get a job on that when I get out cos that'll, like, help me with my drink and drugs, cos you get drink and drug tested, so that'll probably be a good start for me. And it's good wages as well. It's like a proper qualification and stuff. It's good pay and that as well, so I'll be able to pay for a lot of things that I've earned. I'll be living at my mum's house. It's a caravan, static caravan.

If you've got a cold heart and that here, it's easy in here. Yeah, I'd say that's about the main thing that I've learned in here … how to bottle feelings. Took me to 21 to learn it properly.

Wayne, an 18-year-old mixed-race prisoner, was serving a four-year sentence – a very long term for a juvenile. Imprisoned when aged 16, he was serving the remainder of his sentence having been recalled on licence. He felt that he had matured in prison and wanted to live a crime-free life on release. However, he recognised that he needed considerable support and it was not clear that this would be available to him. Returning to the same place and the same friends with whom he had committed his offences, it was less than certain that his hopes for the future would be realised.

I live with my mum, I've got two older brothers. Dad has always been distant. School was all right. I got suspended a few times. I got expelled from primary school but not from secondary school. I went to college for about a year, not even that. After that I just went about my business and from there on to robbery, selling drugs and whatever the crowd were doing. Before I came into jail I was really deep into crime. When I was 14 or 15 I was seeing more money than my parents had seen. I had cars, motorcycles, stupid things like chains worth three grand, four grand, watches.

My mum will come up one month and my girlfriend another month. So one of them comes up every month. I get friends come up every now and then. But the people here constantly are my mum and family members. I've got closer to my mum and girlfriend since I've been in custody.

When I came in I was just turning 16. There was much more conflict than in 18 to 21. [In] Juvenile [prison] everyone is hot-headed, everyone is a coming up gangster, everyone is out to make a name for themselves.

It's crazy in juvenile, just crazy. Juvenile is more like a bunch of wolves looking for prey.

When I was in [prison X] I did the Princes Trust and went to Wales for a week. That was nice. They weren't officers but they worked in the prison. They helped me a lot, they got me town visits and things like that. [And] I had a mentor. He was a cool guy. He was my anchor when I went off course and he really helped me. He gave me time if I had a problem, he'd call my mum for me and things like that. He really helped me to change my ways. He was more like a father-figure. I knew my boundaries with him and he showed boundaries with me. When he said no it was no. I knew this guy was trying to do whatever he could for me. I appreciated it more than anything.

I got my forklift licence in jail, done the Princes Trust award, done first aid, done coaching awards and I've done MORE – thinking and all that – done painting, and a few other things.[5] I wish I had done the MORE course in youth jail. I attended because I had to, to get out of jail. But there are a lot of things that you can achieve from this course if you let it.

When I got out after having been in jail for 21 months, there was no one to meet me at the gates, no one to direct me the right way, I just got out. As soon as I got out it was like I was a little fish in a big pond. I had probation, they gave me a timetable and said, 'This is what you have to do, you have to be there, there, there'. I got back home and all the old faces, all the people that got me in trouble in the first place, they were my comfort blanket, they were my direction. Even though I didn't get arrested once in the whole seven months I was out, I still got recalled, so what's the point in not doing crime when you still go back to jail? I got recalled for being late for probation, I was late three times. I didn't do no crime, I didn't get stopped by the police or anything, I had to take a drug test once a week for probation and they were negative, I was in college but I got sent back to jail for being four minutes late and have to do the rest of my licence again, 16 months.

I feel safer in jail than I do outside. In jail you know what you are doing all the time, there's a schedule, it's like a path you know you can't fail. Jail is my upbringing and jail has taught me about things. I didn't feel that there was anything that could hurt me in any jail because I was more like a ringleader. It wasn't a thing I thought about because in Juvenile jail I was the troublemaker. You do one or two things, and fight with this person and before you know it you are the centre of attention. I wasn't someone who would threaten people and say, 'Give me this'. It was more like I would play pool and I would bet them £20 that I would win and if he bet me I wouldn't pay but if I win I want my money. He owes me money and things escalate. I wasn't a threatening guy but I would do something like bet on a football match and if I don't win nobody gets paid.

In jail everyone is a threat to me. No one is your friend in jail. You can't have friends in jail. Enemies stay enemies but it's impossible to have friends in jail. You can have someone you get along with, someone you really bond with, but at the back you have to know that you are disposable, so they have to be disposable to you as well.

Last time I got out I made a plan to get a job, made a plan to go out and look for a job, but I went out did some CVs, did everything I was supposed to do but nothing showed up. I thought it would work out somehow. This time I will try different but know that things don't always work out to plan. I will try my CVs in shops and whatever, try to focus on whatever benefits me.

I was distracted by everything around. Even if someone called me about a job or directed me that way, there were so many things around me to do, I was lost. I would start off the day and say, I'm going to hand out a few CVs, and then someone would call me and say meet me wherever and I would completely forget what I was going to do. It's really hard when you get out. It's crazy when you get out. There were a few opportunities for me to do good when I got out but it was too much, it's a big world for me and I didn't know where my head was at.

My biggest concern about getting out of jail is coming back, that will always be number one. That feeling of letting everyone down, letting down everyone that has tried to help you again. It comes to a point where people walk away. That's my biggest fear – being left alone in the dark when I get out.

Commentary

Young prisoner accounts in context

The business of interviewing prisoners appears simple but is in practice difficult. Prisoners mostly welcome the opportunity to talk to someone from outside, someone not in authority over them. But they've also been asked the same damn-fool questions by officials so many times that they're often bored by their own story and tempted, as would any of us, to make it more interesting or coherent, or simply wave aside events, issues and relationships that are too near the bone to strip bare.

These difficulties are seldom less likely if the prisoners are very young. On the contrary, young prisoners are developing at a furious pace. Their transition from childhood to adulthood is typically painful, chaotic, lacking in stable relations and hard to make sense of. Their emotions are raw and may oscillate between stunted unresponsiveness and fierce outbursts. Young prisoners have the whole of their lives before them and may unrealistically hope for everything. Yet their existence may also seem pointless and their prospects so hopeless that the future appears to promise nothing. For, as so many see and express it, who gives a fuck? It is precisely this way of putting the matter that represents their greatest risk. If they appear not to know truth from fiction, if they're not able to keep their emotions under control, if their anger is overwhelming, if their ability to communicate their experience is socially so stunted, if their capacity to face the future seems totally lacking in realism or forethought, if their every statement contains what appear to be violent inconsistencies, then how will those adults – prison officers and other front-line residential staff, police officers, magistrates, even youth offending team supervisors, most of them largely untrained in child development or social psychology – how will these adults, meeting and knowing them only fleetingly yet contributing to decisions that will shape their life chances, how will they give them a fair wind, establish meaningful relationships with them and provide them with grounds for hope?

This is why it is vitally important that we listen to young offenders' accounts carefully, reading as much off as on the line. If, for example, one had lost one or both parents either through death, mental health decay or drug-addicted oblivion, if one had been looked after by other relatives or constantly moved from one foster parent to another, if one had run the gamut of every type of residential institution from care home to Young Offender Institution, would one know, remember or care precisely which event had triggered which dislocating decision, when and why? Would one invest much hope or trust in yet another interlocutor, posing the same questions, no matter how sympathetically and politely? It is unlikely one would, and not unreasonably so. So, the listening has to be worked at and the analysis undertaken carefully.

The three young prisoner accounts above are all freighted with stark glimpses of anguish such that it is difficult not to feel sympathetic anger at the personal betrayals and the ill-considered relationships and responsibilities taken on too early. Personal disasters litter the brutally exposed ground, all to be shouldered by limbs presented as broad, but fragile because scarcely formed. The assertiveness and self-confidence is belied by the flashes of fear about the problems to be faced when they get out and the prospects of return to custody.

Personal histories

Our three young men, Ben, Wayne and Jack, are being held at a large Young Offender Institution, built in the 1970s. Jack has the longest experience of closed institutions. His account suggests that he was taken into care when he was around ten and transferred from a children's home to a secure children's home (SCH) when, aged 12, he was sentenced by a court for an arson offence committed in a children's home. Since then he's spent most of his short life in custody, experiencing the full range of penal institutions for children and young people. These institutions include nine relatively small (10–30 beds) SCHs in England and Wales catering for mostly young children in penal custody aged 12 or more; four larger but still relatively small secure training centres (STCs,

60–70 beds, but like the SCHs broken down into sub-units of six beds), run by private security companies for slightly older adolescents, particularly those aged 15 or more considered too vulnerable to cope with a YOI; and 14 YOIs (65–400 beds, generally arranged in sub-units of 30–60 beds) catering for those aged 15–17, mostly run by the Prison Service.[6] Jack almost certainly comes among the 28 per cent of young prisoners who have more than ten previous convictions[7] and who it is virtually certain – a likelihood of 96 per cent according to 2003 Home Office figures[8] – will be reconvicted within two years of release. He has few hopes for the future and when last out he was at liberty for a few days only.

Wayne and Ben, by contrast, are serving their first spells in custody. Wayne served the required first half of his sentence in custody, was released on licence and then recalled to custody, not because, according to his account, he committed a further criminal offence but because he failed to comply with the terms of his licence. Wayne is among the one in five prisoners serving four years or more annually recalled to prison for breach of licence, the overwhelming majority of them for failing to comply with the terms of their licence rather than for committing a further offence.

Ben's criminal career appears to have been triggered by the death of his brother, after which he says his use of alcohol and illicit drugs began and got rapidly out of control. This is an aspect of his personal history he has in common with Jack, who began to experiment with cannabis at a very young age, moving on to 'dabble' with cocaine and heroin. In this respect, Jack and Ben are typical of young offenders in custody, over half of whom report being dependent on alcohol or an illicit drug in the year prior to their incarceration.[9] Bereavement, usually of a parent, in childhood or adolescence has been linked to early resort to alcohol and illicit drugs.[10]

According to Wayne's account, he was 'really deep into crime' by the time he was 14 or 15, part of a group that lived by crime from which, he asserts, he was 'seeing more money than my parents' and owning bling and vehicles worth thousands of pounds. Further, though he stayed at school until 16 and started college thereafter, there were signs of trouble as early as junior school, from which he maintains he was excluded. Over half of all young offenders in custody have significant or borderline learning difficulties. Two-thirds of those serving detention and training orders (DTOs) have been excluded from school at some stage. The overwhelming majority of young offenders in YOIs for 15 to 17-year-olds claim to have been excluded from school and most say that they effectively left school well before the age of 16. Furthermore, four in ten have, like Jack, been in the care of their local authority and 17 per cent have been on a child protection register.[11] The result of all these factors is that children and young people in custody typically have literacy and numeracy ages three to five years below their chronological age. They are typically multiply disadvantaged.

Learning to live in prison

All three of our young offenders have learned to cope with the stresses of custodial life. Their accounts give the lie to those who see closed institutions as potential crucibles for positive change. The few hours spent on the cognitive-behavioural courses that have become part of the core, rehabilitative curriculum of young offender and adult prisons in the last ten years have to be set against the stark realities of 24/7 life on the landings and in the cells where very different lessons are learned.

Jack has had a particularly gruelling apprenticeship. He has learned how to survive the hard way and says he now feels safe, though his apparent calm and sense of security is bolstered by the medication he takes for his 'personality disorders'. During this sentence he has set fire to himself, an act of gross self-harm as much as deliberate destruction, resulting in severe injuries. He is not atypical. Almost one-third of young prisoners have identifiable mental health problems, almost one-fifth with problems of depression, a tenth having engaged in an act of self-harm in the preceding month; similar proportions suffer from anxiety and post-traumatic stress symptoms, 7 per cent suffer from hyperactivity and 5 per cent suffer from psychotic-like symptoms.[12] Jack may *say* that he feels safe but he does not think YOIs provide a safe environment. The latest survey evidence suggests that although safety levels in YOIs for 15 to 17-year-olds have in recent years improved, nonetheless one-third of young offenders have not felt safe at some point, and a majority say that if victimised they would not expect staff to take their report seriously.[13]

YOIs are volatile places in which significant numbers of young prisoners feel that they have to prove themselves. Wayne may be exaggerating when he describes YOIs for those aged 15–17 as 'crazy' places dominated by packs of 'wolves looking for prey'. But it is clear from these accounts that this is no environment in which one should show weakness. Those who exhibit signs of vulnerability, whether it be unwillingness to stand up to exploitative or bullying fellow prisoners or emotional stress, will be ruthlessly preyed upon, their persons abused and their property taken. All three of our young men claim to be assertive men, willing and able to see off aggressors and in Wayne's case capable of being a 'top dog'. But they are generally agreed that one can't really trust anyone in prison, that if one is wise it is not sensible to reveal personal feelings or regard anyone as a friend to be relied on in the way one might on the outside.

Personal futures

All three young men come from fractured families, all living with their mothers when their parents split. Jack appears not to receive visits from his family and gets no practical support by way of money or consumables sent in. He has a long-standing girlfriend who has recently started visiting him again after a lengthy gap, but he is ambivalent about release and his prospects of remaining at liberty. He thinks he's probably 'institutionalised', life now being easier on the 'in' than the 'out'. He doesn't fully trust anyone because, after being taken into care as a young child, 'if you can't trust your mum and dad, who can you trust?' He can't banish the thought that his girlfriend may be 'cheating on him'. He has the offer of a job as an unpaid volunteer when released, but he has no real qualifications or training and he's not looking forward to release because he feels he has 'nothing to go out to'. He concedes that it's going to life in a community he's no longer familiar with.

Ben and Wayne are more hopeful. Ben already has a child (as do 10 per cent of 15–17-year-olds in custody) and although he's broken up with the mother he hopes to regain contact with his son. When he is released he'll go to live with his own mother in her static caravan and hopes to get employment in railway maintenance in preparation for which his prison has a dedicated course. This is an option not available to Jack because his history of self-harm means that he's not allowed to have access to the tools that such work requires. Indeed he's so far been denied release on temporary licence (ROTL) because, as the risk assessment mantra goes, nothing predicts behaviour better than past behaviour, he's 'high risk' and the options left open to him are disturbingly few. Even though Ben robbed his mother of her possessions when he craved drugs prior to his incarceration, he still enjoys her hopes and support. He's convinced that, given employment on the outside, he can overcome his past pattern of drug and alcohol abuse. Wayne is also hopeful, but having already been recalled for breach of licence he is fully aware of the risks that await him. His biggest fear is of coming back to prison, people who currently support him giving up on him, and his then 'being left alone in the dark'.

The problem with prisons, as all three of our witnesses testify, is that you get used to the culture that inhabits them. The demands it makes on its inhabitants are very different from the world outside. Alexander Paterson, that great pioneer of penal reform, coined the aphorism that 'you cannot train men for freedom in conditions of captivity'.[14] All three of our witnesses testify to that contention. They fear the world outside almost as much as they fear a return to captivity.

Reshaping penal policy from the ground

Might things have been managed differently such that these lives could have taken a different course? Jack thinks so. His family provided quite inadequate care for a young child. He was deprived of parental love. It was not good to be locked up so young. There must have been other ways of keeping a young child like him off the streets. Further, when he was locked up, was it appropriate to incarcerate children as young as 10 with youths aged up to 16, as was the case in the SCH where he was held? He does not think so. There was a lot of bullying. Though his experience is that there is bullying in all custodial institutions, it was particularly bad in the SCHs, possibly because he was still learning to cope with patterns of behaviour he now takes as normal.

Wayne exhibits no bitterness about his sentence. Serious, persistent crime had, he confesses, become a habit for him and the youth group of which he was a part. He is, however, critical of the decision to recall him to prison and his criticism is shared by policy analysts concerned about the increased use of custody for offenders for failure to comply with the increasingly onerous conditions attached to community penalties and release on licence.[15] Both Ben and Jack are critical of the lack of control and support exercised by officers. Nor, they assert, do the staff show respect to their charges, a view that is widespread among young prisoners.

Jack is highly critical of the lack of resettlement support he has received. The last time he was released he initially had to sleep rough before being admitted to a hostel which provided no safeguard from getting into trouble, possibly the reverse. Everything is apparently being done to ensure that he completes the custodial part of his sentence without incident, with the consequence that there is little likelihood of his remaining at liberty when released: no risk-carrying investment is being made in his future thereby making a penal future all the more certain.

All analysts are agreed that releasing young offenders to 'bed and breakfast' accommodation is a recipe for disaster and that much more needs to be invested in resettlement support. But it is the testimony of Jack that raises the biggest questions. The youth justice system, substantially reformed by the Crime and Disorder Act 1988, is arguably not working. Though there are about one-third fewer children and young people in custody today than at the population peak a few years ago, there are nonetheless approaching twice as many as was the case at the beginning of the 1990s. Yet grave crimes by this age group have not significantly increased and despite substantially increased expenditure on custody and improved conditions, the recidivism rate has not improved. We now know a great deal about what works by way of early intervention with the families of children who get into trouble[16] and there is arguably great scope for using effective mentoring schemes – like the one that Wayne describes, in highly positive terms – and restorative justice programmes so as to prevent young offenders reaching the serious criminal pitch our three witnesses represent. There is arguably a need for, as a recent, comprehensive review of youth justice puts it, *Time for a Fresh Start*.[17]

Notes

1 'ROTL': release on temporary licence.
2 'Burn': tobacco.
3 A 'nonce': a sex offender.
4 A 'shank': an improvised knife or weapon.
5 'MORE': an offending behaviour programme.
6 For an overview of the administrative arrangements for children and young people in custody, see Morgan R. (2007) 'Children and young people', in Y. Jewkes (ed.) *Handbook on Prisons*. Cullompton: Willan Publishing; for up-to-date details, see the Youth Justice Board website.

7 Ministry of Justice (2010) *Offender Management Caseload Statistics 2009*. London: National Statistics.

8 Home Office (2003) *Prison Statistics England and Wales*, Cm 5996. London: National Statistics.

9 HM Chief Inspector of Prisons (2008) *Annual Report 2006/7*. London: HMIP.

10 Kiernan, K. (1992) 'The impact of family disruption in childhood and transitions to young adult life', *Population Studies*, 51: 213–34.

11 See Harrington, R. and Bailey, S. (2005) *Mental Health Needs and Effectiveness of Provision for Young Offenders in Custody and in the Community*, London: Youth Justice Board; and Parke, S. (2009) *HM Inspector of Prisons and Youth Justice Board: Children in Custody 2006–8*. London: Youth Justice Board.

12 Harrington and Bailey, *Mental Health Needs.*

13 Parke, *HM Inspector of Prisons and Youth Justice Board.*

14 Ruck, S. K. (1951) *Paterson on Prisons: Prisoners and Patients*. London: Hodder and Stoughton.

15 Hart, D. *Children and Young People in 'Breach': A scoping report on policy and practice in the enforcement of criminal justice and anti-social behaviour orders.* London: National Children's Bureau.

16 Hawkins, J. D., Welsh, B. D. and Utting, D. (2010) 'Preventing youth crime: Evidence and opportunities', in D. J. Smith (ed.) *A New Response to Youth Crime*. Cullompton: Willan Publishing.

17 Salz Commission (2010) *Time for a Fresh Start: The report of the Independent Commission on Youth Crime and Antisocial Behaviour*. London: Police Foundation/ Nuffield Foundation.

Further Reading

'Youth Justice' by Rod Morgan and Tim Newburn, in Mike Maguire, Rod Morgan and Robert Reiner (eds) *The Oxford Handbook of Criminology* 4th edition (Oxford: Oxford University Press, 2007) provides a general overview of the recent history and current arrangements for youth justice in England and Wales and the characteristics of the young people drawn into it. It also provides a comprehensive bibliography. The Youth Justice Board and Ministry of Justice websites provide up-to-date statistics on the population in custody and HM Inspectorate of Prisons provides regular survey evidence about the experiences of young prisoners (see S. Parke, 2009 *HM Inspector of Prisons and Youth Justice Board: Children in Custody 2006–8*, London: YJB, 2009). *Time for a Fresh Start* is the 2010 report of an Independent Commission on Youth Crime and Antisocial Behaviour chaired by Anthony Salz and commissioned and published by the Police and Nuffield Foundations. The report is grounded on a survey of the most recent research regarding youth crime and the manner in which we do and might more effectively respond to it, published as a supporting book (David Smith (ed.) *A New Response to Youth Crime*, Cullompton: Willan Publishing, 2010).

8   Ageing prisoners

Natalie Mann

George was a 69-year-old disabled prisoner who had served just over five years of a seven-year sentence for sex offences. He was very friendly and forthcoming but completely denied committing the offence: 'There's loads of innocent people in here, if the CPS done their job in the first place. I mean, I've never been in trouble all my life.' Feeling lonely and isolated, George succinctly conveyed the problems that ageing prisoners often experience.

> I've got arthritis in me hands, lost the strength in me spine and so there's no work for me. The chair don't even come out of me cell; I have to get up on me crutches and that, then somebody has to fold me chair up and put it out of the cell. The doors aren't wide enough, so I don't get to come out and see the other lads, so I'm stuck in there. I read me books, got me television, which is marvellous, it's a great help but you can't watch television all the time. The cell door is shut all the time, that's what gets on me nerves; if the door was open, I could see them all out and about, but they just shut the door behind me. I was doing the stamps here about two and half years but me hands couldn't tear the stamps no more. I was just offered another job about three months ago, but there aren't no stamps in there for me to do, so I can't just sit there and do nothing; if I'm doing a job, I wanna do the job. I can't get up and down the stairs, so I can't get a job out here.
>
> I can't get me own medication, I have to wait for them to bring it over. Terrible, I used to be independent, I used to be able to do things for myself, go out with me crutches, get me shopping and push it back on an old trolley, I felt I was useful. I don't feel useful no more. It's frustrating, so frustrating when you can't do anything. They call your name out, it don't take a couple of seconds to walk out your door, but I've got to fold me chair up, push it out, get back in it, then come up here; 'Oh, we don't want you now'. It's like going out onto the exercise yard, what a palaver. I get out here and I've got to wait for a man to back me up and get me down the steps. It's okay getting me down but if he hasn't got the strength to hold me, then the chair goes *bang*! And

I get upset, so I don't go out there very often, which breaks my heart. I've asked for a ramp but the Governor says NO! I only want a little bit of help. I can't take part in nothing and that's when I get so frustrated; I mean, they want you to go on courses, but I can't do the courses. I've said, 'Yes, I'll do it', but they'll say, 'Well you can't', cos they cannot get me there, it takes a lot of trouble. Where it takes one man about ten minutes to get there and back, it'd take me half an hour. It's the same with the arts upstairs, I'd like to do art, but I can't get up there. Education's down here; it's all right going down once but any more and it's too much. Tuesdays they go upstairs to the library to do their books and sometimes they watch a film but I can't get up there, I can't get up all the stairs, you see?

I have a hell of a job to see anybody. If I put in to see the doctor, I've gotta wait for the doctor to come over and see me because I can't get to see him cos he's on the second floor. Just recently I had an infection in me gums and all me teeth are loose. I've only got five but I couldn't get to the dentist. I put in for it, they called me for the dentist, I sat down there at 1.30, I was still there at 4.30, nobody came to take me over so I went back to me cell. Go down there again Sunday, this time I was only down there a half-hour and they took me over to the lower healthcare – all types of inmates. I'm sitting down there and don't know who's gonna come behind you, someone could slash you or something like that, very frightening. All the medical staff are upstairs, you see. I was waiting there till five o'clock, my dinner is at half past four; five o'clock the dentist came down and said, 'Oh, you've got a gum infection, I'll give you some antibiotics for that', five minutes. He said, 'If they get worse, come and see me'. I said, 'Do you know that it's easier to see God than to see you? I could go and kill meself and see God quicker than I can see you.'

We've got a stair lift in here that hasn't been working for a long time. It's a big old thing and push the button to go up the stairs and it goes *da da da da da da da da* [*judders and jerks*]. Nobody likes taking us down there, sometimes it takes 10 or 20 minutes and then I've got to walk the few stairs to go into the surgery. It's all stairs here, all stairs. There's another prison I heard about a couple of weeks ago, the man has supposed to put me down for it; a man with a walking stick went up there to court, or something, and they put him in a cell in there for the night and he went upstairs and they were disabled and he looked around and there was wheelchairs that could get in and out of the door, they can go to the surgery, get their own dinner. I've never got my dinner in five years cos I can't go down and get it.

This [wheel]chair is an extra four inches back, have you noticed? Cos I used to wheel about here and the blokes used to pull the back of your chair straight over. It happened to me a few times, that's the type of idiots they are. I can't go for a shower when they're there cos they mess about with me chair; I can't afford to lose me chair cos it's me legs.

Sometimes I sit in me cell for hours and don't say nothing. It'd be nice to turn to someone and say, 'Oh, that was a good film', or something. I have always been a loner, so I can always occupy myself, if not, you can always get on the bed and have a kip. But I can't always sleep. I feel wound up and my mind isn't settled. They're pretty good here, the officers; I've only gotta ask them, 'Can I have a shower this morning?' and so they leave the door open, but other days you're banged up and you don't even see the cleaners working; if you see them working, you feel as though you're in the world. I used to be on another block, and I was looking out over grass and a tree and it's lovely to see it out there, a little pond and the ducks; I was there four years looking out that window but then they moved me over here.

They don't want me here cos I'm in denial; I was innocent of the crime they said I committed. I was enhanced in here and then they brought in a new rule, you can't be enhanced if you're in denial. You know enhanced, you have certain privileges, more money to spend in canteen … After all these years I'm still B-cat,[1] I mean if they left me door open, I couldn't go anywhere.

It's like the hierarchy here, you get the hooligans come in on the other block and they think they're hard and they cause a lot of noise and everything else, so I think they moved me here because of the noise, but all I'm looking at now is another prison wall, with a load of windows in, and they shout out the windows, and the language … but I liked to look at the grass and the trees. They put a tree in, when I first came here and now it's a great big thing; it's lovely to watch it grow.

Brian was 55 years old and was serving a five-year sentence for fraud. He was very intelligent, very articulate and had a very positive outlook on prison life, due in part to the continued support of his family. He recognised that he was not 'typical' of the older prisoners and his role as a prison Listener had provided him with a valuable insight into some of the problems that older men face.[2]

In general the youngsters ignore the older people and I think in one sense older people have an easier ride in prison because the youngsters are always jockeying for position among themselves and that leads to aggravation and antagonism, but there isn't much gain in a younger person laying into an old man, and although the old men annoy them intensely, bullying them isn't an accepted thing to do among their peers, whereas it's fine to jockey for position among your peers. Now the interesting thing is, you get that same sort of thing among the older men, you see the oldies jockeying for position among their own age group, but the younger ones do tend to blank and ignore the older men, rather than respect them. In Listener conversations I've heard from older guys who really don't know what to say to the youngsters and if you're sharing a cell, come bang up and you're spending hours with them and you can't hold a conversation because one is speaking a version of English that the other can't understand: 'How's it hangin', Bro?' There can be quite a problem develop.

There are a lot of people in this prison who are old, and not just old but very ill and infirm and they do struggle, and I think it's very sad that they are expected to function normally in this prison. They are genuinely and physically struggling in here with the routine and simple things like stairs. I mean, I'm extremely lucky, I'm fit and well with no serious problems, but I'm not typical of my age group.

I had a minor problem with a vein in my leg and let's just say that a lot of what you've been told about healthcare is true, it's dreadful. I am an old man but fortunately I have all my own teeth, but I have had an absolute nightmare in getting an appointment, weeks and months go by before you hear, and the same with my glasses. For well over seven months my glasses were not the right prescription and I needed them for my work. I don't blame the healthcare staff here; I just don't think it's geared up for 700 people, when a high percentage are really quite elderly. I just think demand is well out-doing supply. When I have finally got to healthcare the treatment I've received has been fine but getting there is the problem. I can't tell you the number of times I've seen the old men struggle to get up there and stand in a queue for hours to get their medication, then get bullied for their medication, get slagged off because of their offence and it's a horrendous experience and I know there are old men who are too frightened because of all that, to even go to healthcare. I've seen men who've had chest pain for three days and been told it's indigestion, and have had a heart attack. I've heard a man telling a doctor that he couldn't cope and was going to take an overdose and he had 36 tablets, and the doctor just said, 'Well, you're in for a bad night then'. The healthcare's overstretched, the staff on the wings don't have time, the old men cannot physically access the healthcare and really you'd have to be in immediate danger of dying before anything was done. I just thank God that I'm in good health. If I was seriously ill or had a degenerating condition, I would be in trouble because those people end up suffering.

Bernard was a 77-year-old life-sentence prisoner who had committed murder. He had approximately ten more years to serve. He was a guarded man who took a long time to open up during our interview. He was seen as somewhat problematic by prison staff and was well versed in the prison complaints procedures.

An older man cannot talk to youngsters because he cannot understand the life he led before he came to prison. I mean there's only three of us older ones on this wing but all I ever hear from them is moaning and groaning, the older prisoners do tend to moan and groan, a lot of these older men shouldn't be, well, not shouldn't be, but would be better somewhere else, but because they're a risk they can't get out and I'm not a risk, so let me out. We have what is supposed to be a lifer unit downstairs, for lifers only, but we've got quite a few determinate prisoners in the cells and they use the unit, which they're not supposed to do, people come on it from other wings, which they're not supposed to do, so all the rules there are, they break. I had a go at one of the officers about other people using our unit and he said, 'I'm not bothered', he don't want to be bothered to fill in the form, so that's what they're like, they're not bothered about people breaking rules.

The younger men take the mickey out of them [older prisoners] and try to bully them but I know how to handle them, keep away from them because they don't know that they'll probably be back in within six months of going out, but all the young blokes are so rude, one new one had a go at me the other day. He called me this and he called me that and I said, 'Are you gonna carry on?' He shouts, 'What you gonna do about it?' So I pushed him up against the wall, threw a few punches and he didn't like it.

I feel sorry for them [vulnerable older prisoners] because they will get bullied: if lifers who are fit get aggro then the frail ones certainly will. But I mean, you get bullying wherever you go; outside you get bullying but you walk away, you can't do that in here, you meet them again and again. It isn't a problem for me because that's what I've been used to. They won't bother me, I mean on the lifer unit we have our own toaster but there's one young lad down there who keeps using it when he's not supposed to and it upsets the old blokes, but while the screws allow it, there's nothing we can do. But if I'm there I'll put my bread in before theirs and they'll ask why and I say, 'You shouldn't even be in here', but they don't mess with me. There's no point moaning about one thing after another because it won't change anything, you just have to live your life as best you can, but all the screws ever say is what that comedian says: 'Am I bothered?'

But you have got some power in here! There's an old saying, 'The pen is mightier than the sword'. I've got a good solicitor. I've made it my business to get to know all the rules and regulations and if I have any hassle, I phone him straight up and he's onto it. They [the officers] just come out with so much bull that they don't understand it themselves, so you have to know what you're talking about otherwise they'll walk all over you. I know my rights. I'll say, 'You can't do that', and they'll say, 'Well, how do you know that?' They try it on, but they'll leave you alone when they see you know what you're talking about.

In prison you can only have acquaintances, just 'hello' in passing and that suits me. I don't wanna get too close because the first thing you find out is that that person wants something from you. I don't have people in and out of my cell all the time. You see, we've been on our own for years and years and we don't want anyone coming into our cell. We don't want people coming in because lifers would not be allowed to talk to the others because a lot of short-termers are scared of lifers, but I don't think we're a threat to anyone. I know someone in Kingston [prison], been there 40 years and now he's in a wheelchair, can't get up, can't wash, can't dress and he committed a crime 60 years ago. I did used to intimidate people, I did that years ago, and I tended to get a bit nasty, so now they keep away. There is bullying in here and I've been bullied but I've always sorted it out myself and I haven't had no nickings [from my cell] for the past two years. If I saw a younger kid bullying an older guy, I'd put him straight. But these young kids can't get it through to their brain that you cannot bully an old bloke because of his age. I was in a fight one day and there were four young kids and six of us [older prisoners] and they threatened to sort us out; what a mistake they made, they were the ones who got sorted out! Ageism, that's all it is. I can still look after myself.

Commentary

The number of male prisoners aged 60 years and over more than trebled in the ten years from 1996 to 2006,[3] making this group the fastest growing population in prison. This extraordinary trend is, in part, the result of recent public disquiet regarding sex offenders which has in turn led to new government policies and legislative changes, but can also be attributed to an increasingly punitive approach to crime in general. With so many older men being sentenced to imprisonment, it is unsurprising that the majority of their experiences are characterised by difficulty. The prison environment is very different from that in which many individuals in wider society find themselves growing old, and the many problems this age group experience are often a direct result of being housed in antiquated institutions, primarily designed for aggressive young men.

The most distressing and depressing account is provided by George, who asserts that a poorly designed and unaccommodating prison, coupled with shortages in staff, resulted in him being shut away for the majority of each day. In this kind of 'worst case scenario', the experience of older prisoners is damaging to them and possibly falls below the legal standards set out in the Disability Discrimination Act 2005, which places a duty on bodies such as the Prison Service to establish practices that positively encourage the needs of disabled individuals.

George's disabilities, which were related to the ageing process and were representative of the types of problems experienced by the older prison population, prevented him from becoming a fully integrated and active member of the prison population. George claims that he had requested the implementation of ramps to aid his mobility on a number of occasions but that these requests had been refused, and so the continued constraints created by poor health and disability, coupled with the material constraints of the prison environment, had resulted in his isolation from other prisoners. His story represents the men who have had all but the most basic opportunities for agency, such as deciding when to go to the toilet, taken from them, and are thus experiencing prison life in highly distressing ways.

With so much time to fill, it is not surprising that for many older prisoners prison work and activities are used as a means of filling time and keeping active. By taking part in leisure activities and pursuing hobbies, ageing individuals can prevent the onset of both mental and physical deterioration. As Crawley and Sparks found in their study,[4] many older prisoners have worked throughout their lives, and not to do so is almost inconceivable. However, the employment opportunities provided for older people in prison are often as monotonous as the time they seek to fill, or there may simply be insufficient work to occupy them. Not only did George find it hard to find suitable employment of a purposeful nature, he also found that his disabilities prevented him from taking part in any other types of prison activity. For George, and many ageing prisoners like him, blocked opportunities to socialise and participate in prison life can lead to boredom and decline.

Healthcare issues may be even more important for older prisoners than for the rest of the prisoner population. As George notes, attaining quality healthcare is often difficult for ageing prisoners, resulting in a lot of time spent waiting around in what can sometimes be experienced as a frightening environment. By stating that it would be 'easier to see God' than the prison doctor, George clearly indicates the frustration and concern about access to healthcare. By describing the time involved in securing a doctor's appointment and the unsympathetic attitude adopted by some prison healthcare staff, Brian also conveys a sense of the powerlessness experienced by some prisoners.[5] Issues such as lengthy waiting periods were experienced by some prisoners as an expression of their 'second class' status, and an assertion that they could not simply 'make demands' for healthcare.

The inaccessible nature of prison healthcare compared to that in the community outside, both in terms of its opening times and its location within many establishments, the experience of the treatment that prisoners receive, and anxieties surrounding the deaths of fellow prisoners can lead to serious fears among many ageing prisoners. By its very nature, ageing brings with it increased incidences of morbidity, infirmity and general decline, yet healthcare provision in prison often remains inadequate, despite the recommendations made in the 1999 combined report by the Prison Service and the National Health Service. *The Future Organization of Prison Health Care* report criticised the existing healthcare system in prisons and suggested that a number of strategies should be implemented, including greater communication between prisons and local health authorities, a review of reception screening, particularly for mentally ill prisoners, a greater promotion of healthcare inside prisons, and the assurance that healthcare centres would be run by qualified nurses. The National Service Framework for Older Prisoners also has a duty to ensure that ageing prisoners receive healthcare in line with that delivered by the NHS in the community. However, as the follow-up to the HMCIP Thematic Review of 2004 discusses,[6] good examples of healthcare practices were mainly seen in isolation, with little evidence of the multi-disciplinary approach recommended in the original 2004 review. Such stagnation of the healthcare services for older people in prison has resulted in a situation where some prisoners feel that they are still, in effect, 'punished for being ill'.[7]

Time is an important issue in the prison experience, and its management can become highly problematic for some prisoners. Some may initially hold on to some sense of time in the outside world, but as their sentence progresses and prison time takes over, this normal chronology is often lost. As Cohen and Taylor discuss,[8] many prisoners 'build their own subjective clock in order to protect themselves from the terror of the 'misty abyss'. For George, the growth of a tree outside the window of his previous cell seemed to serve as a way of 'marking time'. By taking an interest in how it developed over the years, and observing its growth and change, George was able to retain some concept of passing time, without having to relate it to his own deterioration.

Friendship is normally a voluntary act, based on the freedom we have to actively choose our friends, but this is not the case in a closed institution like a prison. For prisoners, friendships are a product of the confined and strained nature of the environment and are often based on necessity; if you do not try to get along with your fellow prisoners then you do your time alone. However, prison friendships can be risky, and Bernard's discussion of prison friendships is typical of the problems associated with close relationships between prisoners.

For older prisoners, friendship needs to be characterised by trust, but trust is very difficult to establish within the prison environment and it is for this reason that older prisoners tend to evade genuine friendship and instead develop a number of acquaintances; as Bernard states, 'you can only have acquaintances, just "hello" in passing ... I don't wanna get too close because the first thing you find out is that that person wants something from you'. Friendship is perhaps more important to the ageing prison population than anything else because of a general lack of opportunities for collective activity. A very elderly or infirm prisoner cannot take part in gym sessions, play pool or even move around the prison unaided; thus having friends who are in a similar situation allows the ageing prisoners to share commonality, mutual support and alleviate the loneliness experienced in the mainstream prison population. However, because ageing prisoners tend to view friendships with mistrust, they often miss out on a whole support structure that could greatly aide their ability to cope with their imprisonment.

George, Brian and Bernard all discuss problems created by their close proximity to younger prisoners, albeit in varying degrees of severity. For Brian, his role as a prison Listener provided him with insight into the difficulties created by the 'generation gap' that exists between young and old prisoners. This is characterised by differences in vocabulary and the difficulties involved in establishing shared interests or common ground. George's experiences of younger prisoners were characterised by childish pranks, such as pulling his wheelchair over while he was in it, and creating excessive noise. However, although extremely distressing for George, these actions were perhaps more juvenile than vindictive, and as such less threatening than those experienced by Bernard.

Bernard's position as a life-sentence prisoner was seen by some younger prisoners as an irresistible opportunity to assert their masculinity and establish their position within the prisoner hierarchy. Due to his outward appearance as an older man, the younger prisoners wrongly believed that he would be physically incapable and therefore unable to defend himself against their threats and intimidation. However, by 'throwing a few punches', Bernard was able to demonstrate his physical capabilities and prevent any future incidences of bullying or intimidation. As gender theorists have argued, violence is a way of demonstrating masculinity in the absence of other resources (such as employment or economic status), but such displays of masculinity become extremely problematic for those ageing prisoners who do not have the physical capabilities to engage in violence, as Bernard acknowledges: 'I feel sorry for them [vulnerable older prisoners] because they will get bullied; if lifers who are fit get aggro then the frail ones certainly will'.

A large percentage of the ageing prison population is housed in vulnerable prisoner units in order to avoid the incidences of 'aggro' which Bernard discusses above. For these prisoners, the nature of their crimes is what separates them from the rest of the prison population; as sex offenders, often child sex offenders, they are considered the 'lowest of the low'. George was highly representative of ageing child sex offenders in that he was serving a sentence for a 'historic' offence. Many ageing men are now serving sentences for crimes they committed decades ago. George was also 'in denial', another common trait among this group of ageing prisoners.

For these men, denial can take many forms and it is perhaps best explained by applying the terminology of 'neutralisation theory'.[9] The first form of denial is the 'denial of responsibility', whereby the individual believes that the deviant actions were a result of forces beyond his or her control. Many ageing child sex offenders seek to justify their actions by transferring the blame from themselves to external factors, such as marriage problems and alcohol abuse. The second is 'denial of victim', where the individual claims that his or her actions have not caused any real harm. Again, this type of denial is common among ageing sex offenders, who maintain that their victims are not coerced into sexual acts by force or violence.

Such denial could potentially make this group of ageing prisoners extremely hard for the Prison Service to control because the use of incentives as a way of encouraging prisoners to conform loses its power, as prisoners in denial cannot enjoy enhancements or privileges. They are also problematic in terms of rehabilitation, as a sex offender in denial cannot take part in the Sex Offender Treatment Programme (SOTP). The result is a static population of prisoners who, like George, remain high category offenders until their eventual release, which comes after having received little or no rehabilitative input.

Some ageing child sex offenders have found ways around this issue; by admitting their offences, 'playing the part' of a remorseful offender and embracing the whole concept of rehabilitation, while secretly remaining in complete denial, they are able to enjoy the benefits of enhanced status and possible early release. 'Working the system' is just one way in which older prisoners can regain small but significant amounts of power.

In terms of their relationships with officers, some older prisoners are able to maintain some sense of power through their knowledge of the system and their personal rights, as Bernard's testimony suggests. For Bernard, knowledge equalled power, and this power allowed him the achievement of retribution via the prison complaints procedure, and also by unsettling the officers' sense of authority. Harnessing the potency of knowledge is a skill that appears to be acquired through experience. While younger prisoners often argue or become aggressive towards officers when they do not get what they desire, older, more experienced men will often declare their rights, contact their solicitor or initiate complaints proceedings. By 'working the system', Bernard was able to take back some power and engage in what he termed 'games of one-upmanship' with officers who, although irritated by the number of complaints he brought against the Prison Service, could not deny him this legitimate form of recourse.

The prisoner now has many more opportunities for redress via wing representatives, committees and prison complaints procedures. These opportunities mean that prisoners now feel less need to challenge the structure in the ways we have seen in the past. However, it could be argued that these procedures serve to legitimise the power of prison staff and maintain control over a population of prisoners whose rights may well be more illusory than real. For power to be both conveyed to and accepted by prisoners, it must be accompanied by the belief that such power is legitimate and fair, thus procedural fairness and a transparent complaints system are extremely important in safeguarding the power of prison staff.

Within the ageing prison population there exists a strong belief that no allowances are made for their age. They are subject to the same regime as younger prisoners, despite some 7,538 men being more than twice the age of an average prisoner. Crawley and Sparks use the term 'institutional thoughtlessness'[10] to encompass the many 'acts and omissions that impinge negatively on older prisoners' as a result of the traditional prison principle that 'one size fits all': in other words, the principle that 'everybody gets treated the same'. As Brian discusses, many of the older prison population are ill or infirm and struggle to function in institutions designed for physically capable young men. For prisoners like George, disability results in isolation and loneliness, which draws the individual deeper into the prison system. These men are a diverse group of prisoners, with particular needs and unique experiences, but while the prison population is viewed as homogeneous, they will continue to struggle within our prisons.

Notes

1 'B-cat': a prisoner deemed not to require maximum security conditions, but for whom escape needs to be made very difficult.
2 The Listener scheme is a peer support system whereby selected prisoners are trained and supported by Samaritans, to listen in complete confidence to their fellow prisoners who may be experiencing feelings of distress or despair.
3 Le Mesurier, N. (2010) 'A Critical Analysis of the Mental Health Needs of Older Prisoners', unpublished report for the National Institute of Health Research.
4 Crawley, E. and Sparks, R. (2005) 'Older men in prison: Survival, coping and identity', in A. Liebling and S. Maruna (eds) *The Effects of Imprisonment*. Cullompton: Willan Publishing.
5 Sim, J. (2002) 'The future of prison health care: A critical analysis', *Critical Social Policy*, 22: 300–23.
6 Her Majesty's Chief Inspector of Prisons (2008) *Follow up Report on the Thematic Review 'No Problems – Old and Quiet': Older Prisoners in England and Wales*. London: HMCIP.
7 Wahidin, A. (2005) 'We are a significant minority: Elderly women in English prisons', *British Journal of Criminology*. Online at: http://www.britsoccrim.org/volume6/001. pdf.
8 Cohen, S. and Taylor, L. (1972) *Psychological Survival: The Experience of Long-Term Imprisonment*. Harmondsworth: Penguin.
9 Sykes, G. and Matza, D. (1957) 'Techniques of neutralisation: A theory of delinquency', *American Sociological Review*, 22(6): 664–70.
10 Crawley, E. and Sparks, R. (2005) 'Surviving the prison experience? Imprisonment and elderly men', *Prison Service Journal*, issue 160. Online at: http://www. hmprisonservice.gov.uk/resourcecebtre/prisonservicejournal/index.asp?id=3833,3124, 11,3148,0,0

Further reading

For a general introduction on the ageing prison population see Azrini Wahidin's chapter *No problems – old and quiet: Imprisonment in later life* in Wahidin and Cain's book *Ageing, Crime and Society* (Cullompton: Willan Publishing, 2006). For a discussion of the policy implications of the current situation see Her Majesty's Chief Inspector of Prisons, *Follow up Report on the Thematic Review 'No problems – Old and Quiet': Older Prisoners in England and Wales* (2008).

9 Women prisoners

Abigail Rowe

Kirsty was in her early thirties. She had been released automatically halfway through a five-year sentence but breached the terms of her licence and had been recalled to prison to serve the rest of that sentence there, along with an additional two-year sentence. She had been in and out of prison for offences related to her heroin addiction for over a decade. She traced the origin of her problems with drugs back to abuse in her teens by a foster parent. Kirsty's youngest child had been born in prison at the start of her current sentence, and 'handed out' to her mother before the end of the full period that the baby could have remained with her.

When I started [my five-year sentence] I was pregnant and I was on the M and B.[1] [I had the baby with me for] five months. They wanted separation before six months because of [the length of] my sentence, [and because] the baby was getting attached. [It was really hard,] but I'm trying to use this sentence to my advantage. I've just done four years of a five-year sentence. It's a long time to be away, especially when my little girl is not that old. She's three and a half now, nearly four, but my mum has had her from five months old and it's just all been taken away from me. Yes, the biggest part of it, I blame the prison system because regardless of what they were saying, I still should have had Katie till she was nine months old. They could have given me that at least. I wasn't asking for 18 months, I was asking for nine months.[2] But then they'd all gone behind my back – my mum, social services, the prison, having meetings without me. I didn't know my mum was coming up, sometimes, to the prison, having meetings behind my back. I wasn't aware of any of that and it made me see some of these people for what they really were. Even the governor was involved in it. And then they were giving me just two days to separate with her.

I wish I was just separated straight from birth because it's caused so much fucking heartache in my life now. That little girl is never going to come back to me now – she's with my mum, my mum has taken over. And I do blame the fucking prison system for that. Girls aren't having a choice whether their baby gets adopted, and they can't do anything about it. Even if you go to a court and fight it, the courts are still going to side with the prison, probation, social services. Nine times out of ten, if you get refused a place on this Mother and Baby Unit and there is nobody to look after that baby, they will not consider long-term fostering. Who's to say that's going to destroy the child later on in life? If anything it's going to fuck that child up more, thinking, well, why didn't my mum ever want me? Care is not always the right thing – I had a really bad experience with my foster dad that I wouldn't wish on anybody – but if you're doing over a 12-month or a two-year sentence, your baby will be adopted if you haven't got anybody to look after that child, and that right has been taken away from you. I've seen that happen on three occasions now in the last few years and it has torn those people apart. Torn them apart. It's no wonder they're going back out there for the drugs – what else have they got? They've lost.

[I think officers' opinions of women in here vary.] Some of them think that we've gone just a little bit fucked up in life, do you know what I mean? They look at us like some of us have had a really sad life, because the majority of us have. I brought most of my life on myself. [I put myself into care], but it was just everything that came with it when I went into care and everything. It destroyed me basically, but there's always somebody else that's got a sadder story to tell than me. But some [officers] look at us like we're scum, we're the lowest of the low. At the end of the day, some people can't help going out there and having to commit crime. Do they really think we like going and breaking into people's houses? Sometimes it's the only thing you can do to survive out there when you've a habit. It's not nice having a heroin addiction because it's not just mental, it's physical with heroin and crack, it's the pain of withdrawal symptoms – you're in agony. But [some officers] just look at us like the lowest of the low. I'm not particularly fucking arsed what any of these prison officers think of me or any of these prisoners – it's just the people that I care about and the people that I've done wrong to, do you know what I mean? I wish I could fucking give them back everything I've robbed off them, but I can't. I know I've done wrong; I'm paying the price for that.

Over the years, my mum and [the rest of my family] have [supported me], but not any more. They've had enough. They thought I'd really cracked it when I came out this time: I got myself a job; I stayed away from everybody. It was only because probation made me do a course that I had to do out there. Once I'd started that course it was game over. I met up with Steve, one of the old heads, and it was back to the old routine. My mum just can't tolerate me at the minute because I've had it and just fucked it all off. And she thinks that she's there to fund me every time I come to prison, like she has done every other time: make sure the money's there every week, make sure my new clothes are there. She's not doing any of that this time. She is making me suffer and it's killing me. She's been to see me once in nearly four months, brought my kids up *once* to see me. And that's hurting me more than any of these can hurt me.

Naomi was a life-sentenced prisoner from a relatively comfortable background, a lone parent whose young child was now living with grandparents. Although she was materially and emotionally well supported by family and friends outside, she was geographically isolated from them, the prison being several hundred miles and a day's drive from home.

A wing like [the one I live on] can change so much. I can phone friends at the beginning of the week and be completely fine, everything's going fine, and by the end of the week it can all change again, so it's very up and down. You tend to find you just start to get to know everyone and then a big influx of other people will come in, new people, and you're like, 'Oh my God, new people everywhere'. I think you can make good friendships [in jail] but at the same time things seem to change so quickly. People sometimes will be there when they need you around and they can change very quickly because it's all about survival, I suppose. I think people get too involved with other people's business as well. The girl I'm seeing was always in trouble and she's really tried [to keep out of trouble] since we got together, [because] I said to her that there was a lot I couldn't put up with because [I'm a lifer and] you're guilty by association in prison. She's really tried, [but] she finds it hard to say no to people. People tried to give her hooch to hide at one point and she didn't want to do it. Rather than say no to them, she [took] it to an officer and [told] the officer to catch her with it, because she didn't want to get in trouble but didn't want to be seen to be letting these so-called friends down. So she's kind of got in trouble but not got in trouble, but then she's done the ultimate sin to the friends by grassing on them but they don't know about it! It's like, rather than do a simple thing like say no in jail, people [find] devious ways around it because they don't want to lose face.

I watch new girls now and I feel so sorry for them because they'll sit down somewhere where they think it's an empty table and someone will come along and just go, 'People sit here, love'. Then they'll get up and sit somewhere else and it will be, 'You can't sit there, someone sits there'. Or some people are even worse. New girls will sit down and they'll come along and go, 'People are f-ing sat at our table! What do you think you're doing?' And then they'll move again, but if you're new you don't know how it works and there's no allowances made for you. I think it took for me to be in my room for a good four days probably, not eating properly, not going out, not doing anything, just being in bed all the time, for an officer to come in. She introduced me to [Sue,] an older woman on the wing, and was trying to sort me out and that really helped, but it was left to another prisoner to help me.

It just feels horrible. It's not like you're in your home town, or you're with your friend and you're lost. You're completely on your own. You don't know anybody, you don't know the surroundings, you don't know the staff, you don't know anything at all and you feel like a little kid again. And perhaps some people can cope with it but I found it really, really hard. Once you are settled in there and you've got your particular little groups of friends, it's very hard to go out of your way to make the effort with somebody else because it's almost you feel like you have to look out for them then and you only get that hour a day to associate. I'm as bad as anyone else, but part of you just doesn't want to do it and it's awful because you've been there yourself and you know how hard it is, but it's just not that easy because people aren't very accepting of just allowing someone else into a group that you're with.

Josie is the first girlfriend I've ever had. I didn't ever think I'd get involved in a relationship in jail but I have, and you don't realise that you're constantly under the watch of everyone. I mean, when Josie and I have had arguments before, you have nowhere to just go off and sit down quietly and sort it out, absolutely nowhere on that wing where there isn't one other person listening in. Everyone always knows everything that's going on – you can't have any secrets in this place. It's a favourite line in here with everyone: 'I'll tell you but don't tell anyone'. You know that ten minutes later ten other people know it. People can't help it. They think they're only telling one other, but then that one other is telling one other and everyone just finds out.

There's one [officer on the wing] that a lot of girls don't get on with. He'll give out warnings for the silliest things, but when he gets funny with me I've learnt to just play it as a joke and he plays along with it then and he doesn't get funny, whereas if someone backchats him he'll then get worse. So a lot of it, I think, is about learning how to be with each officer. There's different ways of being with each one and once you find the way you're generally okay. In here, you have to get them on side to make your life easy. I stand there and laugh at officers' jokes and pretend to listen to them. And they're not funny, and they're not interesting, but if you do that then they're a bit more okay with you than if you just don't. You just have to try and strike up some kind of rapport with them and it's the only way it can work. Some girls just won't do that because they say why should they, but the ones that won't are the ones that get their life made a bit more difficult for them. You just have to bite your tongue and smile sweetly and let them think that they've won. If they always feel that they're in control then they'll be all right with you, it's when you start questioning their authority and it turns into an argument, and then what? That officer that you've had an argument with is the one you then need to do something for you the next day and they're not going to. You're easier just letting everything go and then you might manage to get on okay.

Lisa was a young prisoner, a mother of two small children, who was several years into a life sentence. Although intelligent and insightful, she had had a difficult upbringing and left school early. She had a long history of self-harm. At the time of the interview, her relationships with wing staff were under strain, and she was struggling with the compromises that she felt were demanded by the prison regime in order to progress smoothly through her sentence.

A lot of the time I will challenge things [that seem unfair]. Not in an aggressive way, but if somebody says, 'Do this', and I'm thinking, 'Well, why do you want me to do that?' or 'Why have you done this?'. But I think it is a survival thing as well; if somebody's saying, 'You've done something wrong', you're going to question it when you know you haven't. And I don't see why I should just say 'Yes' when I know that they're wrong. And I find it very hard to just go, 'Yes, it's my fault; lock me behind my door'. I find it difficult not to say – but I know that's something you have to learn.

If I didn't have a parole sentence, I'd challenge everything and probably go to the governor and say, 'This is out of order', but I'm a parolee and everything that I do gets written down. And if these officers decide, 'I don't like you', then they're not going to write nice things in your file. My file's going to be terrible and I've got to think about that when I'm involved in anything; they can write anything and it can mess the rest of my life up. For a lifer as well, every single thing you do gets written in your file and then it gets looked at deeper – I couldn't just have an argument with somebody, a friend, on the wing, it wouldn't just be, 'Lisa had an argument'. That argument would go in my file and would be looked into so deep by psychology and everything as me having a problem with my anger issues: *I'm a risk to society*. So therefore I might not be moved on.

Psychology is a big, big part of your sentence plan. Now personally from me – but this is my comment – I think psychology is a bit overrated, because psychologists can stand there and say, 'Right, I've read this out of a book', [and] this particular person [is] boxed off into [that category]; this person's categorised as being like this, and that's the end of it. And what a psychologist says can have a tremendous impact on that person's life and how they perceive them. If a psychologist says that they think you're manipulative or that they think you're aggressive, for a lifer that can have such an impact and that is just one person's perception of you. Now somebody could describe you as being an aggressive person when you're not necessarily aggressive, that's just the way you're expressing yourself; you're emotional about a situation.

You'd think you'd come into jail and the positive things would be thrown on you, do you know what I mean? They'd be wanting you to do courses; they'd be wanting you to better yourself; they'd be wanting you to do well. If you want to do things the right way, you feel like you constantly have to fight to try and get somewhere. You constantly have to fight to do education; you constantly have to fight to keep your head down and be good, because they're fighting against you all the time. It feels like they're just wanting to knock you down; it is hard to do things the right way and you'd think that it wouldn't be. You'd think if you sat there and went to someone, 'Right, I want to do things the right way, tell me what to do', they'd be like, 'Oh right. Great. Well, there's this course, there's that course, this is what …' No. It's easier to just say, 'Right, well, fuck it.'

When I first came in I used to self-harm. I haven't done it for two years, but [recently] I was having problems at home and on the wing with officers. It was getting on top of me and I self-harmed. I was put on an ACCT, and they ask you in the ACCT,[3] 'What do you think we can do to make things better? Is there anything we can do?' And I said, 'Put counselling down'. I've been to the doctors, I've said I want counselling; no one's come back to me with anything. I've been to the officer and said I want counselling and I've not heard anything back from it. I know I need it soon. I'm not at the point where I'm beyond reason and I'm that depressed that I can't see clearly, but that's why I want it now in case I get like that. Things do get bad before anyone will listen to you. You've just got to chase it and chase it and chase it. I think that's the only time that things do get responded to is when you don't let them drop, but it's tiring on a daily basis. It's tiring and frustrating.

I know there are a lot of people that are struggling [in here]. For me personally, [self-harm] is my way of dealing with stress. Whereas somebody else might go out and they might have a drink, or they might go cry their eyes out to their family, or they might throw something. If things are getting on top of you and you feel like you can't cope any more, and there's no other way, that's why you do it. And it feels like it's a release, and it just helps you get by. So [people] don't self-harm because they always self-harm, they self-harm because circumstances have brought them to self-harm; circumstances in jail; circumstances in the past; but yes, this jail, this environment makes people more stressed out and more likely to self-harm.

I think there should be more support. It all comes down to them giving a shit though again. You can't make people give a shit at the end of the day really, can you? And like I say, a lot of these [officers] don't seem to; they think that you're a hassle, like, 'Oh my God, more paperwork'. You even get the jokes like that, but you know that they're serious. Like, 'Oh my God, you should have seen the amount of paperwork I've had on you today'. And you laugh with them and they're laughing, but you think, 'Yeah. I know that you're being serious about that deep down.'

Commentary

Prisoners arriving in custody are often in crisis: struggling with chronic problems of addiction, or detoxifying from drugs or alcohol; anxious about what might happen to their home and children while they are in prison; traumatised by the circumstances of their offence, or reeling from the shock of arrest or trial.[4] Many prisoners have histories of personal and social disadvantage that heighten their vulnerability in prison. Both men and women in prison are disproportionately likely to have experienced abuse and instability in childhood, to have been in local authority care, run away from home, and left school with few or no qualifications. Concentrations of particular kinds of experience in women's prisons reflect patterns of gender relations in society as a whole. A third of women prisoners have been sexually abused, for example, and over half have been victims of domestic violence. Women in prison are more likely than male prisoners to be a lone parent to dependent children, exacerbating the impact of a sentence on their households and families.[5]

Prison officers who have worked in establishments for both men and women often remark that, 'Men do their time on the inside; women do their time on the outside'. By this they mean that women prisoners seem to remain more preoccupied with the problems and responsibilities of home and family. Although arguably overstated, this perception is perhaps unsurprising, given that a woman's greater likelihood of having sole care of dependent children increases the chance that when she receives a custodial sentence her children will have to be looked after by someone other than a parent. Fewer than 10 per cent of children with a mother in prison are cared for by their father.[6] The scenario of forcible adoption described by Kirsty attracts a special sympathy among women prisoners with children; the loss of children in this way is almost universally regarded as the most serious collateral consequence of imprisonment. However, as Kirsty's experience also illustrates, in order to avoid this prisoners may have to make substantial compromises in the arrangements they make for the care of their children during their sentence. Prisoners often have to rely on people with whom they have either a tenuous relationship (a child's father's family, perhaps, or an ex-partner's ex-partner), or a fraught one (family members who are unsympathetic to their own problems, a child's violent father). Kirsty's access to her children is mediated by and entangled with her chronically strained relationship with her mother, charged with the resentment she feels at what she regards as her mother's collusion with prison and probation authorities to remove her daughter – born in prison – before the full nine months she could have been allowed with her had elapsed. Her anger at what she sees as not just the premature, but the irrevocable, loss of her child is palpable. She perceives this as a harm inflicted by the Prison Service, dovetailing with the perverse effect she attributes to the community-based offending behaviour course she was obliged to attend on her last release from prison, which made it more difficult to desist from drug use by making it impossible for her to cut her connections with others with similar problems.

Entering prison for the first time, it is common for prisoners to describe feeling disorientated and alone; prison routines and practices are often inscrutable and those whose expectations are shaped by the representations of prison in popular culture are often fearful. A larger proportion of female than male prisoners – almost a third – are serving prison sentences for a first conviction, and few women in prison are 'career criminals', for whom the risk of a prison sentence is often an occupational hazard. Most women serve short sentences for non-serious offences; in 2008, most women in prison were serving sentences of six months or less, and in 2007, more had been convicted of shoplifting than of any other offence.[7] A large proportion of women prisoners, then, have little prior experience of the criminal justice system. Recalling their sense of vulnerability on entering prison, for example, first-time prisoners commonly remark that the only time they felt completely safe during their first days in prison was when locked in their own cell. Even established prisoners observe that it is time spent 'behind your door' that passes most quickly in prison, because that is the only time it is possible to be completely relaxed and unguarded. Nevertheless, women serving a first sentence generally comment with surprise on the discovery of warmth and mutual support among prisoners. Prisoners commonly remark, 'You think it's going to be like *Bad Girls* but you get here and it's nothing like that'. For many prisoners, other inmates are a crucial source of practical and emotional support when they first arrive in custody, or at a new prison. It is inmates who understand most precisely the nature of a new arrival's need: the tenor of the reassurances that will answer her fears; the information about the wing routine that she was perhaps not given by staff or was too overwhelmed to retain. Only prisoners are in a position to be able to provide small material comforts and necessities such as coffee and sugar that a new prisoner will not be able to secure for herself until she has her own money and canteen.[8] Even relatively weak ties among prisoners offer important forms of support, and many emphasise that support can exist among prisoners even without deep friendship.[9] It is customary for those being released, for example, to leave behind items such as toiletries, which are valued and difficult to procure, for other prisoners.

At the same time, however, prison relationships can present inmates with a host of risks. Much of day-to-day life for women in prison is concerned with attempting to ensure that the relationships they form in order to avoid isolation and secure support do not bring exposure to a different set of risks. Even those who are grateful for offers of help from other inmates on arrival describe a sense of vulnerability in accepting advice and support from prisoners, who are not just strangers, but often at first assumed to be an untrustworthy source of information. As Naomi suggests, prisons foster cultures of prurient interest in the affairs of others, and a new arrival is likely to have to field approaches from others wanting to know what she is 'in' for, and 'how long she got'. Gossip and rumour spread quickly in prisons, perhaps gathering some embellishment along the way; offences and sentences may be discussed and compared, perceived unfairnesses picked over and resented. Naomi makes a connection between high levels of need and distress among prisoners and instrumentality in prison relationships.[10]

At its extreme, prisoners in need and lacking alternative sources of support, or those who are opportunistic, may view others as a material resource. A woman who has just arrived from court may have drugs that can be bought (or perhaps coerced) from her, or she may herself be in sufficient need of tobacco or drugs that she can be induced to trade desirable items for very little.

Although relationships with staff and other prisoners can be stressful, complex and sometimes threatening, they can also be a vital resource for coping with the collective and private pains of imprisonment. Emotionally expressive and affectionate friendships, and romantic and sexual intimacies between prisoners, are common and accepted in women's prisons. Most women prisoners socialise primarily with a small group of friends, with looser constellations of friendly acquaintances or associates beyond them. As Naomi explains, the boundaries of these social groups are often carefully controlled to protect against the risks of confiding too widely in what is often effectively a 'community of strangers', in which trust is highly circumscribed. Many prisoners argue that the best way of 'doing prison' is with 'just one good friend' to provide support while minimising exposure to gossip, instrumentality and instability. Those serving indeterminate or parole sentences who want to progress smoothly through their sentence also often seek to avoid associating with individuals who are likely to attract negative attention from prison staff. Naomi repeats the saying, common to both staff and prisoners, that one is 'guilty by association' in prison: it is generally accepted that inmates' friendships and associations will be used as an indicator of their own character and behaviour.[11]

Prisoners are divided on the extent to which 'real' friendship is possible in prison. Many describe becoming progressively more guarded in their relationships with other inmates over time. During the course of their sentence, prisoners serving long sentences will see many 'generations' of inmates serving shorter terms come and go. Distress at seeing friends or girlfriends leave leads many to avoid close involvements with others. Repeated disappointments in friends who have promised but failed to maintain contact on release lead many to take a relatively sceptical view of prison relationships, as do the breaches of confidence described by long-term prisoners. Women who have spent long stretches of time in prison often relate stories that are emblematic of the limits to trust in prison relationships, including such grave violations as attempting to sell stories about their offence or family to the tabloid press. Women serving long or repeated sentences, then, more often describe their relationships in prison as 'associations' rather than 'friendships'. For many, the social and spatial dislocation of the prison make it difficult to feel that one can ever 'really know' anyone else. Some, however, do describe deep and sustaining friendships with other inmates, characterised by high levels of emotional and material support, and by markers of trust such as the reciprocal sharing of information whose disclosure entails a degree of vulnerability, such as offence details. For those who have lived with controlling or abusive partners before being sentenced, it might be the first time in years or decades that they have been able to access the friendship of other women. Despite the obstacles to doing so, some prisoners succeed in maintaining contact with friends once they have moved to another prison or been released, and some released prisoners provide important material support to those still inside.[12]

Although staff–prisoner relationships in women's prisons are somewhat freer than in men's, prisoners often comment on their surprise at finding that their relationships with staff are in many respects more ambivalent and harder to manage than those with fellow prisoners, as both Naomi and Lisa describe. There is no blanket injunction in women's prisons on sociable contact between prisoners and prison staff, and interactions are often informal and friendly. For many prisoners, officers and other staff are an important source of practical and even emotional support. While there is no systematic hierarchy of prisoners based on offence type in women's prisons, women convicted of certain crimes, such as offences against children, will generally be at best ostracised by other prisoners, and at worst at such risk of assault that they can only live safely in segregation from the rest of the population. The support of officers and other staff is particularly important for these women. Women prisoners generally regard it as part of the officer's core role to give support when needed. It is not uncommon for women prisoners to solicit support from staff on behalf of other inmates, approaching officers to draw their attention to a friend who is in need or struggling to cope. Similarly, officers co-opt prisoners' informal social networks – for example, to help induct new prisoners onto the wing, as Naomi has described – in order to provide support.

One of the effects for prisoners of living in what Goffman calls a 'total institution' is that social relations can take on a 'panoptical' quality, whereby both prison staff and inmates are highly aware of other people's activities: who is talking to whom; which relationships have been formed or broken off; where and how people spend their free time.[13] The awareness that even private social encounters may be observed and noted by others means that prisoners often become circumspect in the ways they manage their relationships. For example, while friendliness with officers is generally acceptable to women prisoners, 'grassing' is not tolerated. For this reason, many avoid private conversations with prison staff that might be misconstrued by other prisoners. Naomi's account of managing a romantic relationship in prison illustrates not only her awareness that staff are attentive to relations among prisoners, but the heightened sense of caution that stems from having an indeterminate sentence, which means that her behaviour is particularly closely monitored, and with greater potential consequences. This is demonstrated in Naomi's anxiety that her girlfriend's behaviour and reputation may reflect badly on her. The imperative for 'impression management' in dealings with both staff and inmates means that prisoners may need to develop complex strategies, such as that described by Naomi, in order to maintain equilibrium in their social relationships and negotiate conflicting social and moral demands. Thus, although relationships inside prison offer women a crucial coping resource, managing them can be taxing; while relationships with others mitigate the risks of isolation, they are themselves risky, making living in prison in part an ongoing negotiation between two unstable states.

Both Naomi's and Lisa's accounts of their interactions and relationships with prison staff illustrate the inescapably and pervasively social nature of prison life. As both women suggest, the delivery of even very basic aspects of prison regimes is socially mediated, and is therefore contingent on the quality of relationships.[14] Where relationships are good and procedures clear and consistent, transactions between staff and prisoners take place smoothly, without prisoners feeling officers' power; where they are poor, it can be difficult for prisoners to access entitlements and services, from getting a toilet roll to seeing a doctor or a counsellor, or getting information about educational opportunities or housing on release.

Prisoners' need for staff support, combined with prison officers' responsibility for security and reporting on prisoners' progress, can give rise to a degree of distance and guardedness in prisoners' attitudes to and interactions with officers, even where relations are generally positive. It is perhaps worth noting that despite the apparent freedom of staff–prisoner relationships and the relative lack of disruption and violence in women's prisons, there is evidence to suggest that women prisoners are more closely disciplined than men.[15] Naomi's account illustrates the very active ways in which many prisoners manage their relationships with staff, taking care to maintain goodwill as a kind of insurance for a time when they might need staff support. Naomi's sophisticated approach to this extends to developing individualised ways of approaching different officers. She states explicitly that prisoners who are unwilling to ingratiate themselves with staff are more likely to find officers obstructive. Furthermore, as Lisa implies, where conflicts arise between prisoners and officers, prisoners lack the power to hold staff directly to account. Both argue that because officers need to maintain an authoritative persona, many find it difficult to be challenged by prisoners. This can foster a sense among prisoners that they are not treated fairly. More fundamentally, perhaps, this can feel as though the individuals charged with delivering the regime are actively undermining the ability even of prisoners motivated by ideas of self-improvement or rehabilitation to address problems and develop skills, and thereby comply with the professed goals of imprisonment.

Despite the intensely social nature of much of prison life, the experience of imprisonment is understood by most prisoners as an essentially solitary one. As discussed elsewhere in this volume (see Chapter 3), the conditions imposed by contemporary prison regimes exert a significant individualising pressure on prisoners. While this is true for all prisoners to some extent, most agree that the rewards and sanctions available for those serving fixed-term sentences have a more limited capacity to incentivise compliance and regulate behaviour than for those with indeterminate sentences. These prisoners often feel subject to very close constraint, because they cannot progress through their sentence or be released until the parole board – informed by prison staff, especially psychologists – is satisfied that they have 'addressed their offending behaviour' and 'reduced their risk' to society. Although she claims to speak only for herself, Lisa echoes other prisoners, both male and female, when she expresses a sense of powerlessness that her future rests on apparently subjective judgements about her character and behaviour by officers and psychologists. The isolating effects of imprisonment are reflected in the common saying, 'You come into prison on your own, and you go out on your own', which both acknowledges and sanctions a degree of self-interest among prisoners in managing their sentences.[16]

Prisoners' ability to negotiate the constraints and frustrations of imprisonment depends not just on support available in prison, but also on what sociologists of the prison term their 'imported characteristics'. Many prisoners – male and female – have acute and chronic mental health problems that heighten their need for support, and hamper their ability to cope. Over 70 per cent of women in prison suffer from two or more diagnosed mental health disorders, nearly 40 per cent have at some time attempted suicide, and close to a third have had a previous psychiatric admission. The incidence of disorders often associated with immediate environmental stressors is also high; women in prison are twice as likely as those in the general population to suffer from eating disorders and nearly half have a major depressive disorder.[17] Many prisoners, then, are functioning at the limits of their capacity to cope, and rely on support from relationships outside in order to manage life inside.

When Lisa's difficulties inside prison converged with problems at home, she lacked both the power to resolve them and constructive ways in which to manage her frustration. She describes her feeling that self-harm was the only remaining coping strategy available to her. Self-harm is endemic in women's prisons; although women prisoners represent just 5 per cent of the total prison population, they accounted for over half of the incidents of self-harm recorded in prisons in England and Wales in 2008.[18] On some prison wings, prison officers are required to confront and cope with prisoners harming themselves daily. While many officers provide vital support to prisoners at such times, some – as Lisa describes – seem to become inured to prisoners' distress, or distance themselves from it to the point of insensitivity. Many detach the hopelessness that prisoners express in harming themselves from the conditions of imprisonment altogether, which Lisa argues strongly is a misapprehension, or failure of empathy. Her overriding experience is of systems that fail to deliver the support they promise. It is painfully ironic that while she experiences psychological assessment and monitoring as oppressive, she struggles to secure the psychological support she feels she needs.

Both Lisa and Naomi describe coping with a prison sentence as a question of 'survival'. Women's prisons disproportionately house those with chronic problems and in acute distress; they are austere institutions in which to find resolution to either. Imprisonment itself often leads to the fracturing of households and families, and imposes burdens of care and support on others that are liable to place relationships under intense stress. In intervening in what are often complex and constrained lives to punish women's offending, the criminal justice system may deepen the very problems from which it stems.

Notes

1 'M and B' or 'MBU': Mother and Baby Unit.
2 Depending on the length of a woman's sentence and the risk she is seen as presenting, babies can live with their mothers in different units for up to nine or up to 18 months.
3 'ACCT': Assessment, Care in Custody, and Teamwork, the Prison Service's protocol for prisoners regarded as being at risk of suicide or self-harm.
4 For a vivid first-hand account of the personal crisis that resulted in her imprisonment on remand, and the disorientation and disempowerment she experienced on entering the criminal justice system, see Peckham, A. (1985) *A Woman in Custody*. London: Fontana.
5 Prison Reform Trust (July 2010) *Bromley Briefings: Prison Factfile*.
6 Prison Reform Trust, *Bromley Briefings*.
7 Prison Reform Trust, *Bromley Briefings*.
8 'Canteen': goods purchased from the prison 'shop'. Prisoners can order goods weekly from a list determined by prison managers. The order is delivered to the prison by a centrally contracted company and delivered to prisoners on the wing.
9 For a discussion of relationships among women prisoners using 'strength-of-weak-ties' concept, see Severance, T. (2005) '"You know who you can go to": Cooperation and exchange between incarcerated women', *The Prison Journal*, 85: 343–67.
10 Naomi's observation relates both to private, 'imported' sources of distress and need, and those arising a result of institutional conditions. Kruttschnitt and Gartner's important study, *Marking Time in the Golden State: Women's imprisonment in California* (Cambridge: Cambridge University Press, 2005), is relevant to the latter of these, demonstrating a link between institutional and regime characteristics and the nature and quality of women's relationships in prison.
11 For a recent ethnographic account of the life of a women's prison in the US that addresses some of the social pressures discussed in this chapter, see Owen, B. (1998) *In the Mix: Struggle and Survival in a Women's Prison*. Albany, NY: SUNY.
12 For a recent account of prisoner relationships in a US prison that has some resonance with the UK context, see Greer, K. (2000) 'The changing nature of interpersonal relationships in a women's prison', *The Prison Journal*, 80(4): 442–68.
13 Goffman, E. (1961) *Asylums: Essays on the Social Situation of Mental Patients and Other Inmates*. Harmondsworth: Penguin.
14 Little published literature exists on the subject of staff–prisoner relationships in women's prisons. For insights into how the care of prisoners by prison officers is mediated by social relations, however, see Tait, S. (2008) *Prison Officer Care for Prisoners in One Men's and One Women's Prison*. PhD thesis, University of Cambridge.
15 Prison Reform Trust, *Bromley Briefings*.
16 Researchers have paid little attention to the ways in which women prisoners' experiences are affected by regime structures. However, the issues Lisa outlines resonate strongly with those described by male prisoners in Crewe, B. (2007) 'Power, adaptation and resistance in a late-modern men's prison', *British Journal of Criminology*, 47: 256–73.
17 Prison Reform Trust, *Bromley Briefings*.
18 Prison Reform Trust, *Bromley Briefings*.

Further reading

There has been little detailed recent research conducted in women's prisons in the UK. However, Barbara Owen's ethnography of a Californian women's prison,

In the Mix: Struggle and Survival in a Women's Prison (Albany, NY: SUNY, 1998) is an evocative account that resonates across jurisdictions. Women's experiences in UK prisons are perhaps best described in ex-prisoners' memoirs. Audrey Peckham's *A Woman in Custody* (London: Fontana, 1985) offers powerful insights into the experience of imprisonment and the social world of English women's prisons. The statistics in this chapter are taken from the Prison Reform Trust's *Bromley Briefings: Prison Factfile* (July 2010). This snapshot of the England and Wales prison system draws on a wide range of sources and is collated and published online biannually by the Trust.

10 Cultural diversity, ethnicity and race relations in prison

Coretta Phillips and Rod Earle

Barry was a white man in his late forties. He was something of a wing activist, advocating and organising hard for better facilities and services. Originally from northern England, and university educated, he was widely travelled and domiciled abroad owing to his intricate business interests, the failures of which had precipitated his entry into prison. He held the prison in the same kind of contempt that he reserved for the state that he felt had incarcerated and bankrupted him unnecessarily. He conveyed genuine sensitivity and compassion for prisoners' predicaments and was agitated by their neglect, even while sounding, at times, intolerant of ethnic difference. He used the interview to vent his many frustrations but ended it by ruefully remarking that it was 'time he got off his soap box'.

Well, you have ethnicity jammed down your throat all the time, don't you? I'm a Samaritan for the prison, a Listener,[1] so I do have to speak to a lot of people, or rather, have them speak to me. They're sometimes quite distressed. And on a couple of occasions, particularly there was one about six months ago who was trying to kill himself. And he said he didn't want to talk to me, cos 'You're a white racist motherfucker'. And he would not speak to me. So the other racists in here do throw one's Caucasian background down your throat all the time. I had a West Indian girlfriend for a couple of years, I've been out with Indians and I've got no racial problems, no discriminatory issues whatsoever. The people in here are just slightly more ignorant than they are on the out, so they throw it down your throat.

You find that people stick together in here for language reasons quite a lot. If there's three Dutch people on the wing, you'll find they play cards all the time. The West Indians stick together cos that's the way they are. I'm not being racist there, but they are, and they're the cause of an awful lot of trouble in here. They're the most racist bunch of bastards in the world. The Asians stick together.

The one thing that does cement the groups together in this prison in particular is the self-cook.[2] And you'll find that the three or four Asian lads on the wing stick together because they cook together, they eat together. The West Indians all have their – and again I'm not being racist, but this is genuinely what they're like – they have their fried chicken, rice and peas, and they eat it all the time. I'm not stereotyping them. And having the cook area, I think it helps. Except it does cement the racial barriers. There's three or four Italians on the wing and they all eat and sit together and talk together. They probably would anyway, but even more so because now you see them all sat like 'that's the Italian table', 'that's the Polish table'.

It brings back the old question, which is whether the racial and cultural barriers and difference should be celebrated or broken down. I don't think you could ever break them down. And if you celebrate them too strongly then it becomes racism. They have to be accepted and appreciated for what they are. Diversity is always a great thing. It's enriching for everybody who's in the melting pot. But it has to be tempered with reason. On one wing there was a period where the Muslims complained so much about people cooking bacon that it was banned completely from the self-cook. And they tried to make that stick on another wing, and in this one. I wouldn't have it, neither would any of the others: 'Fuck off, if you don't like it, mate'. I'm sorry, we can always fall back to the old baseline that this is a Christian country and if you want to be here, come and fit in. If I go and live in Dubai, I fit in with the Arabs, I observe Ramadan. I don't walk down the street with a beefburger. And you observe the traditions of the country that you're in, you don't try and impose your own traditions on them. I know that sounds a bit hard-line.

With the bacon ban, it didn't last long at all, but that's what they can do, they play the race card, they say, 'He's being racist, he's cooking bacon where I want to'. Fuck off. Everybody has their own pots and pans and if you want to keep them halal that's up to you. But they argue about there might be some bacon grease in the washing-up basin and all that. Sometimes we still get the occasional militant Muslim, who will see you cooking something and he'll stand back and go, 'I can't go anywhere, he's cooking bacon, he's cooking bacon, it's disgusting!' Now he'll get told to fuck off, and quite right too. They try it on all the time, they try and play the race/religion/Muslim card all the time. It has made them so unpopular. I mean, I've heard people on the wing saying openly that they do not want Muslims on this wing. And that's not healthy. I've a feeling that what the screws do is when somebody is known to be causing problems like that, they have a quiet word and say, 'Look, they do cook that stuff on here, if you don't like it I'm afraid all we can do is send you back to your old wing, if you like'. And I think they do try and be diplomatic like that.

On the other wing I couldn't get down to self-cook because the West Indians are the only ones allowed to cook. Nobody else is allowed to. It's the fact that the West Indians are the ones who take over. Again, I'm sounding racist. I'm not at all, it's just an observation. If you're not West Indian you can't cook on that wing, full-stop, that's it, end of the line. You try, you have a fight. If you're not West Indian you have to queue for your dinner as well on the servery. If you're West Indian you don't need to queue, you just go straight to the front, and the officers turn a blind eye because they can't argue with them because they're West Indian. That causes resentment. But the West Indians are a minority obviously, but they're one of the bigger minorities, they are very strong, they're not afraid to have a fight because they pull the race card straight away. If you hit a black guy, you'll get shipped off the wing because you've assaulted him in a racist manner. That's the way it always goes. It's reverse racism.

It's the same as it is outside the prison. There'll always be ethnic intermingling and ethnic separation as well. I had a flat once in Stoke Newington – big Turkish area. Everybody was Turkish round there. I was one of the few English people in the street. And they just stick together, it's a ghetto. You go up to Stamford Hill and it's a Jewish area. It's a funny thing in here and it's a funny thing in society in general. Pure diversity and lack of racism involves not noticing the other person's diversity, the other person's race. It's irrelevant, it's irrelevant that you're black and I'm white, that you're from somewhere else to me. And yet the first thing they do when you come in here is, 'What's your ethnic code?' That's disgusting. How dare they! It's none of their business what my ethnic code is. I put myself down as a black Afro-Caribbean/Chinese cross usually, just to piss them off. It is none of their business. It's disgusting that they even ask. And I always tell them, 'It's none of your business'. 'Make a guess', I say.

Racial tensions only play out because there are undoubtedly prisoners in here who do have racial prejudices, and the system, as it does on the out, the system allows the race card to be played. Most people's way of being racist these days doesn't involve any racist incidents, it involves trying to accuse the other person of a racist incident. That's how racism is used. And the framework is set up in here for people to be able to pursue a racist complaint with no foundation or basis whatsoever. If somebody gets refused some dinner on the servery, you know, for some reason they say they want fruit instead of pudding, and the officer will quite rightly say, 'No, sorry, you're down for a pudding, that's what you're getting'. He'll say, 'If I was a white man you'd let me have it'. Racist incident. Racist problem. And the officer's up on charges and he has to defend himself. They pull that card all the time.

The prison service is not working, particularly because of the social worker input, as I call it. The fact that they're forced to record one's ethnic code and all the rest. Even mentioning that somebody is Chinese or Norwegian should be a sackable offence. Nanny state again. We seem to have somebody from Laos on the wing, so they'll have to reprint every sign in the jail with Laos as an option. Fuck off! This is England. These people, they're all one great big bunch of ethnic foreigners or English ethnic different background, but nevertheless they're in England. Keep the signs in English, supply some translators and pretend not to notice that they're from a different country. That's the only way to do it. And anything beyond that is racism in itself. It's only a problem in England. What is it with the English? And the more these PC idiots try and do to solve the problems, the worse they make them.

Clinton was in prison for the first time having been convicted of property and drugs offences. He was just outside his teenage years, born in central Africa, and spoke French, English and Lingala. Clinton had recently been affected by the death of a close friend and he talked very openly about his anxieties and difficulties in adjusting to prison life. He had found the early months of life in prison emotionally challenging. Clinton was largely sanguine about race relations among prisoners, but was somewhat less positive about relationships between minority ethnic prisoners and prison officers.

Have you seen *Money Train*?[3] It was basically like that. He was the white friend and I was the black friend and we grew up together. Everything together. Very, very close. Like I look at his mum like an auntie. Forest Gate is more … is an Asian community. There is black people there. Asian community, where they think they are better than everyone. Especially when there was a little documentary on Channel 4 about Asian people going to be taking over soon, rair rair rair.[4] That was a negative vibe. Because after that everyone was hating Asian people. And me, it is like I ain't got nothing against them but I can't make friends with Asian people. I've got Asian friends but they have been there from day dot. So I'm not going to try and make new Asian friends. The Asian friends I've got, I don't need to make no new ones.

Yeah, but, you know, I mix with everyone but there is only really two Asian boys I do speak to on my wing, one is from Walthamstow and the other is from Leeds and I speak to him. White boys, I speak to all of them, but there is only two that come in my cell and I can chat to on a regular basis. Tony, Vince and Robbie, they are the only white boys that I can actually speak to. One of them is from Barking. That is not too far from Walthamstow, we go to the same nightclubs as each other and we know a couple of girls, he knows a couple of girls I know, I know a couple of girls he knows, so we have got something to talk about through that. It gradually builds up and so now yeah, he is a friend that I've got in jail, like, tight; everyone else, they don't do it for me. Yeah, I've got nothing in common with them. Everyone from Walthamstow ... that is a guaranteed we are going to stick together. You don't have to do nothing, innit. If anything kicks off then we are all there for each other, innit. Whoever else gets involved with a little scene then we are there for them. Nobody is going to bully you or nothing because they know there is too much of us.

Even in the jail, you don't really see a black person going into their cell but an Asian person could come into a black person's cell. A bit weird. It is what you do before you come in jail. Certain Asian guys, there is an Asian guy from Stratford, he's known because he does a lot of negative things. So if a lot of black guys from that same area know that he does a lot of negative things what they do ... they can easily bond, that is how it is, you see.

There is racism but they don't really want to confess it, innit. I see it all the time. Staff, prison, inmates they are so fucking ... One time where someone was serving someone food, at the servery, serving someone food, and he just ended up giving him a bit more chips, extra chips or something. And he was saying, they give these black people more food than they give us. Why don't they go back to their country? As soon as they heard that they thought, right, leave it to the morning, and then they got his head flushed down the toilet for saying that. That was one occasion and there was another occasion where they [a group of prisoners of different ethnic origins] were having an argument and he just shouted out 'black cunt', so that is how he really felt. And his head got flushed down the toilet and ever since that it has died down but it is still there.

Come Christmas, a prisoner server[5] touched pork with one of his hands and still gave a Muslim prisoner it. He knew that he can't mix pork and chicken because everyone told him you are not allowed to touch the pork. But I clocked him and he done it to about three other Muslim people. I said, 'That is the same hand, you can't do that'. He said, 'So? They don't know'. That is still not right, is it? Everyone told him before, 'Don't do it', but he carried on doing it. There was this other thing when, basically, it was Eid. They wouldn't let him [a Muslim prisoner] go somewhere because it was Eid. Gym or somewhere. And they wouldn't let him go because he is Muslim and they said, 'It is Eid and you are supposed to [be] fasting', or something. I just thought that that was a bit racial.

I got an experience as well, I think it was racial, I got a nicking for it. I told the teacher that someone was smoking, he was white, he was smoking in her classroom. And she said, 'You're getting a Red entry'. And I said, 'Why do I get a Red entry?' I called her a stupid blind 'b' in

French. And she said something about did I call her a prick? And I got a nicking for it. I said, 'No, I didn't', I just called her a blind woman. And then an officer said, 'You can't say that to a member of staff', and then a member of his staff said something about my mum. Nothing happened to him but I got three days nicking for it and seven days 50 per cent, where they take 50 per cent of my money.

Racism is still around. On my wing, there is six large cells and they are only meant to be for enhanced prisoners, cleaners and servery prisoners. Then they moved two of the black people to a normal cell and moved two white people in. One of the white people was enhanced but his cellmate was not, but they kept him in there as well. I asked for one of my friends to come in there, but they ended up moving another white boy, who is not enhanced, not a cleaner, not a servery, in my cell. Every time I ask, 'I don't want him in my cell, can I have another cleaner?' That is just a little racism, that …

Commentary

In the academic literature there are contrasting accounts of prisoner identities and how prisoners relate to each other inside. Most have typically drawn on the now dated US sociological literature. The 'indigenous model' suggests that prisoners' identities are established through the pains of imprisonment – the exceptional isolation and brutalising conditions of the prison environment.[6] This promotes a solidarity that binds prisoners together as a group against prison officers. The 'importation model' poses an alternative account that sees prisoners carrying racial, ethnic and religious identities with them into the prison.[7] These identities reproduce the collective inter-ethnic divisions and conflicts that characterise society outside. In the UK, Genders and Player's 1989 study of race relations, like others in the European context, supported a synthesis, finding elements of both models in the social organisation of prison life.[8]

In the twenty-first century, UK prisons are often ethnically, religiously and nationally diverse. In 2008, 27 per cent of the prison population in England and Wales was of minority ethnic origin and 25 per cent of these were of foreign nationality.[9] Concerns about whether this significant over-representation of black men and women in custody is the result of institutional or individual racial discrimination on the part of the police or courts, or the result of other legitimate factors, is an ongoing issue.[10] Inside prison it is clear that minority ethnic prisoners believe that they receive differential and inferior treatment compared with their white counterparts. In HMIP's thematic inspection of 2005, *Parallel Worlds*, for example, black prisoners reported that prison officers often treated them disrespectfully.[11] They also felt that they had poorer access to the regime, and were more harshly disciplined, and less likely to have their resettlement needs met than white prisoners. As Clinton asserts, 'there is racism

... I see it all the time', but the forms it takes are deeply contested, as Barry's account reveals. Many minority ethnic prisoners described incidents where they believed black prisoners experienced less favourable treatment than their white counterparts. Among these prisoners the belief that white prison officers were suspicious and judgemental of black prisoners' social interactions and cultural styles was widespread. Many were convinced that the almost exclusively white prison staff lacked, individually and collectively, understanding and awareness of minority ethnic cultural practices. Being heavily policed on the wings, or being frequently challenged by officers simply for gathering in groups, were common complaints. Prisoners reported a sense of suspicion falling on their games of dominoes, for example, or their manner of talking and interacting with each other. Each was felt, at worst, as an assault on their ethnic identities, or, at best, as a form of cultural stereotyping.

Like many other minority ethnic prisoners in the research literature, Clinton also talks about prison practices, such as the allocation of cells or the use of discipline, as more often producing a positive outcome for white prisoners. Many minority ethnic prisoners believed that this reflected white prison officer prejudice towards them. Specific incidents, such as a request to an officer that was ignored when made by a black prisoner but responded to in the case of a white prisoner, or the refusal to allow a Muslim prisoner to attend Friday prayers, were frequently, though not always, interpreted through the lens of racism. Stories of fewer black and minority ethnic prisoners getting their D-cat, parole or enhanced status,[12] or the larger number of black prisoners employed as menial wing cleaners, were commonplace. The same perceptions of racial disadvantage were held in relation to increased cell searches and the lesser use of officer discretion resulting in harsher formal disciplinary measures. As the Prison Service itself has acknowledged, there is continuing evidence that black prisoners are more likely to be on the basic regime, to be subject to disciplinary action in segregation units, and to have force used against them, than prisoners from other ethnic groups.[13] Clinton's account of a nicking he got for being abusive in French to a member of the educational staff, while a white prisoner was not reprimanded for smoking, nor was a prison officer for retaliatory comments, exemplifies the concerns expressed by many minority ethnic prisoners. For Clinton, 'it was racial': his original misdemeanour was secondary to the subsequent abuse he received from a member of staff whose actions escaped scrutiny because he was both white and a prison officer. The everyday ambiguities of an exceptionally authoritarian environment throw up countless possibilities of rule infractions, petty, playful or otherwise, which will inevitably be differently interpreted according to the relative powerfulness or powerlessness of the position of those involved. The lens of race, and by extension racism, is a constant presence through which these experiences are filtered, though varying according to circumstance and often by ethnicity.

For example, Barry has a radically contrasting perspective on racism in prison. The paramount issue for him is 'reverse racism', where prison officers discriminate in favour of minority ethnic prisoners. So, 'if you hit a black guy, you'll get shipped off the wing because you've assaulted him in a racist manner'. The prison system, according to Barry and many other, mostly but not exclusively, white prisoners, 'allows the race card to be played'. It can lead to plainly mischievous allegations of racism by minority ethnic prisoners which have to be investigated using the complaints or racist incidents procedures prescribed by the Prison Service. Barry appears to suggest that racism, as it is more conventionally understood, does not really occur in modern society, and that in prisons it has mutated into a tactic or tool in the armoury of minority ethnic prisoners. According to such accounts, minority ethnic prisoners use 'the race card' for personal advantage, 'to get one over on', or even hurt, an individual officer, the regime in general, or other prisoners.

In this perspective there is also a sense of undue privilege being gained through the betrayal of a common (prisoner) condition: a black prisoner asserting his right to be allocated a particular meal, such as a halal portion, steps over the line of his minimal rights to choose afforded to him as a prisoner. By invoking the spectre of racist treatment, he is able to assert power over an individual officer in a way that white prisoners clearly cannot. Instead of a universal prisoner identity based on a common condition, Barry sees modern prison social life as riven with ethnic conflict and division, which is perversely fostered by the prison's management of race equality. In Barry's colour-blind account, racism is the fabrication of do-good 'social workers', twisted and inverted by unscrupulous, self-serving individuals. It stands in stark contrast to Clinton's account of racialised suspicion and systemic disadvantage. In Barry's eyes, minority ethnic prisoners hold a power over white prisoners and prison officers. It is a socially corrosive power that upturns the traditional allegiances that pits prisoners against prison officers. For Clinton, there are no signs of such reversal and white prison officers continue to exert an additional power over minority ethnic prisoners through the medium of conventional racist prejudice.

Interactions between Muslim and non-Muslim prisoners and staff draw correspondingly polarised accounts from both Barry and Clinton. Clinton refers to an episode in which a Muslim prisoner is prevented from going to the prison gymnasium because the officer seemed to be acting on the assumption that, as a Muslim, he should be fasting and not engaging in physical activity or leisure. For Clinton, this was perceived as another example of a stereotypical pigeon-holing of a prisoner's faith, not least because Eid involves the breaking of the fast following Ramadan. Institutionally, there is significant support for Muslim observance, but individual officers may struggle to administer such policies with sensitivity, as was also reported in HMIP's thematic inspection on Muslim prisoner experience.[14] Such misunderstandings and misperceptions were commonly reported by Muslim and non-Muslim prisoners, many of whom shared the officers' relative ignorance of Islam. Barry's story is also littered with references to Muslim prisoners, but his accusatory account again runs in the opposite direction. Barry, like some other white non-Muslim prisoners, believed that Muslim prisoners had a trump card up their sleeves ready to be 'played' at any and every opportunity. His resentment of the prison's accommodation of Muslim observance comes across strongly in his account. It stems from a genuine prison difficulty of sharing very limited space and resources. However, for Barry, this takes shape in his 'recognition' of the apparent privileging of minority ethnic identities, whereas he feels that his white, nominally Christian, majority ethnicity remains unacknowledged and subordinate. This status of invisibility is his benchmark such that 'even mentioning' another ethnicity 'should be a sackable offence'. Barry's exasperation with efforts to differentiate and accommodate difference is palpable.

The antagonism and tensions apparent in both Barry's and Clinton's accounts were not always present in other white and minority ethnic prisoners' accounts. In fact, a significant proportion of minority ethnic prisoners explicitly claimed that racism was not part of their experience of incarceration, perhaps reflecting the impact of the Prison Service's race equality reforms, which set out to facilitate the equal treatment and protection of minority ethnic prisoners.[15] This was particularly the case among younger prisoners. Comments such as, 'I wouldn't agree with anyone who said that they thought that any of the officers in here was racist', '[Racism] ain't really been a big issue', 'I've been in jail for six years, never seen nothing', 'So far as I know there is no racism in prison ... never seen it', were voiced by both black and white minority ethnic prisoners in our interviews. It is important to acknowledge that many of the younger prisoners did not typically jump to assume that particular incidents were motivated by racism, even where they themselves believed that they had experienced unfair treatment at the hands of prison officers. Perhaps surprisingly, they tended to be more circumspect in their attributions of racism.

Among many of the older prisoners, some of whom had spent a considerable part of their lives in prison, there was often rueful reflection on the changes that had occurred in prison race relations. References were made to the past where more endemic racism was prevalent among prison officers, with it much reduced in current times. A white Muslim prisoner, for example, recalled the prejudice shown towards Muslim prisoners in the late 1980s where officers would try to 'beat the Muslim out of you', while others recognised the significant improvements made to non-Christian faith provision in prison in recent years. These provisions were often regarded with equanimity, as a reasonable and welcome recognition of human needs in a place more notorious for doing the reverse.

Ethnic, religious and national diversity is, of course, commonly encountered in everyday life in multicultural Britain. Recent sociological work has emphasised the relative absence of racial divisions among young people raised in large metropolitan urban areas, as solidarities are formed on the basis of class, sexual, and regional or local identities. Among prisoners, as Clinton suggests, there are certainly identifiable elements of the 'multicultural conviviality' that sociologist Paul Gilroy has described.[16] Black prisoners' accounts of the mixing process were generally more positive than those of white prisoners. Many, like Clinton, would offer instances of interactions with white 'mates' or places where common activities were undertaken, such as in the gym or cook area. For other black and Asian prisoners, references were made to white friends with whom they had shared common experiences in the mixed multicultural environment of London and with whom they felt close bonds that erased racialised distinction. Clinton, for example, 'mixes with everyone'. He refers to his white friend as being like the Woody Harrelson character in *Money Train*, to his Wesley Snipes, invested together as partners in crime. Inside prison, Clinton nominates his white and Asian friends, of whom some share his local neighbourhood. These strong, local affiliations are the largely unconditional solidarities of place that many prisoners carry over into their prison lives.[17] Place-based identities provide a means of bonding between prisoners through familiarity with the outside and will likely ensure defensive support in prison disputes. At times, these 'postcode loyalties' usurp racial and ethnic identification, particularly among younger prisoners.[18] As Clinton asserts, for him, everyone from Walthamstow will be 'guaranteed ... to stick together' inside.

Like Clinton, Barry signals his willingness to endorse diversity as a 'great thing' for 'everybody who's in the melting pot'. Such views were widespread and conveyed a conviviality between prisoners, not least because in the words of another prisoner, 'You have to [mix] in here, because there's no choice about it, is there?' While ethnic difference, as Gilroy claims, could be regarded as a normal feature of life in Britain, symbolising the 'liberating ordinariness' of multicultural realities, prisoners' friendship groups and informal gatherings remained largely same-ethnicity inside.[19] Thus, Clinton mixes 'with everyone' but maintained the strongest friendships with mostly other black prisoners. A mixed race prisoner put it this way: 'You see a little bit of a mix and then you see everyone isolated as well, black people stick together, Turks stick together'. Significantly, this did not appear to be out of active hostility or opposition to other cultural groups, but simply because 'it's just who you get on with really'. Barry's account similarly reflects this benign perspective when he talks about foreign national prisoners hanging out during mealtimes and association, for 'language reasons'.

Self-cook areas, although rare in the prison system, provide a unique insight into multicultural living inside. They can condense and reveal the ethnic diversity of the prison as no other prison place can. In one of the prisons that we researched, Cypriot and Turkish men made yoghurt and *kattimeri*,[20] sharing kitchen facilities with black British and Caribbean men who cooked rice and peas and dumplings, African men cooked groundnut stews and white English men fried eggs, grilled bacon, made toast and ate curry. The self-cook area was a place of exchange and sharing, of food, tools, resources and ideas; a prison resource defended as a highly valued but ultimately discretionary facility. As such, while tensions around its use were inevitably present, it also provided a place of multicultural socialisation and interaction. Notwithstanding, as Barry describes, the self-cook area could also be a place of friction which could 'cement the racial barriers'. He alleged that black prisoners used the gas cooker 'rings' to control space in the prison, which caused resentment among white prisoners. For some white prisoners, black prisoners' assertive presence was out of kilter considering their presence as a numerical minority. Accommodating diverse cultural practices, such as observing halal food regulations, prompted in Barry, and many other non-Muslim prisoners, a degree of bitterness and resentment. Nonetheless, given the precious nature of the cooking facility and the way it enriched prisoners' lives, prisoners managed to achieve a constrained con-viviality for much of the time, an accomplishment that should not be underestimated.

Among prisoners, as Clinton remarks, racism 'is still around' but it does not go unchallenged. White prisoners would sometimes get their heads flushed down the toilet for unguarded remarks, as Clinton's account makes clear. Yet for Barry, black prisoners were 'the most racist bunch of bastards in the world'. For many white prisoners there was an awkwardness and an anxiety in negotiating everyday interactions with minority ethnic, particularly black prisoners. For Barry, his attempts to assist a fellow black prisoner were actively rejected on the basis of his white ethnicity, and for him this was symptomatic of the prison's obsessional mismanagement of race, which only endorsed a white racist, black victim mentality. Within the framework of the informal sanctions against racist behaviour, and the prison's formal race equality policies, white prisoners have to tread a difficult path in avoiding claims of racism and in provoking confrontations with minority ethnic prisoners. In the public spaces of the prison, during association, at the servery, while cooking in self-cook areas, for example, the ambiguities of multi-ethnic cohabitation are amplified and the negotiations intensified. So in Barry's vitriolic account of the struggles over the cooking of bacon in the self-cook area, the challenges of the daily negotiation of ethnic difference become explicit. This serves as a useful example of the way in which the prison's faith policies are differentially experienced by diverse groups of prisoners.

Although such talk was relatively rare, some white prisoners spoke of maintaining only a reserved level of interaction with black prisoners. At the same time, because expressing racism in public was generally considered unacceptable, white prisoners had to contend with the effort of self-policing and moderating racist habits of speech. The strain of doing so in the permanently semi-public, supervised social space of the prison, where privacy is limited, was clear, and at times resented, such that racist talk went on 'behind doors' in cells. When verbal slips such as 'you black ...' did occur in the heat of an altercation, black prisoners saw this as indicative of the covert status of racism in prison social relations.

Indeed, for many white prisoners, there is a limit to the active celebration of diversity – 'it has to be tempered with reason', as Barry suggests. This reason has to be founded on the 'baseline' of Britain 'as a Christian country'. Otherwise, there is an unhealthy redistribution of power that is already felt by

Barry and many other white prisoners. They perceive a fundamental shift in power relations, which sees Britain's minority ethnic groups as ascendant. This represents an unsettling of traditional racial hierarchies which has a destabilising effect and manifests through anxious interactions, racialised resentment and occasional altercations. While, on the one hand, Barry welcomes diversity, on the other, he feels uncomfortable and outraged with the specific recognition of ethnicity in prison ethnic monitoring. The tensions between colour-blindness and equal treatment and colour-recognition and unequal treatment are thoughtfully considered in Barry's account. However, he remains deeply conflicted, unable to resolve the ambiguities he feels, and concludes that the mere mention of an individual prisoner's ethnic or national identity should be a 'sackable offence'. Ethnicity is an overwhelming irrelevance because, after all, 'this is England'. For him, the prison inescapably epitomises the politically correct nanny state which privileges minority ethnicities over white ethnicities – 'you have ethnicity jammed down your throat all the time'.

Thus, it can be seen that prison race relations are complex, contradictory and conflicted. Multicultural con-viviality is present, to an extent accompanying prisoners into the prison from outside, but this is not the complete story. The constraints of prison life – the social isolation, continual surveillance and enforced proximal living – promote a desire among prisoners of different ethnicities, faiths and nationalities to make life inside tolerable for each other. This is assisted by neighbourhood affiliations that frequently overlay ethnic identification and division. However, it is also clear that the con-viviality is constrained; it is contingent, managed through everyday negotiation and conflict. Moreover, underlying the surface-level equanimity lies a powerful current of racialised antagonism. For black prisoners there is the suspicion of old-style racism among officers and some prisoners, but this is now more covert than in previous decades. For many white prisoners, understandings of racism have been appropriated and up-ended through talk of 'reverse racism' and the systematic marginalisation of white prisoners by the race equality regime in prisons. Minority ethnic prisoners are resented for playing 'race cards' given to them by this regime, thereby compromising the traditional solidarities of prisoners. These tensions are negotiated in the social world of the prison on a daily basis, resulting in a sometimes brittle, sometimes flexible equilibrium. The efforts required to maintain this under the constraints of prison life generate an uneasy con-viviality.

Notes

1 Listeners are prisoners trained by the Samaritans to provide support and solace to their peers.
2 Here, the interviewee is referring to cooking facilities, such as ovens, grills, gas rings and washing sinks, available in the communal area of the wing.
3 *Money Train* is a 1995 American action/thriller film starring two prominent Hollywood actors, one black (Wesley Snipes) and one white (Woody Harrelson), who decide to hijack and then rob the money train.
4 A slang term meaning, loosely, 'and so on and so on'.

5 A worker serving food to other prisoners.
6 See Sykes, G. M. (1958) *The Society of Captives: A Study of a Maximum Security Prison*. Princeton, NJ: Princeton University Press; and Goffman, E. (1961) 'On the characteristics of total institutions: The inmate world', in D. Cressey (ed.) *The Prison: Studies in Institutional Organization and Change*. New York: Holt, Rinehart and Winston.
7 See Irwin, J. and Cressey, D. R. (1962) 'Thieves, convicts and the inmate culture', *Social Problems*, 10(2): 142–55; Jacobs, J. B. (1977) *Stateville: The Penitentiary in Mass* Society. Chicago: University of Chicago Press; and Jacobs, J. B. (1979) 'Race relations and the prisoner subculture', in N. Morris and M. Tonry (eds) *Crime and Justice*. Chicago: University of Chicago Press.
8 Genders, E. and Player, E. (1989) *Race Relations in Prison*. Oxford: Clarendon Press.
9 NOMS (2008) *Race Review 2008: Implementing Race Equality in Prisons – Five Years On*.
10 Phillips, C. and Bowling, B. (2007) 'Ethnicities, racism, crime and criminal justice', in M. Maguire, R. Morgan and R. Reiner (eds) *The Oxford Handbook of Criminology*, 4th edn., Oxford: Oxford University Press.
11 Her Majesty's Inspectorate of Prisons (2005) *Parallel Worlds: A Thematic Review of Race Relations in Prisons*. London: HMIP.
12 D-cat refers to the security categorisation of prisoners, with 'D' being the lowest and hence most privileged status. 'Enhanced' refers to the status of prisoners in the Incentives and Earned Privileges (IEP) scheme, a hierarchy of 'basic', 'standard' and 'enhanced'.
13 NOMS, *Race Review 2008*.
14 Her Majesty's Inspectorate of Prisons (2010) *Muslim Prisoners' Experiences: A Thematic Review*. London: HMIP.
15 HMIP, *Parallel Worlds*; NOMS, *Race Review 2008*.
16 Gilroy, P. (2004) *After Empire: Melancholia or Convivial Culture?* London: Taylor and Francis.
17 See also Crewe, B. (2009) *The Prisoner Society: Power, Adaptation and Social Life in an English Prison*. Oxford: Oxford University Press.
18 Kintrea, K., Bannister, J., Pickering, J., Reid, M. and Suzuki, N. (2008) *Young People and Territoriality in British Cities*. York: Joseph Rowntree Foundation.
19 Gilroy, P. *After Empire*.
20 A sweet deep-fried paste made of flour, oil, butter, almond and cinnamon kindly offered for sampling to the researcher.

Further reading

Elaine Genders and Elaine Player's *Race Relations in Prison* (Oxford: Clarendon Press, 1989) remains the most comprehensive study of race relations in England and Wales. James A. Beckford *et al.*'s more recent book, *Muslims in Prison* (London: Palgrave Macmillan, 2005) focuses on the experience of Muslim prisoners in England and France. For direct considerations of race in prisons in England and Wales, see HMIP, *Parallel Worlds: A Thematic Review of Race Relations in Prisons* (2005) and NOMS, *Race Review 2008: Implementing Race Equality in Prisons – Five Years On* (2008). The chapter on 'Ethnicities, racism, crime and criminal justice', by Coretta Phillips and Ben Bowling in the fourth edition of the *Oxford Handbook of Criminology* (Oxford: Oxford University Press, 2007) provides further details of the experience of minority ethnic groups in prison and elsewhere in the criminal justice system, while Paul Gilroy's *After Empire: Melancholia or Convivial Culture?* (London: Taylor and Francis, 2004) provides a broad discussion of race and multiculturalism.

11 Rehabilitation, generativity and mutual aid

Steve Barlow and Shadd Maruna

John was a 23-year-old interviewed in an Australian prison in 2006 as part of an investigation into how prisoners indicate their readiness for change.[1] He was nominated by prison staff as an individual who appeared to make positive changes inside prison and he volunteered to be interviewed 'if his story could help others learn from his experiences'. He came from a 'good family' but involvement with the 'wrong crowd' led him into a life of drugs and crime and, eventually, to prison. He recognised he 'probably needed jail' to overcome his addictions and to gain a new perspective – to see 'through other people' what he was like. With clearer vision, the commitment to 'do something worthwhile' with his life, and an emerging sense of purpose, John wanted to help others overcome their problems and avoid the mistakes he so readily made in his own past.

I came from a good family. I was always good at school, just got distracted and started hanging with the wrong crowd. By the beginning of Year 9 I was expelled from school and I went to work. I was working for a while, about a year and a half. I couldn't keep a job. I was still hanging around with the wrong people, doing bad things. I knew what I was doing was wrong but I guess growing up where I grew up, I wasn't at home a lot, I was mostly on the streets with my friends. I ended up getting into trouble with Juvenile.[2]

I got involved in drugs and got addicted, got a habit. That was probably the hardest time in my life. Once you get into that stage everything else just falls apart. It's like a trap. I tried to go straight. Did a couple of programmes to try and better myself – ended up didn't really last long, in and out of rehabs. At the age of 15 I started working again, [but] fell back into the wrong crowd again and started getting into trouble.

Then I got myself clean and started doing a TAFE course.[3] I was doing well, finished the course. I wasn't doing anything for a while and ended up falling back again with the wrong crowd – that's where things started going downhill, and I eventually ended up here in jail.

Since being in jail I've been looking back on my past. My life needed to change a lot, my lifestyle wasn't getting me anywhere. The people I know, I used to look up to them, but looking up to them, it's not the way I want to go. I can't look up to drug dealers and gangsters; it's not what I want to be. I don't want nothing to do with them, and most of the people I used to hang around with are either dead or in jail. If I go that way that's where I'm going to end up, and that's not the life for me. I've got bigger and better things to do than to waste my life. I don't have any contact with them any more and I don't plan to. I'm definitely through with all that. I've had enough of it.

Coming to jail has helped me a lot. I probably needed jail to make that change in me, to give me that push. If I was outside and doing the same things I would probably have kept going, I wouldn't see how I was escalating from bad to worse, but here I can see it for myself. I knew I wasn't living a good life but coming here has opened up my eyes even more. I can see it more clearly. I think it would have been harder to leave that lifestyle if I didn't come here, because being here has given me time to get things in perspective. You don't really notice it until you see yourself through someone else's actions; it's like you can't see yourself. I couldn't see how I was acting, but I can see through other people and it makes me want to change. I can relate to a lot of people here who haven't changed, and that's how I would be.

I'll just keep doing what I can to improve myself and keep my mind focused and busy. I've been working hard, I've been studying as much as I can, trying to improve myself. I don't want all that to go to waste. I want to move forward not backwards. I want to be a full-time student; I want to study and get a degree and do something worthwhile. I want to help people who have been in my position as a counsellor, a drug and alcohol counsellor, so other people won't have to go through what I had to go through. I want to help other people before it's too late and they end up in jail. I just want to make a change and I think of all the bad things I've done, I think I owe it to people to help them.

My family is very important. They are the only ones you find will stick by you 100 per cent no matter what. Friends come and go but your family is always there for you. They've always been supportive, they've always done everything they can for me to help me, they're hard-working people, good honest people. And that's what helps me, gets me through.

I'm not the same person I was before I came here, and I don't think I'll ever be. The chaplains have been a lot of help, I've been seeing them, talking to them, to drug and alcohol workers, and they just gave me encouragement and hope. And that's just completely changed me. I don't look at things the same way, I don't act the same as I used to. If I thought the way I did before, I'd probably be getting myself into more trouble here. It's like, you know, learning to walk for the first time. You've got to work on the beginning again. That's what I'm doing. For me it's like my life's beginning, my journey's just started.

I really don't look at people like I used to. When I was out there before I came here I wouldn't care about what happens to people. But now, if I see someone in trouble I'll be there to help – even though I don't know them, I'd want to help. There's a lot of drama going on here, you see a lot more trouble here than you see outside, you just feel sorry for people and you want to help them out. I don't like seeing that happen any more, people getting stood over, getting picked on – that's not who I want to be; instead of putting people down, I'd rather just help people.

I try and talk to the younger people. That isn't the life! I've been through a lot since I was young, and this is where I've ended up and it could have been even worse. If you want to make a change you've just got to start. You've got to start now, that's what I'm doing. Everyone's got their own opinions and you can't really change what they think, but you can try and influence them in a good way. But it's up to them. Like a lot of the young guys I've brought them to education and I've taken them to a lot of classes I've been doing and it's helping them, so I'm happy with that. But some people are not interested. I guess they haven't been through enough yet.

Carl was a 37-year-old European émigré interviewed in an Australian prison in 2006 as part of the same research,[4] again selected for interview because prison staff identified him as being ready for change. In some ways Carl was not a stereotypical prisoner – he had wealth, 'magic hands for artwork', and a meaningful and profitable career at one point. However, he suffered a severe bout of depression following the loss of his father, and 'went ballistic' on drugs trying to cover his pain. He told a story of brokenness and loss, but also a story of discovery and emerging hope.

I left school when I was 15 or 16 years old and started working for my dad in the furniture shop. That went really well. [Eventually I had my own shop in the same business and was working for myself.] ...

[A few years ago] my dad started feeling a bit sick. My dad used to do all my accounting. I used to make the money and my dad used to do all the bookings and make sure all the receipts were there for tax purposes; at that stage I couldn't do that. My dad used to give me the right opinions, how to run things, how to make the money and without him beside me I feel hopeless. He was everything for me, my dad. We went to the hospital, that's where I heard the bad news. He was going to die from cancer. I was in hospital with him 24 hours a day, watching my dad breathing less and less every day, until he died. That's when I got involved in drugs.

I didn't know what to do; the good side of me was just out of control. It just went, I don't know where, I couldn't find it. It was like my twin disappeared. I was just lost. People used to talk to me and I couldn't register in my head what I was doing, sleeping on the streets; and like, I come from a rich family. But I just couldn't deal with it. I just wanted to kill myself. I just wanted to be with my dad. I ended up sleeping at the cemetery for a month. I just couldn't deal with life any more.

When my dad passed away I went ballistic on drugs, for a year. I got raided by the police. They called it commercial because you're only allowed to have two grams and I had three and a half grams [of heroin]. When the court case came up I breached bail because taking drugs, my mind just forgot where I was. I was on the streets for two or three months. I lost track of time and everything.

When I went back home, the police were there waiting for me. They locked me in here and since then I've been having a hard time really. I'm thinking about my mum, she is dying and I try my best to get out of here.

While I am here in the jail my mind is all cleared out, free of drugs. I realise that I was stupid and silly to do things like that. But at that time I wasn't thinking because of the depression and I couldn't handle my dad gone. Now that I have cleared up my mind I just want to get back into my life like my dad taught me. When I get out of here I want to stay away from drugs. I just want to get back with my wife and my children and be there for my mum. I promised my dad that I would look after Mum.

I accept that my dad is still here in spirit, so I just need to clean up myself and make proud of him that he has a son like me. I just don't want to go back to the street again. I did that, not thinking at all, like just being stupid and childish. In a way it was good for me to come to jail because it really cleaned my whole system out and my mind is clearer than what it used to be on the streets. But I regret what I did. I know I've got to pay the penalty for it. Drugs are not a manner of solving your problems; it just gives you more problems.

I have made up my mind what I want to do with my life, get out of here, go back to my family, open up the shop again and do the usual thing. I have got magic hands for artwork, I create beautiful furniture. All that is missing out of me is my English. If I can improve that then I can make him happy and proud of me. If I do get out I will go to a TAFE, enrol myself and take it from there. I feel really hopeless that I didn't learn from my dad about this paperwork. I realise that it is very important these days. So I need to learn my English better.

I really don't want to get involved any more with drugs. I have lost a lot of money. I was spending $1,000 a day. I had the money, I had no problems but I could have given that to my children to give them a better life. They have a good life but I would never go back on drugs. No way, I will go straight for help. If I can't deal with it I will go straight for help. I just need someone to talk to, to help me out. When I first came in here I looked at myself, I was so skinny I looked terrible, but now I've been doing exercise, eating well, I'm putting myself back together. I would never put myself back in those shoes again. Never again, I can't do that for my children. If any of my children do such things with drugs, I will be very disappointed in them. I will make sure they never touch drugs.

I would like to help people out there to get off drugs if I could. One stage I did help. I helped three people to get off heroin. This girl was on heroin, she was only young, she was only 15 years old and I got her off heroin. And I got another guy off heroin. I made work for them in my shops or on my farm and every time they were hanging out I knew they were doing things behind my back. That's when I checked their arms and I looked at it and they've had a shot. But I love to help as much as I can. I am against drugs now myself. Once I get out of here I will ask to get involved with activities for people who are taking drugs and make a donation to them, to clinics; that's what I will be doing. All the money that I spent on myself on drugs, I could have given that to the clinic to help children off the streets. That's what I would like to do. That's my next step.

Commentary

Carl and John are, by all indications, preparing to desist from crime. This is not at all an uncommon phenomenon among prisoners, as both men are ageing beyond the peak years of offending and crime is widely known to be a 'young man's game'. For most individuals, participation in 'street crimes' like burglary, robbery, and drug sales (the types of offences of most concern to criminologists) generally begins in the early teenage years, peaks rapidly in late adolescence or young adulthood, and dissipates before the person nears 30 years of age (see Figure 11.1).

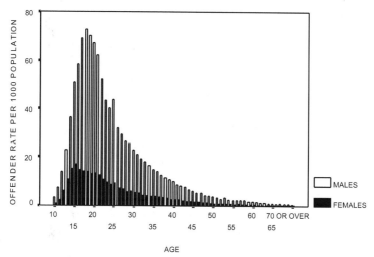

Figure 11.1 Recorded offender rates per 1,000 relevant population by age-year and sex, England and Wales, 2000[5]

Official conviction statistics, like those represented graphically in Figure 11.1 are not easy to interpret and might be skewed by any number of factors (older offenders may be better at avoiding apprehension than young people, might be more likely to die or spend long periods in incarceration, and so forth). However, longitudinal cohort studies such as the Cambridge Study in Delinquent Development (CSDD) consistently confirm that the primary reason that relatively few street crimes are committed by older persons is that they have desisted from these behaviours. David Farrington, for instance, found that for the CSDD sample, self-reported criminal behaviour peaks at around age 17 or 18 and decreases sharply as the young men progress through their twenties.[6] Based primarily on these sorts of longitudinal studies, criminologists estimate that around 85 per cent of crime-involved young people will desist by the time they are 28 years old.

The bad news for John and Carl and other prisoners hoping to change their lives is that desistance involves a good deal more than the desire to change one's life and do good. There is often a considerable distance between wanting to change and actually being able to do so in the face of life's challenges. These challenges, after all, can be considerable. Around one-third of British prisoners are thought to lose their housing while in prison, two-thirds lose their job, over a fifth face increased financial problems and over two-fifths lose contact with their family.[7] This lethal combination of stigma, social exclusion, social learning, temptation, addiction, lack of social bonds, and dangerously low levels of human and social capital (not to mention financial capital) that ex-prisoners face conspire to ensure that over half return to prison within a few years of their release.

The problems of reintegration may be exacerbated by the record high numbers of individuals being processed through probation and the prison system in the UK and US. This strain on the system of release and parole, combined with recent high-profile scandals in England and elsewhere involving released prisoners under community supervision, give the impression of a resettlement process in a period of crisis. Nonetheless, it is clear that the problems ex-prisoners face are anything but 'new' problems; indeed, they have been documented since the earliest days of the modern prison, as evidenced in the Prisoners' Aid Act 1862 and the Gladstone Report of 1895 in the United Kingdom.

For this reason, prisons feature a variety of rehabilitation and reintegration efforts designed to encourage and facilitate desistance from crime upon release. HM Prison Service of England and Wales, for instance, currently focuses on seven distinct 'pathways' for reducing reoffending:

1 Accommodation
2 Education, training and employment
3 Mental and physical health
4 Alcohol and drug misuse
5 Finance, benefit and debt
6 Children and families of offenders
7 Attitudes, thinking and behaviour

These interventions seek to target the key risk factors or criminogenic needs related to reoffending, based on a process of risk assessment and individualised treatment.

Interestingly, though, one of the notable aspects of actual prisoner narratives about rehabilitation (and these two examples above are no exception) is that prisoners are just as likely to cast themselves in the empowering role of being rehabilitation facilitators as they are rehabilitation recipients. Indeed, the line between the two roles (help giver and help receiver) becomes so blurred in rehabilitation narratives that the distinction becomes almost meaningless. If it is true, then, that 'the first step to recovery is admitting you have a problem,' the second step to recovery seems to involve 'admitting' that you also have something to offer the world. Without this, without a sense of purpose, a sense of meaning, the hard work necessary for rehabilitation or 'recovery' is likely to be deemed too onerous.

Without question, both John and Carl recognised that their lives were not going in the direction that they wanted them to go. Carl talks about the 'stupidity' of his actions when he was on drugs and suffering from depression after the loss of his father. John captures the realisation that many former prisoners reach perfectly when he says he looked back on his past and decided, 'I've got bigger and better things to do than to waste my life' in the way he was. Many individuals caught up in crime and drug use regret the harms they have caused others in their lives, but the most frequent regret one hears in interviewing prisoners is the regret they feel for wasting their own lives, for not living up to the potential that they have inside them to make a contribution to the world. The key for triggering this kind of remorse, then, may be convincing individuals that they have something to offer the world in the first place (hence, something to lose by going back to a life of narcotics-induced haze).

For Carl, this inner belief was fairly clear as he had the role model of his own father to which to aspire (he hoped to 'make proud of him that he has a son like me'). Many prisoners lack this sort of male role model in their lives, but some, like John, can find substitute father-figures (and mother-figures, sister-figures, perhaps) among treatment staff. In particular, prisoners frequently encounter former addicts and ex-prisoners working as drug addiction treatment professionals or community mentors to whom they can immediately relate. They see such individuals as reflections of themselves and decide that 'if he (or she) can do it, then so can I'.

This prosocial modelling[8] partially, but not entirely, explains why so many prisoners, like John and Carl, talk about wanting to get involved in rehabilitation work themselves, helping others rather than seeking help for their own problems. The main reason for this, however, is probably that being in the position of the 'giver' of help is actually more therapeutic and more empowering than being a receiver. Although Carl is clear that he 'will go straight for help' if he needs it on the outside, he is also insistent that the reason he is willing to admit to this vulnerability is because he is needed by his own children: 'Never again, I can't [go back to drugs and crime] for my children.'

Both Carl and John exhibit an almost overwhelming 'need to be needed' in their self-narratives. John, in fact, openly recognises this need as a new one in his life. Only a few years ago, he said, he would not have given a second thought to people being victimised, indeed he was often the one doing the victimising. 'But now, if I see someone in trouble I'll be there to help – even though I don't know them I'd want to help'. At the ripe old age of 23, John is especially interested in helping 'younger people' stay away from crime and drugs: a role he has even assumed inside the prison. Carl also has ideas about helping 'children off the streets' as his 'next step' in his recovery, and is proud of the work he has done helping young people get off heroin in the past. Yet, his specific goals are very much about his own family. He wants to reconcile with his wife and children, and support his own ageing mother. 'I promised my dad that I would look after Mum.' John recognises an element of 'making amends' and reparation in these desires the two men share: 'I just want to make a change and I think of all the bad things I've done, I think I owe it to people to help them.'

In the academic literature, following the work of Erik Erikson, such desires to make a difference in the lives of others – in particular, the next generation – are labelled 'generativity'.[9] Generative goals (or, in John's words, plans 'to do something worthwhile') appear to be antithetical to at least much criminal behaviour, which tends towards 'being stupid and childish', according to Carl. Carl has particular regrets about the way he threw away the money that he once had earned, spending $1,000 a day to get high on drugs, when he could have saved that money for his children's futures. He sees little in these selfish behaviours of his past to take particular pride in, but still maintains a sense of clear self-belief, especially in his ability to create: 'I have got magic hands for artwork'. This is the legacy he hopes to be remembered for – his furniture, not his drug taking. Many individuals who are able to desist from crime find similar ways that they can make a worthwhile contribution to their families that can replace the sense of satisfaction they once got from crime and drug use.

John and Carl seem to have reached these conclusions largely on their own, but hardly in isolation. Interestingly, both John and Carl spoke positively about their time in prison, both for the connections they were able to make (to drug counsellors and pastors) and especially as a sort of 'wake-up call' in their lives. John talks eloquently about not realising what he was acting like until he saw his own behaviour reflected in the young prisoners around him. 'You don't really notice it until you see yourself through someone else's actions'. Such sentiments are not uncommon among prisoners, but it is also important to remember that these may be selection effects. John and Carl were nominated by prison staff as individuals they felt had made a real change in their thinking. Although this certainly appears to be the case, the two might also have stood out in the mind of prison staff on the grounds that they were particularly uncritical of the facility and its staff!

The more pertinent lesson to be gained from stories such as these is that even prisoners need opportunities to be useful to others, to discover their own hidden uses, and recognise the rewards of this sort of generative activity. John has already discovered that helping others is not easy. While he claims a number of successes – young people whom he has convinced to come with him to education or other programmes – he also admits that there are others who 'are not interested' in the help he wants to give (and somehow one imagines these others did not phrase their disinterest quite that politely). Carl surely already knows these frustrations from being a parent. At the same time, many individuals eventually discover that despite such difficulties there are distinct rewards involved in productive, creative, supportive roles such as teaching, coaching, counselling, parenting and mentoring.

Prisons worldwide recognise these processes, and, to a greater or lesser extent, do provide opportunities for prisoners to become involved in volunteer and mutual aid work. Prisoners donate their time and abilities in workshops repairing bicycles and wheelchairs for the disadvantaged, training guide dogs for the blind, and even volunteering to fight forest fires in places like California. Other prisoners volunteer to be 'Listeners' for fellow prisoners who may be suicidal, 'carers' in hospice wings for terminally ill fellow prisoners, or peer counsellors to those struggling with addiction issues. Even more work can be done by individuals outside of prison on parole or sentenced to community penalties as they are better able to make visible contributions to their own communities or direct reparation to the victims of their actions.

Indeed, a growing movement, associated with 'restorative justice' and 'justice reinvestment' concepts, has sought to channel the potential strengths and contributions prisoners and probationers can make towards crime reduction efforts – in particular addressing some of the visible signs of community breakdown (such as 'broken windows', graffiti, litter) thought to exacerbate crime problems. The idea is that justice should be about transforming individuals from 'part of the problem' into 'part of the solution' and facilitating acts of reparation rather than the simple retribution of a harm for a harm.

One of the most innovative projects along these lines is a long-standing Canadian Correctional Services (CSC) programme known as LifeLine, which utilises the experience and hard-earned wisdom of 'lifers' – those individuals sentenced to life sentences – who have been released from prison and are successfully living on the outside. As is inherent in the name, lifers remain under surveillance and supervision their entire lives, which can be a rather demeaning situation. However, the CSC also recognises lifers as 'resources, role models and successes'.[10] The LifeLine project puts released lifers in the position of counsellors for newly sentenced life-sentence prisoners. The volunteers offer current prisoners support and advice, based on their own experiences, to help them survive a highly stressful sentence and re-emerge as productive citizens upon release. The well-respected programme is therefore meant to be a lifeline for current prisoners, but it also serves an important function for released former prisoners, offering them a rare chance to utilise their expertise as help givers and not just help recipients.

Unfortunately, prisons are by their nature security-conscious institutions and many similar schemes bringing ex-prisoners back inside prisons are deemed too risky to allow. What if, for instance, the ex-prisoners were secretly smuggling drugs or weapons into the facility? Indeed, research by the Prison Reform Trust, published in the report *Barred Citizens*, found that prisoners and former prisoners are prohibited from doing a wide range of volunteer work for fears of community safety.[11] Even with years of crime-free behaviour, former prisoners can find themselves prohibited from doing just the type of work that John and Carl hoped to get into upon leaving prison – counselling young people involved in crime and drugs. Indeed, one of the conditions frequently put on individuals released from prison is that they do not have contact with other ex-prisoners in their daily lives, making it nearly impossible for ex-prisoners to 'give something back' to others in their same situation.

Such concerns make sense at some level, of course, yet there is certainly something ironic about prohibiting ex-offenders from helping people in the name of community safety, especially when this seems to play such a central role in the rehabilitative process of redefining oneself as more than just a criminal.

Notes

1 Barlow, S. (2009) 'Identifying the Indicators of Individual Readiness for Positive Life Change Amongst Defenders within a Remand Setting', unpublished PhD thesis, Australian Catholic University.
2 'Juvenile': Department of Juvenile Justice.
3 TAFE: Technical and Further Education.
4 Barlow, 'Identifying the Indicators'.
5 Bottoms, A., Costello, A., Holmes, D., Muir, G. and Shapland, J. (2004) 'Towards desistance: Theoretical underpinnings for an empirical study', *The Howard Journal of Criminal Justice*, 43(4): 368–89.
6 Farrington, D. P. (1992) 'Explaining the beginning, progress, and ending of antisocial behavior from birth to adulthood', in J. McCord (ed.) *Advances in Criminological Theory: Vol. 3, Facts, Frameworks, and Forecasts*. New Brunswick, NJ: Transaction.
7 Social Exclusion Unit (2001) *Reducing Re-Offending by Ex-Prisoners*. London: Home Office.
8 Trotter, C. (1999) *Working with Involuntary Clients: A Guide to Practice*. Sydney, Australia: Allen & Unwin.
9 McAdams, D. P., Hart, H. and Maruna, S. (1998) 'The anatomy of generativity', in D. P. McAdams and E. de St Aubin (eds) *Generativity and Adult Development*. Washington, DC: American Psychological Association Press, pp. 7–43.
10 http://www.csc-scc.gc.ca/text/prgrm/lifeline/1-eng.shtml
11 Farrant, F. and Levenson, J. (2002) *Barred Citizens: Volunteering and Active Citizenship by Prisoners*. London: Prison Reform Trust.

Further reading

For a theoretical discussion of these issues and the role of personal narratives in helping to understand the rehabilitation process, see Shadd Maruna. *Making Good: How Ex-Convicts Reform and Rebuild Their Lives* (Washington, DC: American Psychological Association, 2001). For a book-length autobiography that perfectly captures many of the themes above, see Mark Johnson, *Wasted: A Childhood Stolen, An Innocence Betrayed, A Life Redeemed* (London: Sphere, 2007).

Afterword

Jason Warr

We live in a society that incarcerates roughly 120,000 men, women and children per year, and have a standing prison population of 80–85,000. Why do we so rarely hear their accounts? Are prisoners shouting in the dark, or are we choosing not to hear them?

To say that the prisoner voice is never heard is a fallacy, for there are numerous accounts out there detailing what life behind bars is like. However, barring an exceptional few, these tend to be salacious accounts designed to feed the cult of infamy that surrounds criminality and incarceration, and to titillate the prison voyeur. By and large these tales are authored either by self-aggrandising narcissists or those pushing some form of agenda.

The likes of Jeffrey Archer, Charles Bronson or Norman Parker, whose accounts of prison life dominate this field, are not representative, and they are the portrayals of a privileged few. They do not reflect the prison world that I spent much of my early adulthood navigating nor, I would argue, do they reflect the carceral world recognised by the majority of those souls who find their way 'inside'. Further to this, there are a number of problems with such accounts: they perpetuate myths and misconceptions concerning prison life and prisoners; for instance, older prisoners are turned into 'lags' whose prison craft is to be envied and aped, the 'villains' or 'faces' are the good guys and the 'nonces' (a more perfect example of reified othering you will never find) are the enemies of the piece. In doing this, they obfuscate the most important issues – the harms of incarceration, the deprivations and mortifications, the forms of disculturation and marginalisation, the bullying, suicide and self-injury – that need to be addressed, and drown out the voices that try to raise awareness of those issues, such as serious academics, documentary film makers and investigative journalists and charities; and they glamorise the prison experience. Prison is not glamorous. It is a place of oppressive tension and stultifying mundanity, which is populated by the lost, broken, marginalised and forgotten of our society. It is a place that, like all hostile territories, needs careful navigation. There are pitfalls that dog every step you make on your journey through your carceral career, whether that be a week or a score of years. It is a place where you are watched, examined and judged; where every utterance, facial expression, emotion and sense has to be weighed and carefully managed. Being in prison affects every aspect of your being. In short, prison damages you.

So, beyond these purveyors of what we might call 'nick-lit', why do we not hear the voices of the majority? One problem is that although we inflict prison on so many of our fellow citizens it is still largely hidden. When people are 'banged up' they are sent away, locked behind walls and fences. The language of being imprisoned – 'locked up', 'sent down' or 'put away' – denotes this removal of the person to someplace else, where punishment is enacted. As a consequence of this 'removal', what happens to prisoners is rarely witnessed by the rest of society, resulting in societal and cultural ignorance about the prison world. Even among those who have friends, family members and loved ones behind bars, the same form of ignorance is found. More surprising is that this ignorance exists among many academics who are actively engaged with the literature on prisons and imprisonment. Very few students or academics with whom I have contact have any understanding of what truly occurs behind the bars. For the period that they are away, the incarcerated become forgotten. The poet Joseph Campbell, writing in the early twentieth century, makes the point that prisoners are like 'so many pieces taken, swept from the chessboard' and are only remembered or noticed on release, when 'a new game is started'.[1]

One issue that compounds penal ignorance is the 'othering' that occurs when a person is imprisoned. As scholars like Goffman have detailed, when taken away to prison you become a 'prisoner', an 'offender', a 'convict' – no longer a member of society, as if, by going to prison, you have given up your membership of the club of society. Consider the rhetoric surrounding current debates on prisoner voting rights in England and Wales. While the *legalistas* proclaim that voting rights are the mark of a democracy, and that it is a contravention of human rights law to deny prisoners these rights, the political consensus seems to be that once sent to prison, you have forfeited your right to vote. The Prime Minister stated that he 'could see no reason why prisoners should be enfranchised', and in responding to Dartford MP Gareth Johnson during Prime Minister's Questions, even went on to say that the thought of giving the vote to prisoners made him 'physically ill'. Some backbench MPs have gone so far as to say that you actively forfeit your rights as a citizen by choosing to be outside of the law. I find it disturbing that within a modern democracy duly elected representatives can hold the view that some members of the citizenry should be denied all their rights and not just their freedom. Such sentiments evidence a distinct lack of care with regard to not only the rights of prisoners but their personages too. It is no wonder that with such anti-prisoner rhetoric resounding so strongly in the social conscience, the plight of prisoners is an unpopular focus of attention.

The popular press plays a pivotal role in contributing to this general malaise in the popular conscience. More often than not, they hold up the prisoner as some form of 'folk-devil' upon whom the ills of society can be hung. Prisoners' rights are reported as infringements upon the rights of society. Prisoner privileges are reported as coming at the expense of the elderly, or of heroic forces fighting in foreign fields. The problem is that the prisoner is constantly shown in a bad light and the realities of prison life are overshadowed by the popular misconceptions that the press perpetuate – perceptions that are consistent with the misrepresentations regurgitated by the 'nick-lit' brigade. This negativity compounds the marginalisation that prisoners suffer, the ignorance and disregard with which they are beheld, and the silencing of their voices.

Why, then, is it important to hear the prisoner voice? Why should we want to know, or care about, what happens to those who are sent down? Perhaps most fundamentally, it behoves us as a society to understand what we inflict on so many of our fellow citizens. If, as the Prison Service claims, one of the aims of imprisonment is to rehabilitate prisoners, then we need to understand the various forms of damage that prisoners suffer and which hinder any attempts to help them turn around their lives. One of the most corrosive elements of incarceration, which is little understood outside academic circles, is the impact that it has on you psychologically and as an emotional being. In describing the changed nature of punishment in *Discipline and Punish*, Foucault notes the transfer of the focus of punishment from the body of the accused to the nature/mind of the convicted.[2] This transference, and the subsequent entrenchment of incarceration as the dominant form of punishment in society, have resulted in a form of punishment that is more profound and psychologically penetrating, and can have deep and long-lasting effects on the prisoner. Like Ewan (see Chapter 3), during my 12 years in prison, I found that I had to constantly hide what I was feeling from everyone – officers, probation staff, psychologists, fellow prisoners and even family. I spent so many years managing my emotional state that, seven years after release, the effects of that process are still with me. While I can empathise with people, the leap to sympathy does not occur unless I am already emotionally invested with someone. I became aware of this while I was still incarcerated, but to have discussed it would almost certainly have seen me 'killed off' on file. Becoming emotionally selective was a survival technique to adopt while I was 'away', but its results have persisted in my lack of care for people who are not my nearest and dearest. This is something I continue to work on, but it is something that I do alone.

Reducing penal ignorance requires that real stories of prisoners, such as those detailed in this volume, are given a platform. It is only through such a medium that accurate information about the prisoner experience can be relayed. Part of the reason for this is the very survival strategies that prisoners adopt or create for themselves. As Jewkes (Chapter 4) notes, one aspect of the prison experience is the effect it has on one's personal and social identity – how one portrays oneself in both frontstage and backstage scenarios. Often prisoners will formulate some form of *masque* which they employ to navigate both the official and social world of the prison. This poses a problem when it comes to learning the truth about the penal experience, as much of that experience is translated through these types of façades. This even extends to one's family and one's interactions during prison visits. I know that during my 12 years in prison I became aware of the misdirection that underlay all my interactions with my family. Not wanting them to worry about some of the bad things that I was going through, once, having flinched after hugging my mum, I told my parents that I had injured myself playing football, rather than the truth that someone had tried to chiv (stab) me and had scored a line along my ribs. They did similar things. Whatever problems they were suffering, they did not wish to burden me with them. The result of this was that while I did not really understand what my family were going through, they did not truly comprehend the prison world in which I existed. If such dissimulation exists even among those who are close and dear, it is no surprise that there is much wider ignorance.

These façades, or fronts, play an important role in the prisoner experience, and are discussed in several of the chapters in this volume. Whether it be George (Chapter 4) talking about the superficiality of the prisoner experience, Ewan (Chapter 3) talking about the necessity of having 'to hide your feelings from everyone' or female prisoners (Chapter 9) talking of hiding the pains of child separation, the common theme is the concealing of what lies beneath. I once heard the prison experience being described as an enforced life of fantasy, and its stresses as the result of conflicts that arise due to competing fantasies. This struck a bell with me, for the simple fact that I remember the 'narrative' that I constructed and emitted was often challenged by those of my fellow prisoners. For instance, part of the 'persona' that I portrayed to the prison world was as a calm and stoic man, but this is difficult to maintain when confronted by a fellow prisoner 'masquerading' as the 'Big-Gangster-I-Am' when you know that he was more Mr Bean than Br Big outside prison. Of course, in this instance I presented a threat to his 'fantasy', as I knew the reality that he had spent years hiding from the world around him, and thus had to be defeated socially in some manner. This resulted in some petty and undignified confrontations that were challenges to my own 'fantasy'. A further challenge occurred when having to engage with the prison authorities, the report-writers, teachers, and the more pro-social visages of visitors, family and friends. After so many years of living with an adopted persona, it is hard to distinguish a backstage identity from a frontstage mask, the constructed from the real.

This book raises many other important issues. What understanding do we have of the plight and difficulties brought about by the infirmity of an ever-ageing prison population (see Chapter 8)? Likewise, how can we learn of the pains and harms suffered by women and their babies on mother and baby units when enforced separation occurs unless someone takes that time to relay the stories of those who suffer (see Chapter 9)? There are other examples throughout this volume, such as the troubles and traumas of those who are struggling to rehabilitate themselves (see Chapter 11). How can we understand the difficulties and complexities of desistance, of 'what works' and what doesn't, without the kinds of accounts provided in this volume?

There are, however, other aspects of the prisoner experience that still need to be explored and might form the basis of future volumes of this kind. The first of these relates to Cohen and Taylor's seminal study of 1972 of psychological survival among long-term prisoners.[3] Prison research would benefit from a thorough re-examination of their work in the context of modern penality, but should explore the emotional experiences of prisoners beyond the high-security estate. A wide examination like this would allow for a greater understanding of the psychological and emotional burdens, and the coping mechanisms, associated with the contemporary prison experience. A second area of interest would be the power relations that dominate the social world of prisoners – not just in adult, male prisons, but also in Young Offender Institutions and women's prisons, where – as this volume suggests – currents of power differ from those in the adult male prison estate. A third topic would be prisoners' perceptions of and attitudes towards physical and sexual violence, in the context of both prisons and the outside world. I say this because within the context of the prisoner social world, there is a very different moral perception of violence than in wider society. An example of this is the sort of violence that is visited upon perceived sex offenders or informers, who are generally reviled by other prisoners. I once described to a friend an incident I had witnessed in which a known sex offender had been doused in petrol and set alight while he was locked in his cell. My friend could not understand the moral motivation behind this act and was not satisfied with my 'prisoner' response that the victim was a 'nonce'. Their reaction made me aware that, 15 years after that event had taken place, my prison experiences had made the moral justification for such an act implicitly understandable to me, but yet this understanding was not something that I could communicate to my friend. He felt that since all the people involved in the incident were prisoners, all convicted of serious crimes, there could be no moral justification, based on form and nature of offence, for such an act. When I argued that the victimisation of such individuals can often act as a form of defence against feelings of hostility and powerlessness, he was all the more horrified by such a utilitarian justification. I realised that imprisonment had skewed my moral tolerance in certain ways, and I am not alone in this. Many of those who find their way into prison have to shift their moral perspective, and adopt a more pragmatic approach to ethical dilemmas, in order to survive the environment. This begs a number of questions: are the normative behaviours which demand a moral shift endemic to the carceral experience, or are they imported into the prison world? If they are endemic, what does this mean for the rehabilitation of violent offenders in prison? What is the impact of this moral shift on staff–prisoner relationships and on the long-term character of prisoners, including their lives after release?

Fourth, why does the modern prison environment make extremist politics and religious expression attractive? In the early 1990s, many of my contemporaries in a Young Offender Institution were increasingly being drawn to the more radical and extreme versions of Christianity and Islam that had started to proliferate in our world. Others embraced extreme right-wing politics, including those that had friends and co-defendants who were of multi-ethnic backgrounds. Many years later, I ran into four prisoners who I had known from that time, all of whom were back in prison for crimes relating to the beliefs they had adopted or had inculcated a decade earlier. What purposes do such beliefs serve for prisoners? How do they relate to the deprivations and mortifications associated with the prison experience, and to feelings of marginalisation and the need for group acceptance? Are there other, more prosaic, forms of identity expression, beyond the grand narratives of religion and politics, which can engender similar sentiments?

Finally, we would benefit from knowing more about how prisoners perceive the outside world. During my incarceration, the outside world retreated to some kind of fantastical landscape, shaped by my memories and the input of second-hand sources (the media, visitors, and so on). The world beyond the stone walls became unreal and idealised, leading to the development of goals that were painfully false and unrealisable. Many of the prisoners in this book express similar forms of ignorance or appear to hold fantastical expectations of what the outside world will offer them. These distortions might hamper desistance, while understanding them would provide the Prison Service with a further means of preparing prisoners successfully for release.

In many regards, I have had a successful transition from prisoner to member of society. I have achieved an undergraduate degree at the London School of Economics, a Masters degree at Cambridge, and am now in the latter stages of a PhD. Many people ask me where I would be today if it were not for the time I spent in prison. The question presupposes that it was the prison experience that turned my life around, as if 'going away' was a positive thing. I cannot deny that going to prison afforded me the time and opportunity to read as much as I did. Likewise I cannot deny that serving an indeterminate sentence and coping with the constant liminality that was forced upon me has enabled me to navigate the uncertainties of the world in a more mature and patient manner than I would otherwise have been capable of. I cannot deny these things. However, as Clemmer notes, rehabilitation occurs in 'spite of the harmful influences of prison culture' and only to those who remain largely unaffected by the processes of 'prisonisation'.[4] I have fought to overcome the effects of my 'prisonisation' and my successes are mine and mine alone; they have come not because of being imprisoned but despite it.

Prison damages in so many ways. The real difficulty of doing time is realising the harms you have suffered and trying to overcome them. People often comment that I seem so well balanced after having done so much time at such a young age. That is something that I work at constantly, for I know that if I do not then the harms that I suffered and have yet to palliate will rise to the surface and cause me to stumble. A stumble for me would mean a recall to prison, where I would be confronted with all those things that I have spent the last seven years trying to undo and overcome. On a personal level, a book like this one is important as it can explore, analyse, unravel and relay many of the issues that I have experienced and struggled with in a way that the 'nick-lit' pulp can never do. It lets me know that my experiences were not mine alone, that other people have experienced them in many of the same ways that I did. It also means that there are people who are willing to look behind the walls, who wish to understand and who wish to listen. For the prisoner still inside me, this makes the world a less lonely place.

Notes

1 Campbell, J. (1963) *The Poems of Joseph Campbell*. Dublin: Allen Figgis.
2 Foucault, M. (1977) *Discipline and Punish: The Birth of the Prison*. London: Penguin.
3 Cohen, S. and Taylor, L. (1972) *Psychological Survival: The Experience of Long-Term Imprisonment*. Harmondsworth: Penguin.
4 Clemmer, D. (1940, 2nd edn 1958) *The Prison Community*. New York: Holt, Rinehart and Winston, p. 313.

Index

reparation 138, 139
reputation (prisoner) 33, 36, 47
resettlement 77, 90, 136
resilient prisoners 23
resistance 51
respect
    crime and search for 9
    officers' lack of 20
    for prisoners 65
    within the prison community 33
responsibility
    denial of 100
    prisoner roles, and relations with
        officers 20
    see also diminished responsibility
restorative justice 139
retribution 101
reverse racism 123–4, 128
rewards 113
risk factors, targeting of 137
role models 137, 139
rule enforcement, sudden 20
Ruth 55–61, 63, 65

safety, feeling of 64
saving face 48
Schmid, T. 46
school exclusion 87
Scottish prisoners 8
secure children's homes (SCHs) 86
secure training centres (STCs) 86–7
self
    loss of sense of 19
    masking of true 46
self-belief 138
self-cook areas 126–7
self-destructive psychiatric disorders 46,
    51
self-doubt 62
self-hardening 35
self-harm
    attempts 46, 51, 63, 88
    as a coping strategy 114
    prisoner view on 108
    see also Mark
self-regulation 37, 113
self-reported criminal behaviour 136
A Sense of Direction 65
separation, from family 74–5
Sex Offender Treatment Program (SOTP)
    101
sex offenders 32, 97, 100, 101, 146
    see also George
sexual intimacy, between prisoners 111

Sharon 13–14, 19, 20, 21, 22, 23, 24
'shedding of a skin' 47
sociability of officers 19, 23
social capital 136
social deprivation 7–8
social disadvantage 8, 109
social distance, staff-prisoner 18
social exclusion 8–9, 136
Social Exclusion Unit report (2002) 8
social inclusion 11
social learning 136
social nature, prison life 36–7, 113, 124
social needs, and criminality 11
social networks 50
social stigma 8
socialisation
    amongst mixed-race prisoners 37
    between women prisoners 111
    inverse correlation between
        prisonisation and 51–2
    multicultural 126
    with officers 34–5
socio-economic system, illegal 51
Sparks, R. 98
specialist support 64–5
speech difficulties (prisoner) 64
staff composition, and attitudes to care 24
staff-prisoner relationships
    ageing prisoners 101
    women prisons 112, 113
    younger prisoners 101
    see also custody, care and staff-
        prisoner relationships
stage of sentence, and prisoner loyalty 36
'standing up', for friends 36
state policy/practices, and criminality 10
status
    criminality and 9, 10, 11
    jostling for 47
    reinforcement of prisoner's 19, 20, 98
    within prisoner community 32, 33
    working the system to gain enhanced
        101
Stephen 27–30, 33, 34, 35–6, 37
stigma
    faced by ex-prisoners 136
    within prisoner community 32
    see also social stigma
stoicism 33, 34
street crimes 135
stress (prisoner) 35
structural disadvantages 9
subcultures (prison) 50
subjective clock 99

mutual support among 110
negotiation of frustrations and
    constraints 114
perceived as victims 24
preoccupation with home problems/
    responsibilities 109
prisoner accounts
    Kirsty 103–4, 109
    Lisa 107–8, 112, 113–14
    Naomi 105–6, 110, 111, 112, 113, 114
relationships between 110–11
relationships with staff 112, 113
self-harm 114
solitary experience of imprisonment
    113–14
suicide prevention *see* Ruth
suicide thoughts/attempts 24
see also Nancy; Ruth; Sharon
women's prisons 24, 146
'working the system' 101
worthlessness, feelings of 19, 22, 24

yoga 65
young offender institutions (YOIs) 38n,
    87, 88, 146
young prisoners 79–91
    learning to live in prison 88
    penal policy 89–90
    personal futures 88–9
    personal histories 86–7
    prisoner accounts
        Ben 81–3, 86, 87, 89, 90
        in context 85–6
        Jack 79–81, 86, 87, 88–9, 90
        Wayne 83–5, 86, 87, 88, 89, 90
    and suicide *see* Adam
younger prisoners
    proximity to older prisoners 100
    relationships with officers 101
youth justice system 90

Zamble, E. 65